AF269971

Two Roman Revolutions

Two Roman Revolutions

The Senate, the Emperors and Power, from Commodus to Gallienus (AD 180–260)

John D. Grainger

First published in Great Britain in 2024 by
Pen & Sword History
An imprint of Pen & Sword Books Limited
Yorkshire – Philadelphia

ISBN 978 1 39903 718 1

A CIP catalogue record for this book is
available from the British Library

Typeset by Mac Style
Printed in the UK by CPI Group (UK) Ltd, Croydon, CR0 4YY.

Pen & Sword Books Limited incorporates the imprints of After
the Battle, Atlas, Archaeology, Aviation, Discovery, Family History,
Fiction, History, Maritime, Military, Military Classics, Politics,
Select, Transport, True Crime, Air World, Frontline Publishing, Leo
Cooper, Remember When, Seaforth Publishing, The Praetorian Press,
Wharncliffe Local History, Wharncliffe Transport, Wharncliffe True
Crime and White Owl.

For a complete list of Pen & Sword titles please contact:

PEN & SWORD BOOKS LIMITED
47 Church Street, Barnsley, South Yorkshire, S70 2AS, England
E-mail: enquiries@pen-and-sword.co.uk
Website: www.pen-and-sword.co.uk
or
PEN AND SWORD BOOKS
1950 Lawrence Rd, Havertown, PA 19083, USA
E-mail: uspen-and-sword@casematepublishers.com
Website: www.penandswordbooks.com

Contents

List of Maps

List of Illustrations

Maps

CLODIUS
ALBINUS
BRITANNIA
THE CAMPAIGNS OF 193 AND 197
SEPTIMIUS
SEVERUS
197
193
PANNONIA
LUGDUNUM
ROME
PESCENNIUS
193 NIGER
NIKAIA
194
ISSOS
SYRIA
CAMPAIGNS 193, 197
PROVINCES OF PRETENDERS 193
0
580 km

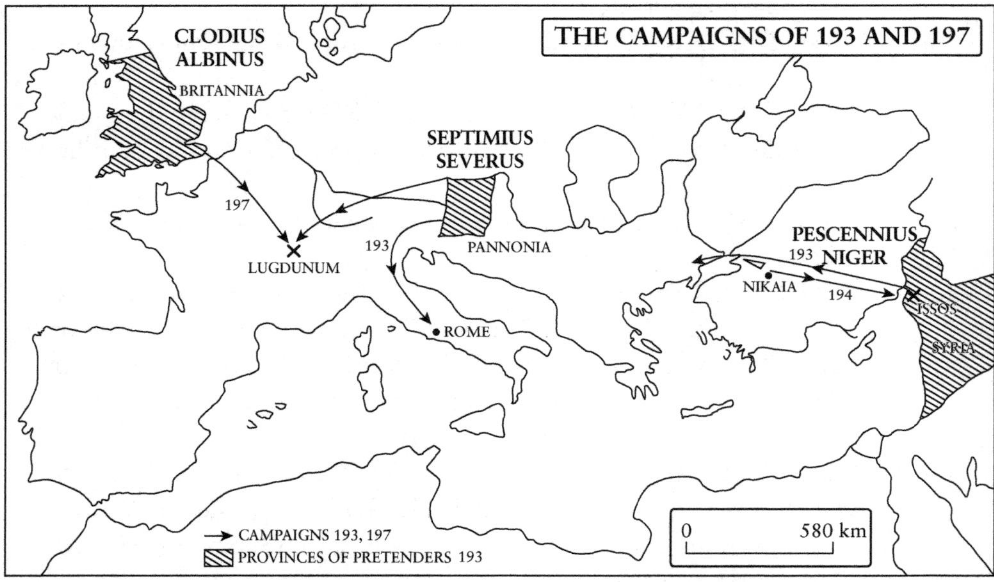

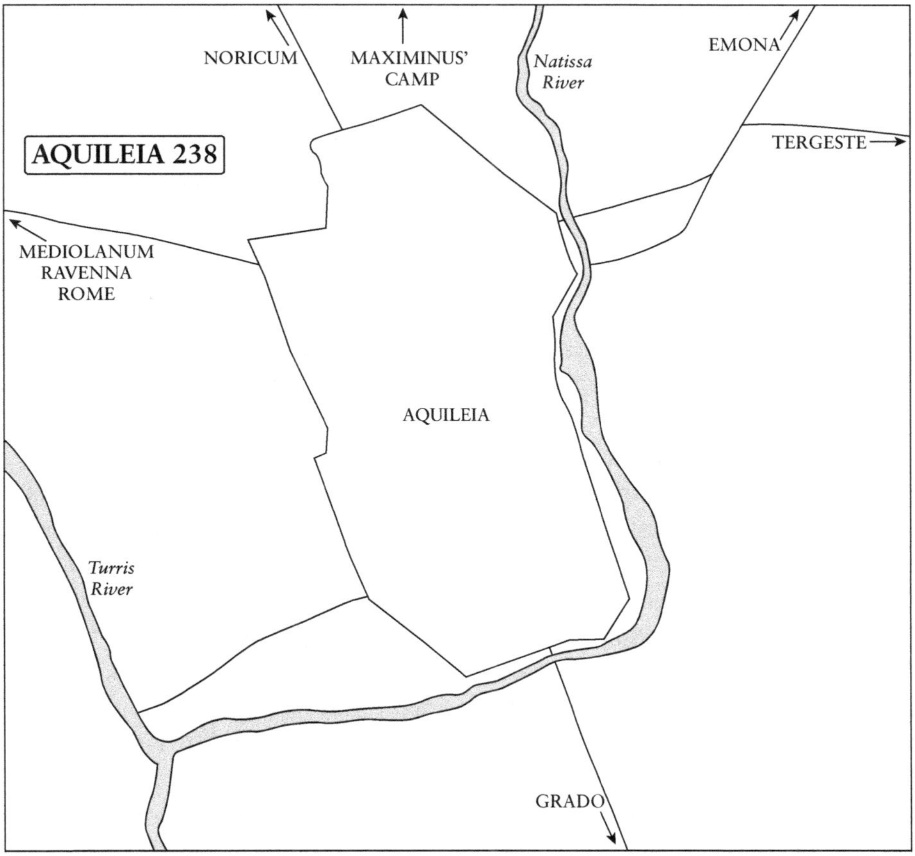

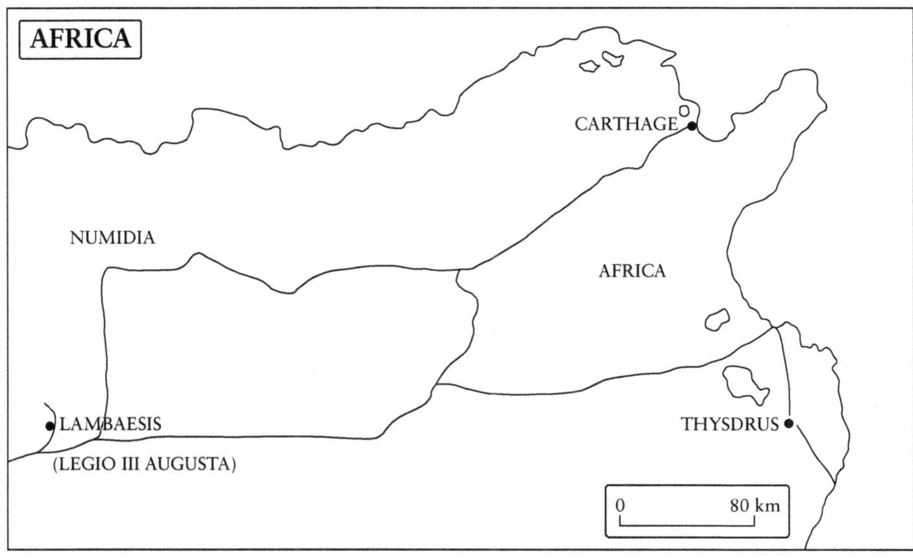

AQUILEIA 238
NORICUM
MAXIMINUS' CAMP
Natissa River
EMONA
TERGESTE
MEDIOLANUM
RAVENNA
ROME
AQUILEIA
Turris River
GRADO
AFRICA
CARTHAGE
NUMIDIA
AFRICA
LAMBAESIS
(LEGIO III AUGUSTA)
THYSDRUS
0   80 km

Introduction

The history of the Roman Empire from the death of Marcus Aurelius in 180 saw a shift from the relatively sedate rule of the 'Antonines' into the autocracy of Commodus. This brought on his assassination in 192, followed by the revolution which occupied the first part of 193, including the murders of two more emperors, but which ended with the accession of another autocratic emperor, Septimius Severus, and the continuing pretenderships – or rival emperors – of the Pescennius Niger and Clodius Albinus. Severus' rule included a campaign against the Senate, which reduced that body to near impotence for the next four decades. Only Alexander Severus of the Severan dynasty was more or less accommodating to the Senate, but he in turn was succeeded by the autocratic military man Maximinus.

Maximinus' deliberate ignoring of the Senate, and of the city of Rome, after the relative relaxation of the Severan autocracy under Alexander Severus, finally triggered a new revolution, in 238. As in 193, the revolution consisted of attempts to find a new emperor who would abate the former autocracy and govern with, rather than against, the Senate. The matter was difficult, producing a succession of emperors – three Gordians, Pupienus, and Balbinus – and repeated assassinations. It did, in the end, result in a rough approximation of the former Antonine system, but by that time the only knowledge of that system was anecdotal, since no one could recall it personally.

The result was a new dispensation, a new relationship of emperor and Senate, which lasted for a couple of decades. It was destroyed by the next imperial crisis when, almost simultaneously, the Emperor Valerian was captured by the Sassanid enemy, and the imperial frontiers were broken open by the assaults of large numbers of barbarian invaders, clearly one of the results of the disaster of an imperial capture. The crisis was an experience that threatened the very survival of the empire, which lost provinces and suffered secessions; the Senate had little to contribute to any possible solution to this crisis. Imperial autocracy returned, in the person of the captured emperor's son, Gallienus, who had to cope with the imperial crisis; this time the autocracy arrived as much with senatorial agreement as by an imperial will.

This then is an attempt to describe the two revolutions and the period between them as a distinct and particular period in the history of the empire, as distinct as that of the Antonines or the Julio-Claudians. The two revolutions are rarely examined in detail, and study of the period between them is usually preoccupied with such matters as the autocracy of Severus and his violence and that of his son Caracalla, and then with the weird experience of the empire being ruled by the extraordinary Elagabalus. By concentrating attention on these extraordinary men, the history of the empire and of the imperial regime tends to be subsumed into discussions of imperial personalities. But given the attention paid to the events of 69 and its 'year of the four emperors', it seems worth talking of 193, a year of six emperors, and 238, a year of seven; for if the revolution of 69 is worth repeated attention, so are these.

Chapter 1

Commodus Emperor

The Emperor Marcus Aurelius died on 17 March 180, after a short illness, which may have been cancer, or the plague, which was rife in the empire at the time. Given that he refused food for a week before he died, it may even have been suicide. He had sent his son Commodus away from his bedside earlier, which implies that Marcus himself believed that he was infectious. It may be that Commodus himself was also ill,[1] or at least threatened by Marcus' illness. However, Marcus' health had never been good, and at fifty-eight, he was already an old man.

It was the end of a chequered reign. Marcus had been emperor for a little less than two decades (161–180), and for much of that time, unfortunately for a man devoted to philosophy, he had been at war. The first had been a war with the Parthian Empire, actually conducted by his joint emperor, Julius Verus, who had died not long after concluding it. Marcus had then spent the rest of his reign, from 166, fighting on the northern frontier, aiming, as Domitian had intended a century before, to bring into the empire the Marcomanni and the Quadi of Bohemia. But he had a different aim than Domitian in the north. Domitian's aim had been to secure a strategic position from which to dominate all Central Europe, with the ultimate aim of extending the frontier of the empire to the Baltic and to the Oder River (at least); this would have produced a shorter frontier line and would then free up some Roman forces for further conquests, as well as extending the empire over all Germany.[2] Marcus' aim was much less ambitious. He was intending in part to solidify the frontier, by creating an open space that the Northerners were forbidden to enter. He also aimed to secure sections of the population of the tribes and transplant them into the empire, and so refresh the empire's population, which had been reduced seriously as a result of the plague – which had been brought back into the empire by soldiers who had campaigned into Babylonia during the Parthian War. So Marcus had been attempting to repair the damage caused by the Parthian War by conducting another war. Towards the end of the fighting, the late 170s, he seems to have switched to Domitian's and Trajan's aim of annexing the Bohemian lands, at least. Had he aimed to do this from the start he might have succeeded. But he had failed.

The first German War, from 166 to 177, had not produced a clear result, and the peace had broken down after only a year. It had looked as though one final campaign in the north would finally succeed – but this is ever the case. Commodus did not like the war, which was still continuing when he inherited the throne. The legacy of father to son was thus mixed, both the plague and the political problem that the young emperor faced as soon as he took power.

Commodus was the youngest man to become emperor since Nero. He had been prepared for the role since soon after birth. He was entitled Caesar at the age of five (in 166) and Augustus at fifteen. He was as well educated as any emperor had ever been, and of as high aristocratic descent as most of the Roman aristocracy. When his father died, he had been the obvious heir to the throne for almost two decades, and the sole heir for a dozen years. His childhood had been scarred, as had most Roman families, by deaths – his twin brother died when he was three, another brother when he was seven and his uncle, the Emperor Julius Verus, when he was eight. His mother had died when he was fifteen, and now his father had died.

When Marcus died, Commodus was already equipped with the necessary titles and powers to exercise his imperial office. He had the titles; he was in the presence of the largest concentration of Roman troops in the empire; he had around him his father's *consilium*, a group of men of almost as high aristocratic descent as Commodus himself, and with vastly more experience. One more ceremony would ratify his accession. He presented himself to the available troops on parade in a ceremony called *adlocutio*. He then did as they expected – made a short speech and promised a reasonable donative to add to their pay.[3] That was all it took.

He was faced with the problem of the war his father had been fighting. The old emperor's advisers had to some extent a vested interest in the war's continuance, because they had long advised so, and some of them had commanded during it. Commodus, much less involved, was also less convinced of the war's continued utility. He remained on the frontier for the next campaigning season and continued with the war with some success. One of the enemy tribes, the Buri, were driven into surrender, but the other two, the Marcomanni and the Quadi, continued to fight, and by October 180, the end of the campaigning season, they were still fighting. One more year was expected to be sufficient – but then, every long campaign requires 'one more year'. That was a decision for the council during the winter.

Meanwhile, the change of emperor, and especially the accession of an untried teenager, had brought the usual problems elsewhere in the empire. There was trouble on the British frontier, where the northern barbarians broke through the Wall, killing a commander, either a legionary legate or the provincial governor newly appointed. An experienced governor, Ulpius Marcellus, was rapidly dispatched to contain the situation. This war lasted for two or three years and further troubles could probably be expected on other frontiers.[4] In addition, it would soon be necessary for the new emperor to be present in Rome, where the population expected to be able to acclaim him, and to enjoy games and entertainments at his expense in the process.

There were thus several serious problems pressing on the emperor besides the northern war, the British war, and the anticipation of wars on other frontiers. The answer was to finish the war on the northern frontier, and then redistribute the legions to be in readiness to combat any new invasions elsewhere. He consulted his *consilium*, of whom most appear to have wished to fight on in the north for 'one more season', when victory would be accomplished. But casualties had been considerable (several thousands of prisoners were held by the tribes, and there had been as many deserters; the troops were weary and not easily motivated any more. Perhaps crucially, the cost of the war, and of the expected imperial donatives, had drained, would drain, the imperial treasury.

At the very least, a pause in the fighting for recovery was indicated. But Commodus was personally unhappy with the war, and, though campaigns in his name were conducted with some success, he was personally less than involved. He had thus good personal as well as political reasons for bringing the war to an end. The *consilium*, or at least a majority of it, was persuaded, and it was agreed to make peace.[5] This the Marcomanni and the Quadi were happy to do. They had sent a delegation as soon as they heard there was a new emperor, and so were now no doubt much relieved. They agreed to terms that theoretically made them Roman subjects of a sort, and had their activities overseen by centurions, but this ended the fighting, and left them without Roman military occupation.

The terms were in fact very much in the Roman favour, so long as it is accepted that conquest and annexation were no longer intended. Dio Cassius provides a summary of the terms, but interprets the result differently, in accordance with his prejudices against Commodus. It seems that the Buri were the first to ask for terms. What they suggested was not regarded as submissive enough. Taking the request for terms as a clear indication of Buri weakness, the Romans attacked once more. The Buri reiterated their wish for peace, which was again rejected; another Roman attack followed. Commodus is credited with this war, but it seems that its conduct was in the hands of the governor of Dacia. Finally, defeated for the third time, the Buri agreed to the Roman terms. They were to release their prisoners – said to number over 15,000 – and return Roman deserters; they agreed to leave a 5-mile-wide strip of land along the border with Dacia unoccupied, used neither for pasture nor for dwellings. The governor of Dacia, C. Vettius Sabinianus Julius Hospes, appears to have not only fought the war, but also negotiated these terms; he also persuaded a band of Dacians, who were preparing to join in the fighting, to settle inside the Roman frontier instead.[6]

The need of the Romans for infusions of manpower was becoming increasingly important. A group of 5,500 Sarmatians had been settled at Ribchester in Britannia as reinforcements for the Roman garrison.[7] Now 12,000 Dacians were accepted by Sabinianus. When the terms of peace with the Marcomanni and the Quadi then were finalised they included many of the same terms as those agreed with the Buri – return of deserters and prisoners, delivery of arms – and added a requirement to deliver stated quantities of grain and 13,000 Quadi and 'a smaller number' of Marcomanni, who were to be recruited into the Roman forces. They were forbidden to attack their neighbours to the north, and of course, the treaty imposed peace with the empire; as with the Buri, a strip of land along the frontier was to be left deserted and unused.[8]

The terms are those of the victors, imposed on defeated and exhausted enemies, so long as the aim of the victors had been reduced from annexation of enemy territory. When Commodus returned to Rome, he celebrated a triumph, quite rightly, even if most of the major fighting had been undertaken under his father's command. But unless the whole territory of the enemy tribes was to be annexed and occupied, there was little more the emperor could demand; there was, for example, no surplus Roman population available to occupy the whole of Bohemia, nor could the empire afford the large garrison that would be needed in the new provinces after annexation. It was a peace dictated by the victor in his own interest, using traditional Roman formulas. The only item missing was formal annexation, otherwise the conquests of Gaul and Britannia and Dacia had included much the same results – return of prisoners, surrender of deserters, the recruitment of large numbers of young men from the conquered provinces into the Roman forces, to be used on a distant frontier far away, and so not likely to take part in any rebellions at home.

In fact the terms as finally agreed were much the same as those proposed earlier by Marcus, and it is probable that it was Commodus' senatorial advisers who engineered them, at least those of his advisers who favoured making peace. There was still a voluble group who wished to go on fighting. It would seem from reports that it was Sabinianus in Dacia who had conducted the wars against the Buri and who concluded a peace with them, doing so along the lines, again, that Marcus had been pressing. Dio Cassius implies that this part of the war was conducted by Sabinianus personally, no doubt using the forces he commanded in Dacia. It was also Sabinianus who deflected the large group of Dacians who were intent on joining Rome's enemies, and who arranged for their settlement inside the imperial frontier. He would seem to have been one of the peace party.

Commodus has been accused of 'haste' in concluding this peace.[9] Yet the war lasted more than a decade, and there was a period of seven months between

Marcus' death and Commodus going to Rome after making peace. There was time for Sabinianus to conduct two campaigns against the Buri, and to conduct three sessions of negotiations with them, and for Commodus to be consulted each time and in the end to agree to the final terms. There was plenty of time also for negotiations to take place with the Marcomanni and the Quadi, and for terms to be discussed and agreed by both sides. This was not something done in 'haste', especially since the groundwork for the peace terms had been done by Marcus before he died. It is likely in fact that a good deal of time was spent in the *consilium*, arguing over whether to fight on, and on the terms of peace.

These arrangements were evidently ratified by the emperor's *consilium*, and perhaps by the larger number of senators who had gathered at the imperial headquarters at Vindobona, because that was the centre of power in the empire for the moment.[10] The *consilium's* members had apparently been appointed by Marcus as Commodus' 'guardians', which would seem to have meant his supervisors, once he realised that he was dying, and that his son was unready to be emperor.[11] The aim was presumably to continue Commodus' education, but particularly in affairs of state. How effective this group of grandees could have been once Commodus was sole emperor is not known, though one may perhaps accept that their influence was strong in the peace terms as agreed. But, as 'guardians', they had a major problem.

The emperor was very self-conscious that he was the emperor. 'I am both man and emperor,' he had announced to the parading soldiers at his *adlocutio*. That is, he was stating that his position and the power and authority attached to him did so by the fact that he was born the son of an emperor. He had after all been styled Caesar, the term now used to distinguish the heir to the throne, since the age of five, and Augustus, the term for an emperor, for the past four years. He had therefore in effect been called emperor for all his life; this can only have inflated his ego and made him impatient of advice. He must have regarded the passing of his father as a mere incident in his life, one more death of a relative, and the guardians he would see as no more than advisers, whose ideas were to be accepted or rejected as he chose. The *adlocutio*, with the soldiers on parade, was an occasion for making clear to all just how he came by all this. The soldiers, after all, saluted him as *Imperator* at the end of the meeting.

The guardians, or the *consilium*, as the historians termed it, were thus put in their place from the start. The decision for peace with the emperor's. Their only chance of prevailing against this imperial wind of power was to stand together, united and consistent in their own authority. They did not. They were divided over the issue of peace and war, other than which there could be no greater issue. And that meant that Commodus had the initiative. He went along with the war party for the campaigning season of 180, perhaps partly persuaded by the argument that the conquest was almost completed, and that to complete it would be to end the problem of the northern frontier. But he switched to the peace party in the autumn, when peace feelers came from the enemy, and when it had become clear that the war had not been completed with a grand submission of the tribes during the 180 campaigning season. In a military sense, this meant that the winter, when campaigning ceased, would be available for their enemies to recover, and the war would last at least another year. The war party was thus discredited. Peace would be made.

Commodus had been fair. He had given the war party a chance to succeed – 'one more campaign'. And he had taken the opportunity to understand the problem, and of several months' fighting, to gauge the competence and opinions of these 'guardians'. It will have been his decision to make peace, given the divisions amongst his advisors, and to decide on the terms. There is one hint that he was active in ratifying the peace. In the terms imposed on the Marcomanni, one item required them to deliver a contingent of grain to the Romans; Commodus relieved them of this obligation, no doubt partly to avoid angering the enemy even more, but also to display his own authority; he also decided not to collect 'the annual levy', which would again be a cause of anger, perhaps as a result of further negotiations, but he did so in exchange for an agreement to recruit tribesmen without conscription.[12]

The division amongst the emperor's senior advisers had wider implications than just a matter of war and peace on the frontier in the north, and depending on whether it was continued after the peace was agreed. The war party could point to the fact that fighting in the lands of their enemies continued the next year, 181, and could claim that the peace had failed. No doubt there were discontented groups amongst the tribes over whether to submit or to fight on, and the latter might well do so; defeat will have weakened the authority of the tribal leaders, who in turn may well not have been sorry to see the remaining young men carrying out unofficial raids. Commodus had prepared for this, with written instructions to the commanders on the frontier to be ready to repel raids; he was preparing to reply partly by force, and partly by treaties of alliance and many subsidies, presumably directed at sub-tribal groups, a process which would weaken chiefly authority even more. Subsidies to the chiefs would help restore their authority, but render them dependent on the empire.[13]

The soldiers had to campaign again in 181, but on a smaller scale than before, and on the frontier, not far into the tribal territory. This would exacerbate the divisions among the advisers, and no doubt it spread to the other senators who were present at Vindobona – many had automatically gravitated to the seat of imperial power. The emperor returned to Rome late in 180, reaching the city on 22 October. His reason was obvious: it was the home of the imperial government, and his presence was clearly required; as a new man in power, it was necessary that he show himself in the city, to the people, and to the Senate. But it could be, and was, portrayed as deserting the army while it was still fighting.[14]

The army in fact was also a problem in itself. The prospect of staying on the frontier for another winter while the emperor and the senators returned to the comfort and pleasures of Rome was a source of discontent, voiced in resentment at having to go on fighting for another campaigning season after the peace was agreed – no doubt the recipients of Commodus' letters had announced the fact. The men were also missing the celebrations of the triumph, which they had won by their own efforts and the deaths of their comrades. How far this was to be characterised as a mutiny is uncertain – Herodian merely calls it 'unrest' – but they did go out to fight again the next year, and most of them did miss the triumph, though most of them would have done so in any event – the whole army could not go to Rome to celebrate, so perhaps it was little more than noisy grumbling, such as would be normal in any army.[15]

In Rome, the emperor had further problems to deal with. He had triumphant progress on his journey from Vindobona to Rome, greeted by revelling crowds as he approached every town and city, celebrating both the youth and beauty of the emperor,[16] and the return of peace.[17] No doubt such acclamations went to his head; they could convince him he was much more popular than he really was. In fact, the welcome he was witnessing was more or less standard practice, not demonstrating support for him or his policies particularly, though no doubt peace was welcome. In Rome, he carried out the expected offerings and obeisances to the usual gods. But he then faced not yet another cheering and happy crowd, but the less welcome stern visages of the senators and the administrators of the empire.

These men had much longer memories and more relevant information than did the people of the towns and cities of Italy, who might see an emperor once in a lifetime, if at all. The great men in Rome knew him. Some of them had known him since he was a baby. Many of them were unhappy at the prospect of seeing him as emperor. The indecision of Marcus in his last days, and the news that the new emperor was surrounded by advice-giving guardians, had no doubt spread. The situation was guaranteed to both annoy Commodus and sap any senatorial confidence in his judgment. Marcus had in fact created a situation in which Commodus had no chance to succeed as emperor. Either he became a puppet in the hands of the guardians or he broke out of their confinement and rejected their advice; defeat would be blamed on him, victories credited to the guardians.

The general senatorial distaste for him had become clear a few years before, when Commodus had accompanied his father on a journey to the eastern provinces. Marcus was going there to settle the situation in Syria where the powerful governor, Avidius Cassius, who had had wide responsibilities for the whole east as a replacement for Lucius Verus, had rebelled. Avidius was killed by soldiers loyal to Marcus, but it was clear that Marcus had to go to see that other participants were identified, rooted out, and executed. The emperor had moved through Syria executing any man he found who had supported the rebel – a hideous lesson for the teenage Commodus.[18]

Marcus returned to Rome without the empress, who had both participated in the rebellion and supported the rebel, and had died on the return journey. He then appointed Commodus joint Augustus. By this time, Marcus in fact had little choice in the matter; it was past time he needed to acknowledge his son as his successor, especially in view of the recent rebellion. Commodus was his only surviving male child, though he had five living daughters. Family piety and practice dictated that Commodus was automatically Marcus' heir, and therefore heir to the empire. Marcus had just faced a failed rebellion by a man he had thought of as his friend; his wife had just died, under suspicion of treason. Had Avidius Cassius succeeded in gaining control of the imperial administration he would have had no choice but to order the deaths of both Marcus and Commodus, and possibly Commodus' sisters. But by making Commodus his joint emperor with the title of Augustus, Marcus was at least creating a further barrier against another usurper; in the event of another *putsch* the two would need to be separated if they were to preserve the imperial authority.

Now that Marcus was dead there was just one Augustus once again, and rebellions and plots had only a single target. And that target was widely despised within the governing group. Many of those who were with him in Rome had got to know the new emperor in the east or on the northern frontier, and they did not like what they saw. It was all very well that the people of the Italian towns might cheer him, but they only saw him; they did not know him. Those who did know him had the greatest doubts about his competence, his capacity for work, and his likely policies. And when Commodus reached Rome, with the long train of suspicious senators following him, he was moving into dangerous territory.

The danger came precisely from those senators. They included the emperor's relatives, notably his five sisters and their husbands, the two praetorian prefects, who controlled the Guard, the city prefect, and a group of men with no particular tasks, but with the prestige of one or more consulates in their past, and a series of governorships and/or military commands behind them; some of these were 'guardians'. These men, having achieved the consulship, were at a minimum twice Commodus' age, and some of them were three times that. It is hardly surprising that he found the company of sluttish young freedmen or slaves, male and female, more enticing. In his chariot in the triumphal procession celebrating his victory and peace, he was joined by Saoterus, his *cubicularius*.

Saoterus was from Nikomedia in Bithynia, a freedman, and his function in the chariot was to hold a gold wreath over the triumphator's head and tell him to 'remember thou art mortal'; in reply, Commodus is said, in one source, to have kissed him several times; at this the oldsters claimed to be shocked, though probably not at the act, but at doing so publicly.[19]

The five sisters of Commodus had been married at Marcus' direction, to a set of carefully chosen men. The firstborn child was Arria Aurelia Galeria Faustina, fourteen years older than Commodus. She was married to Cn. Claudius Severus, a distinguished commander and twice consul.[20] The next sister was Annia Aurelia Galeria Lucilla, who had been married to the Emperor Lucius Verus, and then, after his death, to Ti. Claudius Pompeianus, also a formidable commander and double consul.[21] These husbands, despite their consular careers and achievements, were a contrast in origins. Severus was from Asia Minor, the descendant of kings in that region, and had a noble Roman ancestry going back through three generations. He was part of the important aristocratic network that covered all Asia Minor, an alliance of Roman immigrant families (by now they had been domiciled there for two centuries and were extremely wealthy) and Greek and Galatian royalty. Faustina could not complain about marrying beneath her; there was scarcely a man in the empire better born than Severus. On the other hand, Pompeianus, also an easterner, from the city of Antioch, was the son of an *eques*. His name indicated that he was descended from a man who became a Roman citizen in Tiberius' reign. This ancestry appears to have angered Lucilla, daughter of an emperor and widow of an emperor.[22] However, like the marriage of Faustina, the decision was Marcus', and he had a plan.

The third sister was Fadilla, married to M. Peducaeus Plautius Quintillus, a nephew of the deceased Emperor Lucius (who had been married to her sister), consul in 177, and so now in his mid-thirties.[23] Cornificia, the fourth sister, was married to M. Petronius Sura Mamertinus, who became consul in 182. Like Pompeianus, he was the son of an *eques*, who had risen to be a praetorian prefect.[24] The youngest daughter, Vibia Aurelia Sabina, was married to L. Antistius Burrus. She had been born in 164 or 165 and was probably married to Burrus in the last year of Marcus' life, when she was fifteen or so. Her husband was another distinguished man, according to his achievements, but he was also another with a less than stirring ancestry, though he was the son of a consul; the family came from the Thibilbis in Africa, one of an increasing number of Africans reaching the consulship in this period.[25]

The lesson from this odd collection of husbands is that Marcus was doing his best to favour men he himself had raised to prominence; he appreciated their achievements and assumed that they responded with automatic loyalty to him and his family. At the same time, the less-than-noble men, Pompeianus, Mamertinus, and perhaps Burrus, would not be considered well enough born to challenge for the imperial throne, and this would cleave them to loyalty to the emperor. If this was in Marcus' mind – and it is certainly in the minds of some modern historians who are obsessed with social distinctions – it made little sense. A man's birth origin did not dictate the level of his ambition: witness Augustus, Vespasian, Hadrian and, as it happened, several of these imperial husbands, and, in the near future, Septimius Severus, Pertinax, Clodius Albinus, Pescennius Niger, and Elagabalus, none of whom could boast of a seriously lengthy Roman aristocratic ancestry, or in some cases none at all. Hadrian in the 130s had gone to a great deal of trouble to design the future inheritance of the throne, and it had worked for two generations; both Antoninus Pius and Marcus were his choices of successors. And so Commodus could be said to have been the third generation in Hadrian's plan; Marcus may have had a similar plan to extend the line further, either through Commodus, recently married, or by the children of his sisters and their husbands, who were already producing offspring. There were therefore plenty of human materials for Marcus to play with, but to expect any of his sons-in-law to pay any attention to such a scheme was to live a dream. In theory, Marcus could have done the same as Hadrian, and selected an experienced man as emperor in place of his unsuitable son, or even as joint emperor with equal powers – possibly Avidius Cassius might have filled that role, until he rebelled. But heredity was built into Roman society and to disinherit a son was hardly to be thought of; if he had done so, it may well have brought on a civil war, perhaps even before he died. Commodus was inevitable as emperor from his birth.

Commodus was married to Bruttia Crispina, a daughter of C. Bruttius Praesens.[26] She was a few years younger than Commidus, about fourteen or fifteen at her marriage. The match may have been hurriedly arranged when Marcus realised that he was dying. Her father would normally have been consul in the year of their marriage as part of the celebrations, but the list for 179 was already arranged so he had to wait until 180 for his second consulship; hence the suggestion of a speedy marriage, one perhaps unexpectedly arranged. Her family had certainly been aristocratic for the last three generations, but the evidence suggests that Commodus paid little attention to the Roman aristocracy. There is, for example, no indication that he paid much attention to her, though the marriage was clearly intended by Marcus to begin the production of the next generation of future emperors. But such plans normally fail.

If Marcus really thought that the less than exalted aristocratic birth of some of his sons-in-law would render them suitable as guardians and yet ineligible as emperors, he was wrong, as any consideration of imperial origins would have shown. Further, if he thought that a supposedly lower social rank would prevent them from feelings of ambition he was also wrong. And he was wrong in supposing, as Vespasian had shown, that it was not possible that a man descended from an *eques* father would get support in a grab for the throne. If he was really attempting to control the inheritance for the future, as Hadrian had done, his biggest mistake was to die when he did; he needed to have lasted at least another ten more years to ensure that his son grew to some maturity, and to show his fitness for the post. As it was, Commodus quickly demonstrated his unfitness as emperor, to the accumulated misery many of his aristocratic equals.

Chapter 2

Work, a Plot, and Survival

A Roman emperor had a lot of work to do. Petitions in their hundreds were addressed to him, and needed to be answered. Judgments in difficult legal cases had to be made. Consultations over internal and external crises had to take place. All of these involved the emperor. The Senate had to be heard and addressed and individual senators carefully listened to, and watched. The emperor regularly met informally with assemblies of hundreds of people, many of whom he had to greet individually. This was the *salutatio*, a regular occasion held in the atrium of the palace, a space capable of holding a thousand people; it was one of these meetings that Domitian had just concluded when he was murdered, inside the palace, in 96.

The emperor had to supervise the administration of the whole empire, beginning with his own household, in which Saoterus was his *cubicularius*; such body servants had a greater familiarity with the emperor than any attendee at any *salutation*, or any senator. Appointments to governorships, to magistracies in Rome, to commands of armies, had to be selected with extreme care, with attention paid to the appointees' capabilities and to the politics of choosing them; the emperor consulted amongst his senior administrators and the Senate in determining these posts. There was quite enough work involved in all this to swamp a conscientious ruler, or at least to fill every hour of every day – if he let it.[1]

As a result, since the work he had to attend to could easily overwhelm him, he delegated. The petitions, for example, were examined first by a staff of clerks of his household, who drafted the replies. Attending to petitions was important and if neglected could easily produce considerable unpopularity. There was a story told about Hadrian that he tried to put off the petitioner, usually described as an old woman; she replied that he should then stop being emperor.[2] That the story was also told of at least two earlier rulers in Greece is not relevant;[3] it is relevant that the accusation stung, and was remembered and repeated in an effort to ensure that later kings and emperors did their job. (It was probably a well-known saying amongst those who were all too subject to the whims and inattention of rulers.) Hence the clerks. Even then, the emperor had to read both originals and replies and indicate his approval – Commodus wrote 'Farewell' as a signature.

It is quite correct to refer to these clerks as part of the emperor's 'household', for many of them would be his own slaves or freedmen, living in the palace. The imperial bureaucracy had developed out of the emperor's personal staff, and had grown immensely in numbers under the pressure of working for an emperor, but still largely composed of slaves and free men, selected and trained from youth. This was an inevitable consequence of a slave society, and could hardly be changed so long as slavery continued. By Commodus' time, it had become embedded in Roman society, and was probably unchangeable without major governmental disruption. Also by this time there was a clear set of officials, who can be called secretaries of state. These might be *equites*, or freedmen or even slaves, but their quality and abilities were what counted.

The origin and composition of the imperial administration is important since the parallel institution of solicitation for favours, by men of all ranks in society, meant that these imperial slaves and freedman were the intermediaries between the emperor and the rest of the Roman population. This meant that caste-conscious senators had to ask freedmen for favours, a practice the former found extremely distasteful, and the latter could exploit for personal enrichment (which, of course, was in many cases the object of those doing the soliciting).[4]

Solicitations for office, from consuls to commanders of auxiliary regiments, and the concomitant selection of men to be consuls and governors, were thus almost as frequent as petitions. These posts were often, however, regulated by a system of promotion and seniority, and there were legal guides for the emperor's choices; senators, for example, were only eligible for magistracies, as praetor or consul in particular, once they had reached certain ages, and having progressed through earlier, junior, offices. Even so, there were plenty of men, up to and including senior senators, who expressed their own claims to choice offices, those in particular where they could profit financially; they were perfectly willing to ignore the legal requirements if they could benefit in doing so, but complained if someone else did. In fact, most magistracies were occupied by men as they became eligible for them. Soliciting may have been no more than pointing out their eligibility. For an emperor, the importunities of such wealthy men, often only seeking ways of increasing their wealth, and basing their demands on their social position and expectations rather than their abilities and achievements, could only become wearyingly annoying, and the perhaps less pressing attitudes of his household staff would be a distinct relief from them.

Commodus was plunged into this life as soon as he reached Rome after leaving the scene of war in the north. He had enough experience of seeing his father at work to know that this would happen, though seeing someone else doing the work was a very different matter than actually doing it himself. The evidence is that he was reasonably competent and conscientious in tackling the problems, attending regularly to the tasks and dispatching the work with reasonable promptitude. If such an argument may be addressed, the fact that they do not complain that Commodus avoided such work may be taken as a testimony that he generally attended to it, reasonably diligently. We can assume that the freedmen and secretaries did most of the actual work, but that was what they were there for; the decisions were always the emperor's.

In fact, it was not the work he did and the judgments he made that were the main problems of his reign, but the senators and their demands, requests, and complaints. These were conveyed to the emperor through the household servants, and through personal meetings at *salutationes* and imperial dinners, and whenever and however the senators and others could conjure it. It seems probable that these importuning senators sought to take advantage of the new emperor's youth and inexperience; blocking them would be a useful use of the secretaries' time. Since these were usually oral decisions, there was clearly plenty of room for corruption to set in.

The imperial office was on the edge of shifting from the consultative method of rule developed by Augustus, in which the Senate had a major role in parallel with that of the emperor, into a full-blown autocracy in which the emperors made many of the decisions that had originally been the responsibilities of the senators. The process had been gradual and had largely been a response to the need for speed and efficiency. Nevertheless, the Senate clearly understood that its powers had been constantly traversing across to the emperor. The empire required, as a necessary part of its government, an ever-larger bureaucracy to see to the detailed administration, staffed by men who had been theoretically trained to that administration, and the emperor controlled the bureaucracy.

Commodus was thus caught between the period when the old 'household' system staffed by slaves and freedmen had reached the stage where it was overburdened, and the subsequent period when the necessary reforms that professionalised the bureaucracy as a response to the pressure of work that was too great for the household system had not yet been instituted. The old system was creaking under the pressures imposed on the emperor and his limited time and attention, and was complicated by the corruption of household and Senate, which was one of the consequences. But it took a long while before the new bureaucratic system could be developed, and even then it was regarded with the same resentment as that raised by the emperor's freedmen and slaves, since clerks were of low social standing. The empire had to go through the agonies of the third-century wars before the new methods could be established. In the process, and beginning particularly with the period of the civil war at the end of Commodus' reign, the Senate would be even more comprehensively sidelined, and the senators would have fewer duties and much less power.

This change had been coming along for two centuries, and had been implicit in the imperial system ever since Augustus took power by military conquest between 42 and 30 BC. Since then each emperor had struggled with the role he had taken on, and gradually the imperial powers had expanded, his household similarly, and the tasks of the Senate were diminished. This went on until a new governmental system was so obviously required by the overloading of the old – and by Commodus' reign it was clearly reaching that point. It was expecting rather too much to expect a twenty-year-old emperor not to feel aggrieved at the unbalanced proportion of work to leisure he was now facing.

The senators, needless to say, did not like this, either the old corrupt system or the change, but the Senate was composed of several hundred ambitious men, some of whom had merely inherited their position without working for it; others, at least later in this reign, owed their membership to bribing the imperial freedmen. As a body, the Senate was rarely able to reverse the accretion of power to the emperor. The last serious attempt had been under Nerva, but this was abruptly ended by the army coup that brought Trajan to power. The Antonine emperors were generally considerate of the Senate, and did not bruise the senators' feelings too obviously, but did continue to enlarge imperial responsibilities at the Senate's expense. Commodus, however, proved to be less thoughtful, and the knowledge that the movement of power was irreversible could only lead to resentment and complaints.

It did not help that ever since the death of Augustus the issue of the imperial succession had been determined neither by the Senate, as was theoretically its duty, nor by the hereditary system, which was preferred by the emperors and was the general social expectation, but by the army, which is to say, the senior commanders of the army. This was inevitable since it was by conquest that Augustus had won power, and then he based his authority to rule explicitly on command of the army throughout the empire – *Imperator*, to be precise. Under the camouflage of the imperial household, the Senate, and the administration, the empire was, in reality, a military state. This would only be revealed by a crisis, typically a succession crisis, but it was there all the same, all the time.

Tiberius had found that the Senate, faced with the question of choosing a successor for Augustus, could not and would not decide, and forced him to, in effect, take the power of decision to himself.[5] The Senate's role from then on was restricted to accepting whoever seized the throne on the death of a predecessor. Claudius went first to the Guard, and only then to the Senate, for ratification of his coup; the Senate, that is, simply ratified the Guard's decision. In 68–69, it had taken a year-long civil war to decide who should become emperor in succession to Nero, and, though all the candidates were former consuls, their effective offices at the time were as provincial governors, and each of them used his own provincial army to stake his claim; in 96–99, civil war turned out not to be necessary, but it was the military power at Trajan's call that prevailed against the Senate's choice of Nerva. The Senate had been manipulated, by a group of its own members, into installing Nerva, a hapless aged emperor, and it then succumbed without a whimper to the mere suggestion of armed intervention; not a sword had been drawn, only a message sent from the frontier, where an army of ten legions had been gathered.[6] Since 99, the imperial succession had been determined by dying emperors, or in their names; sometimes, as by Hadrian, this only took place by killing possible contenders so as to leave one man standing. It had become all too easy for emperors to order awkward men, especially challengers, to be executed without trial – a military procedure.

So this was the way emperors had been installed, either by force (Trajan), or by subterfuge (Hadrian), or by a dying man choosing as his successor an experienced man, usually a senator, of course (Antoninus Pius, Marcus Aurelius). Until 180. For the first time in well over a century, the succession in that year went by heredity, and to an inexperienced youth. Twice before had inexperienced youths succeeded – Caligula in 37 and Nero in 54 – and only twice had the succession gone by direct heredity – Titus in 79, and Domitian in 81. In the first case, Caligula was murdered within four years; in the second, Nero's reign ended in his suicide and the civil war; in the third, Titus lasted only two years before dying, and he was followed by his brother, Domitian, but he had seized power first through army acceptance and then that of the Senate, even as his brother lay mortally ill – on the model used by Claudius.[7] Titus may or may not have indicated that Domitian should succeed him, but Domitian made the decision himself, and Domitian was eventually also murdered.

Every succession since the death of Augustus had been accomplished by a *coup d'état* of one sort or another, and frequently – seven times – by the murder of the previous emperor. There was, in fact, no recognised 'system' of succession, a consequence of the brutal seizure of dictatorial power by Augustus; he left his successors with no alternative but force. It had begun to seem as though the problem had been solved when Hadrian and then Antoninus Pius had successfully nominated their successors, and those successors had smoothly glided into power. Marcus, of course, had done the same, the difference being the succession was also by heredity, and Commodus had had no apparent difficulty in taking over the imperial office. But the previous practice by Hadrian and Antoninus had been to lay the weight of choice on experience and obvious ability, not on heredity – they certainly both had had the possibility of choosing an heir of their families. This was what was different in 180; Commodus was inexperienced, and largely unschooled for his task, but had inherited the position by hereditary 'right', and this he emphasised.[8] This had been inherent in the position of emperor since the beginning, but most emperors had had no direct heirs to whom they could pass their powers. But the assumption always was that if an emperor had a male child, that person would inherit; the hereditary principle was part of the general assumption of Roman society.

The succession of Commodus, therefore, was highly unusual. If there really was a system for selecting emperors it was by nomination by his predecessor, followed by a ratification of the choice by the Senate and the army, though that was a formality. It had also been normal to choose a successor with experience of government. Commodus had been trained by his father, to be sure, and performed adequately, but he clearly had less personal authority and very little experience in dealing with the wily, corrupt, and greedy members of the Senate; also by abandoning the war in the north he could not alternatively count on much military legitimacy, acquired via victory, except perhaps at a distance. He might do his daily administrative work conscientiously, guided by the clerks and his *consilium* members, but he had also to be a politician, making deals, smoothing down annoyed men when he could not gratify their demands, and in this, he had no skill. He had to appoint clever and able men to suitable governing positions, and it is not likely he had developed the judgment to be able to do that, though the Roman system of senators reaching an age when they were entitled to become commanders of legions of governors helped. He was also, at least late in his reign, all too ready to accept the recommendations of servants who had been bribed. As a result, he was very much in the hands of his advisers, and another result was that, due to nervousness and inexperience, he was very liable to use his executive powers to beat down opponents.

The question of the succession and how it was to be organised was dangerous, of course. Only a brief and superficial consideration of the history of the last two centuries will have demonstrated that. An hereditary system might land a country with a fool or an idiot in control, or not in control; the quasi-hereditary succession amongst the Julio-Claudians had produced Caligula and Nero, and the Severan hereditary system, if it can be called that, is a prime example of the possible consequences. And, of course, a family can die out, which usually results in a disputed succession. Yet the system the Romans had contrived had been even more disastrous. It may have produced a line of four competent emperors since Nerva had been shoved aside, but it could not be taken for granted that this would continue, and it could not be said that the succession 'system' that produced them had been either open or straightforward, still less was it predictable. The succession of Commodus is therefore best seen as a decisive shift to an hereditary succession, with all its imponderables, uncertainties, and difficulties. It has to be confessed that no method of succession – selection, heredity, election – has ever yet proved to be a guarantee of quality; any system is liable to be trumped by incompetents.

The new emperor was vulnerable and a sitting target. Commodus had no heir, other than the husbands of his sisters, and his family was less than supportive. His wife, Bruttia Crispina, gave him a link to an important senator general, and was perhaps pregnant within a year or two of the marriage,[9] but she never did produce a living child despite, it seems, more than one pregnancy. If Commodus died, or was killed, there would be no obvious successor who would be able to take control in the emergency that would inevitably follow. The most likely would be Lucilla's husband, Ti. Claudius Pompeianus, but she disliked him, and despite the consulships and considerable administration and military ability, he was an *eques* originally and came from Syria – three strikes against him, and if he were excluded, there were no obvious other candidates.

The whole of Commodus' reign was therefore a succession crisis, and as a result, the question of the succession was a constant issue during the reign; no doubt Crispina's repeated pregnancies kept everyone on edge. Not only that, but the emperor must have been conscious of the fact as well. It made him an obvious potential victim for an assassin. Crispina is known to have survived at least until 191,[10] and, despite his frequent infidelities, Commodus did not divorce her until near the end of the reign; he was clearly loyal to her, for whatever reason, and probably her to him.

Any Roman emperor lived very much in the public eye, meeting many people, holding audiences, being available. The practice had been the death of Caligula, on his way to the amphitheatre,[11] and of Domitian, in the palace returning from a *salutatio*,[12] while Claudius and Domitian both fell to a household conspiracy, as probably did Tiberius; Nero killed himself when abandoned by all, which left him obviously vulnerable to any casual killer. And now Commodus, with no successor in view, was living in public, in a corrupt and greedy court, with many senators who distrusted and detested him. And then there was his own family, probably the biggest threat of all.

Commodus' sister Lucilla had been married originally to Lucius Verus, joint emperor between 161 and 168, and the supervisor of the Parthian War. He had performed adequately there, but had also very much enjoyed himself; as a devotee of physical pleasures, he found the atmosphere and facilities in Syria more than adequate. Lucilla had not been at all pleased when, within a year of Verus' death, Marcus Aurelius had arranged for her a second marriage. Given that she had been overly conscious of her position as an emperor's wife, and had been allowed to continue with the title Augusta, which she had retained after his death, to find that she was now being married to Ti. Claudius Pompeianus was a severe blow.[13]

Pompeianus was a distinguished general, and had been consul in 162, two years before Lucilla's marriage to Verus, and for the second time in 173. The age difference between the two was perhaps thirty years. He was also, in senatorial terms, a *novus homo*, the son of an *eques*. He was, furthermore, a Syrian, though since he came from Antioch he was more probably mainly of Greek or Macedonian ancestry.[14] But all these qualities were a collection of unpleasantnesses so far as Lucilla was concerned. She opposed the marriage, as did her mother, but Marcus insisted, and it took place in 169. It seems that his purpose was to put her in a situation where she was under a husband's protection; in the event it was Pompeianus who suffered, humiliated by his wife's infidelity, contempt, and plotting. And by the time her brother became emperor, she had by no means mellowed. Her complaints were personal, above all related to her social status, but because of her political position, her complaints were magnified beyond their petty origin.

Commodus' accession should have improved her status still more, but she found that Crispina, Commodus' wife, expected to take her place as the senior lady of the court, pushing Lucilla down one stage. If Crispina was pregnant, as it seems she probably was in 181, Lucilla was going to move even further away from power. For her complaints about status were really about her lack of access to power, which related to her closeness, personal and social, to the emperor. So the personal grievances became political as well; this made Lucilla a valuable tool for others.[15]

Commodus paid no heed to her complaints. In this he was clearly being reasonable, no doubt dismissing them as complaints by a disappointed woman, a matter beneath his notice or attention, though he might have done more to conciliate his sister. There was no solution he could arrive at which did not insult someone or other he was close to – wife, sister, brother-in-law, his other sisters, several senators. So he did nothing. But Lucilla's attractions, whatever her personality and appearance, remained. She was an empress, who, if the emperor was removed, would be in a decisive position to influence the succession, and, given her poor relations with her husband, the field was wide open.

Who enlisted who in the plot that developed is not known, but the man chosen to attempt the assassination of the emperor was Ti. Claudius Pompeianus Quintianus, Lucilla's husband's nephew, and betrothed to her daughter. This would seem to identify the people who began the plot. They brought in Claudius Ummidius Quadratus, born the son of Cn. Claudius Severus, brother-in-law of Commodus, by an earlier marriage. Severus was a highly distinguished general and governor; his son had been adopted by M. Ummidius Quadratus, consul in 167; Severus was probably originally married to Ummidius' sister. The younger Quadratus is also credited as one of Lucilla's lovers. The plot, being limited to a few closely related people, had in fact therefore begun very well, since none of these were likely to leak the plot to outsiders.

Lucilla therefore had collected a set of ambitious men around her, supposedly being mistress to one of them, of course – but all historians and critics of these events were male, so how accurate such reporting was is not clear. The plot was formed and her discontent fuelled their's. They may have discussed who the successor would be, but it is virtually guaranteed that whoever was chosen would not last long. They may have included Quadratus' adoptive father for the role of replacement emperor, but equally possibly, they may not have got quite so far. The executant was to be Quintianus. It does not seem that Lucilla's husband was involved. Maybe he had already withdrawn to his country estate, where he is known to have stayed for much of the next ten years,[16] though it is possible that part of Lucilla's ambition was to make it seem that he was in the plot.

The procedure of plotting against the emperor was now well understood. First, a small group of malcontents was assembled, a successor was nominated, and an executant was chosen (who was actually disposable, being very liable to be killed in the process, or in the immediate aftermath). Then some men in public office were to be brought in, preferably praetorian prefects who had force at their disposal, and who commanded the Guard around the emperor; in this case one of the prefects is directly accused of being part of the plot. How much wider the plot extended is not known, but at least some senators were probably involved, as Herodian states. It seems that the presence and power of the *cubicularius* Saoterus was one of the grievances that propelled men into the plotters' camp.

All these elements had been familiar in such plots since at least the assassination of Caligula and had reappeared in the murder of Domitian, and in the plots against Nerva, and no doubt in later plots, most of which had not succeeded. The problem for the plotters, of course, was that the emperor and his guards also knew the procedure, and could take measures to disrupt or counter it. The only possible method of succeeding for the plotters therefore was to keep the number small and act so suddenly and quickly that the Guard and the emperor could not react in time to prevent the assault. That was the crucial part. For if they failed to kill the emperor, the whole plot automatically failed, and retributions would follow.

And this was what happened. The executant Quintianus concealed himself in the tunnel leading into the amphitheatre, dark and with niches where he could be concealed. (Shades of the killing of Caligula.) It was late in the year, probably December, and Quintianus was wearing a dark cloak, which allowed him to conceal his weapon. His eyes will have adapted to the darkness, whereas those coming into the tunnel from the bright daylight had their sight perception reduced. So far so good. The narrowness of the tunnel compelled the royal procession to spread out along the tunnel. It was probably a fairly informal group, but it certainly included armed praetorians, or possibly men from other units. Conditions were thus perfect for a suicide mission by the perpetrator.

The emperor entered the tunnel. Quintianus sprang out, with his dagger in his hand. He shouted 'This is what the Senate has sent you', and waved the dagger. This was the theatrical gesture that guaranteed his failure. The emperor could react defensively, probably by turning away and retreating, and the guardsmen could react in the other way, by attacking the attacker.[17]

Retributions followed the failure. The plot has been often blamed on the petty social complaints of Lucilla, her quarrel with Crispina, her lovers, her dislike and disdain for her husband, her social complaints, and all these were part of it. But for the serious political players involved all this was no more than a set of unimportant pretexts. The men involved were using her and her petty complaints as a vehicle for planning the assassination. Her high social position inevitably attracted the ambitious and the discontented, and she was known to be herself discontented and ambitious. Some of those who were gathered in were ambitious to attempt to succeed the emperor, and his death was the only way they could see to realising that ambition. Some were resentful at the prominence of freedmen and slaves in the imperial household and administration, and assumed that the killing of the emperor would change that; if they were supporters of the plot, they might expect rewards. Some focused specifically on the influence of Saoterus, which was assumed to be bad, though this was an assumption based on social prejudice, not necessarily on close acquaintance. Some were annoyed that the Marcomanni War had been abandoned, as they may have thought it unfinished.

A great deal of this was hardly new. Much of this anti-Commodus attitude had actually originated under Marcus, who could not have been the easiest emperor to serve. He had relied, like Commodus and like his predecessors, on freedmen and slaves as his administrators. He had been the one to set out the terms of peace that the Marcomanni and the other German tribes eventually agreed with Commodus, which some resented as being less than a clear victory. Lucilla's resentment dated further back, to her second marriage, enforced by her father, with the intention of providing her with powerful male protection, which he assumed that an imperial widow would require. Commodus had continued his father's policies, social, administrative, military, familial, under the guidance of the surviving members of the old man's *consilium*, of whom Pompeianus, his brother-in-law, was a prominent member.[18] Therefore, he reaped the accumulated resentments of Marcus' reign, to which was added some generated by the new emperor himself. The news of his accession had been greeted in many parts of the empire with public celebrations of pleasure.[19] This was in part the expected reaction, and so in part the formal one, but it would also be partly due to his making peace, partly to his youth after two rather elderly emperors, but mainly because it was naïvely assumed that matters would improve simply because there was a new emperor. So one more of the resentments at Commodus as emperor was probably that they did not change.

These problems had been already clear with the rebellion of Avidius Cassius in 175. In the aftermath, Marcus, with Commodus at his side, and while proclaiming that he would not order the killing of any senators involved in the rebellion, had not flinched at killing others who had failed to act against Cassius when he rose in rebellion. Such a 'campaign' could only deepen the resentment, particularly in the army, since most of those victims were military men, particularly, it seems, centurions. (This item is regularly omitted in accounts, both ancient and modern, but the *Historia Augusta* includes it.)[20] But to blame them for accepting orders, or for simply staying at their posts under a usurper, was to damage the established military command system, as well as to fail to investigate adequately the response of those deemed guilty, presumably without a trial. And any senators involved were thus shielded.

This was the pattern of behaviour that Commodus had seen in action under his father, the revered philosopher king, in Syria. It is not surprising that he reacted to treachery in his family in the same way. The two praetorian prefects may or may not have been involved in the original plot, but in either case, they now had no option but to root out all the plotters and all the plot's ramifications. They had the assassin Quintianus, who had been captured, and was probably tortured into volubility. Quadratus, the potential new emperor, and Quintianus were both executed. Lucilla was exiled to Capri, and later executed.[21] They could hardly have expected any lesser punishment. (Nerva had faced down Calpurnius Piso, and then exiled him to Tarentum, whence he returned to Rome in the new reign and plotted against Trajan, who exiled him more rigorously. Hadrian did not wait to be threatened; he had Piso killed within a few months of his accession; it did not pay to be lenient in such a case.) Several people who were probably of the households of one or other of these executed people were also killed; presumably they had known of the plot and had not revealed it.

Quintianus had implicated the Senate by his words as he waved his dagger, but he was regrettably unspecific. This was where the praetorian prefects entered the business. It seems that P. Tarrutienus Paternus was the leading investigator, but the prefects' involvement in the plot is claimed by the *Historia Augusta* alone, not necessarily reliable on all details, and avid for scandal;[22] the other sources for the period, Cassius Dio and Herodian, raise no such accusation.

Paternus' investigations were not very successful. This may be because he was part of the original plot, and was protecting his co-conspirators; alternatively, he was attempting to avoid making too many accusations, hoping that the number of those to be punished would be limited, and disruption minimised. The larger the number of victims, the more longlasting and wider the resentment.[23] He and his colleague Sex. Tigidius Perennis identified Saoterus as a major issue, and decided that by removing him they would remove a major irritant in the body politic. He was decoyed to a sacrifice by the two men, but then murdered by some soldiers who were not of the Guard, in the hopes of the prefects avoiding responsibility. So says the *Historia Augusta*; Cassius Dio lays the blame directly on Saoterus' successor in office, Cleander; the case in the *Historia* makes this the more credible.[24]

Needless to say, this further blow to the emperor – he was said to be more angry over Saoterus' killing than by the original plot – had further ramifications. Perennis betrayed Paternus to the emperor, accusing him of involvement in the plot, and perhaps laying the blame for Saoterus' death on him as well. In order to remove him from the protection of the guardsmen, he was promoted to senatorial rank by adlection, then arrested and executed as a conspirator; his promotion had made him vulnerable.[25] No doubt, he fully understood this and yet acquiesced. This political plot also saw the emergence of Cleander, another freedman, into prominence as an imperial favourite, but for the next couple of years it was Perennis whom the emperor mainly trusted; he remained as praetorian prefect, but without a colleague.

The removal of Paternus meant a more rigorous search for members of the original assassination plot, if only for Perennis to demonstrate his own innocence of everything. Two main locations emerged as problems and centres involved in the plot: Rome and Syria. Rome is hardly surprising, since that was where Commodus was, and where the known plotters lived, and where the senators could gather and talk. The guilty were thus more widely identified: besides Paternus, Vitruvius Secundus was a close colleague of the emperor, as his *ab epistulis*; by his position he was no doubt able to intercept and so ignore any warning messages; P. Salvius Julianus, a former governor of Germania Superior and probably other provinces, and consul,[26] had betrothed his son to Paternus' daughter, and the whole family were assumed to be involved and were executed. This was not necessarily direct proof of involvement, but if Paternus was executed, the whole family had to be executed as well, in order to prevent feuds festering for years – a Roman legal practice. Sex. Quintilius Condianus and his brother Maximus[27] were tried and executed; their sons were therefore also condemned, though one of them, Condianus' son, went on the run for some time – eventually, he was probably found and killed. He was accused of aiming in this period to foment a rebellion in Syria, so it is likely that he was not being hunted and condemned merely for being his father's son.[28]

This brings in the Syrian connection, for Condianus was on duty in Syria at the time of his condemnation. This was a restless province, having been the host to the army in the Parthian war, and having seen the failed usurpation of Avidius Cassius, also a Syrian, and the punishments meted out to those deemed involved. The city of Antioch had received a collective punishment, which left it aggrieved. D. Velius Rufus, a senator from Heliopolis, was executed; he had been consul in 178.[29]

P. Salvius Julianus the younger was involved in some way, and he and his father were executed, the latter for the same reason that Paternus' relatives were. But it may be that the elder Salvius did know something of the plot and chose not to say anything; this would be construed as guilt, just as Vitruvius Secundus was probably involved. Egnatius Capito may well have been the most prominent victim of the purge, after Salvius Julianus. He had been consul in the early 170s and *magister* of the Arval Brethren in 176. He was executed but no indication survives of how he was involved in the plot.[30]

L. Aemilius Iuncus, from Tripolis in Syria, and M. Atilius Severus were both exiled. They were consuls in 183 and their punishment was presumably for not detecting and preventing the plot, or possibly for not pursuing those involved with sufficient rigour.[31]

The anti-Commodus historians imply that many more died.[32] But no names are mentioned. This might mean that they were not prominent enough to be noted, and so were beneath consideration; or it might be that the wider accusations were merely rhetorical, to cover the possibility – the probability – that the historians did not know them by name, but simply assumed many more were killed. Ignoring this vagueness, therefore, and considering only what is actually known, the cull was notably light. Most of those killed were actually involved, numbering eight senators (plus five named non-senators), and two others (the consuls) were exiled – plus Lucilla, exiled then executed. It is clear that all those executed were either certainly involved or were close relatives of those involved, which in the Roman system condemned them. It is thus a relatively small number who were punished.

On the other hand, those who were punished were prominent men, and senators. It may have been the case that it was also a family plot, but the presence of senators may well have been at the base of Commodus' disdain for senators as a class, and for the Senate as a political colleague.

Chapter 3
Commodus' System

The defeat of the plot to kill the emperor brought the destruction of the group of experienced men, the guardians, who had been set about Commodus by his father. The executions removed the most prominent men of the group and silenced, scattered, or intimidated the rest; the involvement of Lucilla further convinced Commodus that he could not trust his own family. He turned once more to Saoterus, and then, when he failed and was assassinated, to Perennis, who may have had the main part in bringing down both Saoterus and Paternus.

The office held by those men – Paternus, Perennis, and the later Cleander – was that of praetorian prefect. In theory, this was the office of the commander of the Praetorian Guard, but it had developed in the last two reigns into an administrative and legal role. Paradoxically, it had then shed some of its military baggage, but had gained considerably in prestige and authority. The prefect – there were in fact normally two of them, but the second was often much less visible than the first – thus reinforced the emperor's power, by taking over some of the emperor's duties, which had probably become too much for one man, and yet they still commanded the Guard. This was thus one of the changes that had been taking place in the administrative system.

Commodus' appointments were therefore not always soldiers, implying that military command was no longer an essential requirement for the post. It is characteristic of a dual office like this that one of the officers was more influential than the other, and several of those who held the office under Commodus are little known, and were easily dispensed with; and, of course, Perennis held the office alone for two years. This office was clearly a major centre of power even without the emperor's overt support.[1]

The actual individual players in the game of power were usually less important than the general situation that had resulted from the plot's failure. The emperor had been frightened – he was still only twenty years old – and had lost faith in those who had been closest to him, family and senior senators alike, and in fact in any senators. As a result, the centre of power now lay decisively with the court, even more clearly than before. These were the people living in the palace alongside, and serving, the emperor, consisting of freedmen, freedwomen, slaves, and concubines. These, especially the *cubicularius*, controlled access to the emperor, which meant that they excluded many of the senators – though this was clearly the emperor's decision. By extension, this also meant that the palace had become the imperial government, with the praetorian prefects passing out orders in the emperor's name to the provincial governors and the commanders of the armies. In the city and facing the Senate, the prefect and his Guard held obvious power, which was added to that of the palace staff. Indeed, Commodus appointed one prefect out of that staff.

This change, of course, could only have happened because Commodus allowed it, or willed it. He had always been lazy, at least intellectually, addicted to play and pleasure, so that it was easy for his staff to take the lead in affairs and lift the weight off his shoulders, especially when it was the praetorian prefect who took up the burden. But Commodus knew what was happening. He had seen how his father had worked, administering the Roman system, and he had attempted in his first couple of years as emperor to do the same, prodded on by the circle of old men around him. He knew what was expected of him. Having been betrayed and threatened by them, he ceased to attend to their advice, or to that of the Senate, placing his trust in the men he appointed as praetorian prefects. This, which may have been a condition of affairs that had developed gradually over decades, was nevertheless Commodus' decision. It marked a decisive shift in the imperial government system, pushing the Senate even more into powerlessness.

Such evidence as exists shows that the emperor was fully involved in governmental decisions and administration, at least in the major issues, such as the construction of the annual consular list, the main law cases, and decision on the military campaigns. He was, of course, no expert in any of these matters, which might have been his excuse for leaving them to the governors and prefects. At least he made no attempt to command in war, sensibly leaving that to the experienced commanders, with some success. This was a division of tasks – between major decisions taken by the emperor, and mere administration by his staff – which was one that had developed ever since Augustus. It was not necessarily a matter of the emperor neglecting his duties.

The effects of the situation in Rome was of little importance and effect on the rest of the empire, at least at first. The administration of the empire continued. Problems on the frontier – there were frontier wars in Britannia until 184, in the Balkans in 185 and 189, and in North Africa – were dealt with by the provincial governors, with adequate support from Rome, resulting in clear Roman victories.[2] This, of course, was also the usual condition of responsibilities. A mutiny in Britannia was solved by the imperial reception in Rome of a large delegation of mutinous soldiers. The *cubicularius* Cleander (an old boyhood friend of Commodus') used the situation to convince the emperor that the problem lay in large part with the praetorian prefect Perennis; he was the object of the soldiers' ire also, and Commodus calmed them by simply handing him over to the soldiers to be killed. The governor Ulpius Marcellus was also blamed, and put on trial for the crime of letting the soldiers become undisciplined, which gave him his reputation for harshness in particular. The cause of the mutiny is not recorded. Cleander surely took this as a lesson and a warning.[3]

It is evident that Commodus was gullible, easily influenced, liable to make important decisions based on poor evidence, such as Cleander's accusation against Perennis, and was fearful of further plots emanating from the Senate and the court. Hence came his promotion of Cleander to praetorian prefect a couple of years after discarding Perennis; the intervening prefects were of little account because they did not last long enough to master the office. And yet it was still the emperor who made the crucial decisions, and here he clearly maintained his grip on affairs. It was his decision to cause the purge of his senior advisers and his family in 182, and it was his decision to have the soldiers kill Perennis as a palliative to their mutiny. And it was also his decision to erect a barrier of freedmen officials between him and the senators and *equites* who by their rank in society claimed the right to have access to him and advise him.

The three men who operated as praetorian prefects for Commodus – at least those three who clearly wielded substantial power, Paternus, Perennis, and Cleander – demonstrated that the court, when allied with the Praetorian Guard commanders, was a very potent source of power, quite independent of the other centres of power in the empire, including the Senate, and even including the emperor, if he was negligent or absent, or if he deliberately ignored the prefects' activities.

Commodus' regime from 182 onwards was revealing a possible new distribution of power in the empire in which the court dominated effectively over the Senate, sometimes in alliance with the plebs (who could be organised in several ways). Until Marcus' reign the balance had been fairly even between emperor and Senate, though the events of 68–69 and 98–99 had suggested a predominance for the emperor in combination with the army; but the emperors from Nerva onwards had been restrained, and had operated the system that emerged from the civil war of 68–69, and the balance continued. Commodus, by contrast, deliberately allowed the court to grow in power at the Senate's expense. He had set in train a major power shift, but also a contest that lasted for the next century between these authorities.

The precariousness of the situation, and its tentativeness, however, was evident when the emperor casually discarded his praetorian prefects – he got through at least a dozen in his reign, but the three notable ones held office for seven of those years. The death of Perennis did not change the system Commodus had thus set up. By his plots, Perennis had removed and succeeded Paternus, who had earlier removed Saoterus, and it was Cleander's plot that removed Perennis, and who then took his place for the next several years. It was evidently an unstable system in Commodus' unsteady hands, though it worked effectively on and off for a decade. It also cut out those who presumed themselves to be entitled to advise the emperor. For a time this might be acceptable, but not in the long term.

The Roman politico-governmental system was flexible within certain limits. The essential point to note is that there were several loci of power within it. Normally, under a skilled emperor, such as Commodus' father, these elements worked in harmony – though even Marcus Aurelius had his problems, largely brought on by his command in the German Wars, which removed him from Rome for years at a time. This was one thing Commodus clearly learned, and he made it his business to stay in the city, which, given his lack of military training or experience, made sense, leaving the conduct of wars to his generals. And yet, though he was in Rome all his reign, he made himself almost as unapproachable as his father on the frontier – and his father had been accessible there for senators who chose to make the journey.

The emperor was the main centre of power, of course, but he was limited in the range and extent of his powers by dint of his physical limitations – that is, his power depended to some degree on his personality, his office, and his presence. It was here that the growth in authority of the praetorian prefect was so crucial, since it magnified the imperial authority, and provided legal and administrative expertise, which individual emperors would not necessarily possess. Commodus' praetorian prefects were clearly capable men, able to make the administration system work, and that applies to Paternus, Perennis, and Cleander.[4] Physically and crudely the emperor's power relied, as Augustus had shown, on his command of the army – hence the emergence of the prefects, commanders whose unit, the Praetorian Guard, was stationed in or close to the city when the emperor was there, and who therefore worked in Rome with the emperor. And yet the army, or armies, could act as distinct centres of power themselves, either in defiance of the emperor, or, if there was not one, autonomously.

But armies would not do this without being moved into action by their commander. They might mutiny, but really the issue would be less political than personal to the soldiers – shortage of pay, for example, or lack of provisions, or an unpopular commander – it was not normally a question of power for them. This was nevertheless another, multiple, centre of power for the commanders of the armies of the empire, and others were also the governors of provinces with authority over the army included. Such men might command several legions and auxiliary regiments, and govern one or more large and rich provinces. Marcus had faced a major rebellion by Avidius Cassius, governor of Syria and over-governor of the eastern provinces, in which office he controlled half a dozen legions and the equivalent in auxiliary regiments – no man who was not emperor was ever allowed such power again. The British army was three legions strong, other frontier provinces had two, Dacia had three, and in each case there was an auxiliary force of the same strength. The governors-cum-commanders of these provinces or groups of provinces were power brokers only a little less potent than the emperor – if they chose to exercise that power. In the last century or so, emperors were propelled into power at Rome from armies in Syria (Vespasian), Germany (Vitellius), and Spain (Galba), and the ancestor of the present dynasty (Trajan) had been hoisted to power by the commanders of that huge ten-legion army in Pannonia.

The most obvious alternative source of power, in addition to the emperor and the army, was the Senate. Of course, all these institutions overlapped, the emperor appointed senators as the governors and army commanders, and appointed the consuls and the subordinate senatorial officials (and therefore the members of the Senate), and had been a senator himself in most cases. (Commodus was the first emperor since Nero who had not been a senator before reaching the throne.) The senior senators theoretically had the right to see and speak to the emperor, and some, those who were patricians, could constitute his *consilium*, his council of advisers, by right of social rank. The Senate as a body had a big role in the government system, composed as it was of men who had plenty of experience in the empire's problems, and its members were the obvious men to be chosen to be provincial governors and army commanders, and to control various departments of the administration. It had a role as a court of law, which linked it with the emperor and the praetorian prefect, who also had a legal role. All this gave the Senate great authority, but it was not, as a collective institution, directly involved in the government of the empire, though, as noted, individual senators were. It had always delegated that function to the consuls and praetors, governors, and the emperor. Its real authority was negative, a matter of criticism, or after-action approval, often after the fact. This gave emperors the real power of action; the Senate could therefore only influence and criticise, which did not make for popularity with emperors.

The Senate was thus liable to complain loudly at something the emperor might do that displeased the senators, and any emperor subjected to loud senatorial complaints would be wise to pay attention. As the power of the imperial court grew, the senators were the only group who could voice informed criticism of imperial policies; there were always senators who had experience of every province and in every department. The only other source of potent criticism was the Roman crowd, or mob, whose conduct, particularly at the games, could constitute a major source of disapproval. And, of course, the crowd could always be manipulated by an interested party – by employing a claque to shout prearranged and rehearsed, and sometimes lengthy, slogans, for example.

The emperor, the Senate, and the army were linked in the operation of the Roman political system. The greatest weight of decision lay with the emperor, now magnified by the staff of the court, and here was the source of power that was exploited by Commodus, and had grown. The court's senior members were employed by the emperor as his agents and messengers. This was not new, for such men of the court had been employed in such ways ever since Augustus' time. The Senate had repeatedly expostulated about these men, who were seen as intruding on senatorial powers, but the emperors had found them necessary, and more likely to be loyal, since they depended on imperial favour exclusively, than the soldiers, who might flaunt their freedom to disobey or oppose. Therefore, the court's members were not a real problem for any emperor who was fully in control of his court.

Commodus, however, was quite willing to see his court become a source of power. He steadily ignored the Senate, and the senators' repeated complaints, employing his *cubicularius* (this was Cleander's initial post) to prevent the senators reaching him. He was, consciously or not, setting up a new governmental system, an open autocracy such as had hardly been seen since Augustus' victory in the civil war that finished off the Republic, but had been cloaked by that emperor by his enlistment of the (purged) Senate as his 'partner' in government. This development had been hinted at now and again with some of the more impatient emperors – Gaius, for example, or Domitian – but it had been more comfortable for most emperors to revert to, and exploit, the by now traditional system developed by Augustus; if it operated as intended the Senate could act as an extension of the emperor's powers. Commodus was thus replacing the Senate in this role by his palace staff under the praetorian prefects, and maintained this version of imperial powers for a decade, which was unprecedented. He was pointing the way to the autocracy which emerged from the disturbances of the third century.

The Senate, of course, did not like this alternative government system, though criticism was couched in the traditional complaints of the past. Commodus did show that it would be possible to rule the empire by means of the members of the court, so long as the appointed governors or army commanders could be relied on, even though they were senators. Such men were often eager for such posts, for many reasons, including the responsibility of power and the chance of acquiring wealth, increased prestige, even though this now depended directly on the emperor, and less so than on their position in the senatorial ranks. This is evidently the origin of the claim in the *Historia Augusta* that Cleander promoted freedmen to the Senate, recalled and rewarded exiles, and the appointment of twenty-five consuls in a single year.[5] This is interpreted as Cleander's corruption at work, but one might alternatively note that he may well have been selecting able men rather than unimportant senatorial nonentities. But the rise of the court also opened the way for such offices to be filled by non-senators. The next generation boasts examples of the position of emperor filled by the son of a freedman, by an *eques*, and by a child-priest from Syria, and women exercising the imperial power on behalf of their children. Eventually, under a later emperor, senators would even be forbidden to command armies, at least in theory; but that was after a long generation of civil warfare. Cleander, for example, used P. Helvius Pertinax to solve the problem of the British war-cum-mutiny, and to deal with disturbances in Africa; he was not a man who earlier would normally have been so employed.

The interest of members of the Senate in their ability to gain unrestricted access to the emperor was partly altruistic, in that they existed, as senators, to serve the empire, to govern and defend it, and at times to extend it (and, of course, exploit it). Since it was the emperor who appointed them to provincial and military commands, it was reasonable to solicit such appointments. But they had personal interests as well. It was from the emperors that they could solicit favours which would increase their influence and their wealth, and through whom they might extend their access to offices of power, to patronise others and to build a useful political clientele, which would be a source of greater influence, just as the rise of the court power increased the emperor's heft.

Probably most senators did not distinguish between their own mixed motives, and often one aspect was hardly more important than the other, but it was one of the ways the empire functioned, and when Commodus began to ignore the senators he was reducing his ability to influence and order events. He handed the task over to his servants in the court, whose judgment might, like that of the senators, be more personal than public spirited – that is, they were notoriously open to bribery; Cleander apparently simply sold public offices, a subtle distinction from 'bribery', since the product mostly went to the treasury, not into his bank account.[6] Abdicating his imperial responsibility by the emperor had adverse effects on many aspects of the empire, down to the ordinary citizens and peasants who might be subject to oppression.

In a sense, the selection of provincial governors could be a near automatic process, since as they took up the succession of offices – the *cursus* – senators became steadily more entitled to greater responsibility, or one might say, they had become equipped to take on particular governmental tasks. In any one year there was a fairly limited number of senators who had the seniority and experience to assume such jobs, and those who made it clear they did not wish to be considered for them, for whatever reason – illness, political enmity, weariness, distaste –

would reduce the number further. It did not need the emperor to decide who would take up particular positions, and indeed it is likely that the bureaucracy worked out well in advance who could do particular jobs and suggested a list to the emperor, for his approval; in many cases it may have been only one name – Pertinax, for example, seems to have been the personal choice of Cleander for Britain and for Africa, a choice no doubt validated by Commodus. The change caused by the rise of the court therefore was in many cases minimal, except that it excluded representations from senators hoping to score points against their fellow senators and jump the queue, so to speak. The fact that senators as a group did not like the new system does not necessarily mean that it was not both efficient and effective. It could cater for emergencies such as that in Britain in the early 180s, when a war broke out and the experienced Ulpius Marcellus had to be sent to the province as emergency governor – and then Pertinax had to be sent there to sort out the mess Marcellus produced.

This is not to say that the general policy of the empire was left to the court. Commodus may have dispensed with some irritating and time-consuming meetings with individual senators, but he did not dispense with advice. His *consilium* still met and could include a variety of experienced and distinguished senators, but they were there because of their experience and ability – military, governmental, political – not because they were members of the Senate; indeed the praetorian prefects were surely members of this group, and none of them in Commodus' reign were senators. The membership of the *consilium* fluctuated, as ever, and may have included men who were expert in some aspect of policy – Britannia, for example, or finance, or Syria and relations with the Parthians. The main point, however, is that the *consilium* existed, in whatever form, and met and advised throughout the reign. It was one of the most flexible parts of the system. In a sense the men who had been put around Commodus by his father were his original *consilium*, but Commodus found them too overbearing, and no doubt they were arrogant and all too insistent that they knew better than the stripling emperor. Once he had got rid of this group, he could at least enlist his own men – and if they included freedmen and servants that was his choice.

Some of these men were family, but this, as the plot in 182 had shown, could not guarantee that they were his supporters. The power and influence of Cleander was inevitably regarded as dangerous. The emperor's brother-in-law, L. Antistius Burrus, husband of his youngest sister Sabina, and ordinary consul in 181 alongside the emperor, was still in the *consilium* when Cleander held power, suggesting that this body was fairly stable in membership. He emerged as the leading critic of Cleander amongst the group. And yet Burrus' career is a blank except for his marriage and his consulship in 181. Since he had been selected as Sabina's husband by Marcus, we may assume he had some achievements to his credit, but they are unknown.[7]

The quarrel between Burrus and Cleander was centred on Cleander's custody of monies collected in taxation. Some may have been siphoned off into Cleander's pockets, or it may just have been simply a shortage; the finances of the empire were primitive, and expenses were heavy at the time, but it is clear that Commodus' imperial finances were benefiting from Cleander's distribution of the tax money, and that he knew well how Cleander was operating. The dispute gradually involved others. An ally of Cleander, P. Helvius Pertinax, whose languishing political career Cleander had rescued, was the agent who levied accusations against Burrus – the charge was that he aimed for the throne.[8] The emperor judged the case, though it is not certain that he was fully aware of the intrigue that had lain behind it. He judged Burrus guilty and ordered his execution, and that of others who had supported him, including later another senator, Arrius Antoninus, who appears to have developed a legal case against Cleander. To do so in the circumstances was to accuse the emperor.

Commodus must be seen as correct here, for to accuse the emperor of peculation and financial dishonesty, however indirectly, was to threaten his position; such an accusation was lethal, though given the distribution of power between the two men it was inevitably lethal for the accuser. It is notable that, despite this, Commodus' reply to the threat was by means of a legal decision, not a sudden strike. The issue was political, and perhaps the judgment was expected, but Commodus here was not acting outside the legal system.

This result would suggest that Cleander had convinced Commodus that the problem was not only a quarrel between two officials, but consisted in a threat to Commodus personally. This would mean that Sabina was being used as a vehicle to threaten him. But again, Commodus' reply was relatively moderate: Sabina was not executed, as Lucilla had been five years before, but she was married off to a man of less than stellar ancestry – L. Aurelius Agaclytus, an *eques* who was the son of a freedman, who had earlier been married to Fundania, the widow of a consul. Sabina went, or was sent, to live at Thibilis in Africa, her former husband's home town, where she was generous and received numerous honorary inscriptions from the community.[9] The choice of her new home was clearly a statement of support for her first husband, and an implicit criticism of the emperor. Where Agaclytus lived is not known, but Sabina was apparently safe. At that distance from Rome, she was apparently judged to be no threat to Commodus – and of course she had probably had nothing to do with the quarrel.[10]

Commodus was especially nervous of threats at the time because he had faced another the year before. An internal war in Gaul, the 'Deserters' War', had lasted for several years and had finally been brought to almost complete suppression by 186. This suppression was a useful case study in the ability of the imperial government under Commodus and Cleander to cope with a difficult issue. Many of the 'deserters' were clearly trained soldiers, and had a capable leader, Maternus, an ex-legionary who had been decorated for bravery. They operated in central Gaul and spread confusion from the Rhine to Spain. It was the sort of war that grew only slowly in the governmental consciousness; no doubt, this was seen at first as only a minor local problem. Maternus' deserters were joined by other malcontents, criminals and desperate peasants, and he broke open jails to recruit more. With no fixed base – Maternus collected quantities of loot, which was then quickly distributed among his followers – he was difficult to catch.

Spreading through several provinces the rebels were no doubt successful in foxing the Roman reply for a time, since provincial governors were forbidden to operate beyond their borders. The provinces of Gallia Lugdunensis, Narbonensis, and Aquitania were thinly garrisoned and so were vulnerable to such an unorganised horde. In the end, though, the several governors learned to cooperate, perhaps having gained imperial permission to cross boundaries. In Lugdunensis was L. Septimius Severus, praetor in 178 after a fairly slow career; in Narbonensis was L. Fabius Cilo, who later was a notable supporter of Severus; in Belgica or one of the German provinces was D. Clodius Albinus, fresh from a successful governorship in Dacia. And with a roving commission in command of an *ad hoc* force of auxiliaries and volunteers was Pescennius Niger, an *eques*, who was adlected to praetorian rank as a result of his prowess in this war. Not only is this an interesting collection of future emperors, rivals, and imperial contenders, but their cooperation was successful in containing the rebellion.[11]

Maternus, however, was a clever, one may say inventive, commander, and had another trick available. After the apparent defeat of the main body, the surviving rebels infiltrated in small groups through Italy to Rome with the aim of murdering the emperor during the Hilaria festival in March 187, when he would be out among the crowds. Normally Commodus felt – and was – safe amongst the people, with whom he was always popular. The plot was betrayed by some of the infiltrators and suppressed relatively easily,[12] but Commodus could no longer think of public crowds without thinking of the danger they might pose, and this was now added to the dangers from his family and from the Senate. Paranoia had a convincing cause. His new fear of crowds, of course, played into the hands of his court, notably Cleander, who was made praetorian prefect in that year (187).

The senators may have been discontented at the behaviour of the emperor, and at the power he had permitted his court to wield, but they could have no real complaints about their access to the highest office, that of consul. These were recruited from the same set of men who had taken up the office for the previous two centuries. The *ordinarii* – Commodus held seven of these posts during his reign, not an inordinate share, leaving seventeen for the rest of the aristocracy – were mainly men whose ancestry had been senatorial. Nine of their seventeen *ordinarii* had three ancestors or more who had been consuls, two had two consular ancestors, and one had one; one of the consuls, M'. Acilius Glabrio, traced his consular ancestry back to the old Republic.[13] Four consuls cannot be classified in this way, but two others had risen through the *cursus* of *equites* to consul. This is, if anything, an unusually heavy balance towards the most aristocratic of senators, Commodus' social equals, in fact, who were evidently being favoured.[14]

We have the names of all twenty-four *ordinarii* for Commodus' reign. Of the suffect consuls, however, we have less information. Only eighteen can be assigned to a particular year, but thirty-one more are known to have held the office in Commodus' reign, though the exact dates are unclear for them, but most can be assigned to a short period of two to four years. There are thus forty-nine suffects known by name, but sixteen of these are no more than names, with no further information about their lives and careers. This is not unusual by this time: they were likely to be promoted *equites*, or *novi homines*, but the loss of their careers and offices is unfortunate. Of the identifiable men, two suffects had two ancestors of consular rank, and eight had at least one; four were originally *equites*; eight certainly appear to be new men, who had worked their way through the *cursus*, though their earlier posts are not known.

This distribution of officials by their ancestry is very like that of every other reign, at least in the century since the civil war of 68–69. Consuls were always a selection of men which included, as expected, a high proportion of those who could insist on their right to hold at least one consulship because of their ancestry, and of those appointed to consular office, more than half were *ordinarii*, the most prestigious post. At the same time, it was the duty of emperors – who were responsible for constructing the consular list every year, at least formally, though it was probably done by their staff – to bring forward men of talent and accomplishment who had demonstrated that they were capable, above all in provincial governorships, of holding military or civil offices; the promotion of Pescennius Niger, an *eques*, to an adlected praetor, is a good example. These were men who might be termed *novi homines*, and most had no known consular ancestors, and might be of *eques* rank, but of equal capability with any aristocrat. These were men who might be the ancestor of a future aristocratic family – there were at least two such families founded by a consul in Commodus' reign, the Ragonii and the Triarii.[15]

So we may say that the consular list of Commodus' reign were fully in accord with the expectations of senators, a mixture of high aristocrats, who floated into the office by right of birth, new men, promoted *equites*, who worked hard to earn this promotion, and men of whom we know little or nothing – all of whom had also had to work their passages through the subordinate ranks. It was by this time normal for consuls to hold their office for two or three months only, which would mean that there would be between 120 (if the term of office was three months) to 168 (if it was two months) consuls during Commodus' reign of twelve years. The size of the annual lists under Commodus is not in fact known except in one year. This had been the case since at least Hadrian's reign; there are frequent gaps in the lists as known now. Emperors were always willing, and able, to change the term of office and so the number of consuls in any particular year. Half of the known senators in Commodus' reign cannot be assigned to a precise year, and the gaps mean it is hardly possible to determine the length of the terms because of the small numbers known for any year. These short terms, of course, had reduced the office to little more than honorary status, with little effective power (though it had been a consul-plus-senators plot that led to Domitian's murder).

Then there is the notorious year 190, when twenty-five consuls held office, paradoxically the only year with a precise count. This may be put into some sort of perspective by these numbers. First, the term of office in this year was clearly a single month – two consuls every month (twenty-four) plus one imperial *ordinarius*, which takes up half of January. Commodus held an ordinary consulship for the first fortnight, as usual, and his first suffect filled out for the rest of January; the other twenty-three were then in office for a month each. Twenty-five was, in other words, simply an unusual number of consuls, a case of imperial manipulation of the consular list system. No doubt those who held the post for even a single month were pleased, even if the great number in the year was a cause for complaint and ridicule.

Why this anomaly occurred is not so clear.[16] The assumption has been that it was in some way the result of bribery, corruption, greed by the courtiers, and contempt by the emperor, all of which can be seen in other reigns. But it might also be a result of pent-up senatorial demand. If the corruption of the court had interrupted the expected, and accepted, sequence of senatorial appointments to the consulship in the recent years, a number of senators would be making a fuss, and if they complained loudly enough, and were numerous enough, the emperor would certainly hear about it. There is a suggestion that the selling of consulships had resulted in men holding the office who would not have been appointed otherwise, or at least not yet, which would mean that those men who were theoretically entitled to become consuls had been shifted out, or back in the queue. When the complaints became too loud to be ignored the delayed candidates were added to the list for 190; it was also a question of interest to the emperor, who clearly knew what was happening. It was, further, a clear indication that the office of consul was by now purely an honour, not a post of action.

Setting this particular case to one side, the sequence of consuls is quite normal, so far as our information goes. It was disrupted only by the interference of the delayed appointments and the government's hasty attempt to rectify matters by the extra consuls for 190, which was blamed on Cleander, who fell from power soon afterwards. For the first half or two thirds of the reign, from 181 (the first year Commodus was responsible for the list) to the later 180s, there had been no cause for complaint; the anomaly arose under Cleander's influence, as the delayed or overlooked men increased in number, and was solved, shortly before he was killed, by the mass consular promotion. The description of the position in the histories is, of course, an exaggeration combined with outrage, which may in fact be synthetic. But these accounts came later; it is doubtful that such comments were being made in Commodus' last years.

For in this period the emperor's tendency to condemn enemies to death suddenly became very active. The removal of Cleander in 190 also removed the man who had dealt with such problems earlier. He may have been corrupt and greedy, but that was scarcely news to politicians in imperial Rome, where corruption was endemic. His corruption was certainly more obvious and open and greater than usual, or perhaps by enraging senators, the complaints of his corruption were louder than usual. Interfering in the consular lists would no doubt enrage some senators and could be another cause of complaint. Some senators, of course, benefited from Cleander's dealings, and reached posts they might not normally have attained; others did not care, and still others hoped to benefit later. But then, without his standing between the complaining senators and the emperor, the emperor himself would become the recipient of the complaints; this was the lesson of the fall of Burrus a little later.

Cleander fell victim, however, suitably enough, to a plot that had nothing to do with senatorial outrage or complaints. Clearly, the senators put up with his manipulations, probably because they had benefited from them, or expected to. His fall was triggered at the Circus Maximus during the chariot races. There was a famine in 190, and the supply of corn from Egypt and Africa failed to arrive, leading to all sorts of accusations. Cleander had been given responsibility for the arrival of the ships, so he could be blamed. The most obvious official who should have taken responsibility was the Prefect of the Corn Supply, Papirius Dionysius. Possibly to evade that responsibility and perhaps persuaded by other anti-Cleanderites, and certainly desirous of deflecting any blame away from him personally, Papirius plotted with others to blame Cleander. He organised a group of children, who entered into the circus in the interval of two of the races, led by a tall statuesque woman in the guise of a goddess.[17] They chanted a series of accusations and insults directed at Cleander.

This was a practice that was usually countered by supporters of the target with their own chant, since it was clearly an enjoyable pastime for all concerned, in the interval, except perhaps the victims. It was also something, like Papirius' demonstration, that was organised and rehearsed well in advance. There was nothing spontaneous about it. But perhaps because it was the appearance of a group of children, the chant roused the crowd, who began to riot. Cleander, the praetorian prefect, sent in troops to combat the riot, unsuccessfully – perhaps the troops were unenthusiastic – but their rampage was countered by the appearance of the city police, who drove off the guardsmen.

At that point, with exquisite timing, Dionysius' co-conspirator Marcia, Commodus' current concubine, who was with the emperor in his chosen palace in another part of the city, probably the Quintilian Villa, told him what was going on. Commodus, possibly fearful that the rioters would turn on him, reacted as he had with Perennis five years before (at Cleander's suggestion). He ordered Cleander's death, which is now what the crowd had come to demand.[18]

The killing is depicted by Dio Cassius as a sudden decision by Commodus. It has also been suggested that the *consilium* was convened to discuss the matter, with a further suggestion that it consisted almost entirely of members of the emperor's own family, sisters and brothers-in-law, plus the praetorian prefects. This, it must be said, seems rather unlikely in view of the situation, with the chanting mob assembled just outside the villa, and quite clearly in a threatening mood. A rapid execution was probably the best way to persuade the mob to go away; after all, Commodus had reacted in the same way with the accusation against Perennis, and that had worked.[19]

Cleander's killing was followed by that of his son (or sons). Not surprisingly Marcia's co-conspirator Dionysius was also executed – no doubt he was now clearly and publicly blamed for the shortage of grain.[20] Commodus' reaction is also very interesting. He appears to have been gripped by panic at the news of a popular riot. In the absence of support from the Senate, he was clearly relying on his popularity with the plebs, but this was something that was fickle and chancy, and the episode with the deserters a couple of years before had been a warning. And then by dispensing with a successor to Cleander, he gradually lost control of the court. He executed a number of his concubines, who had supposedly been seduced by Cleander and had produced children; the children died first, followed by their mothers. This would send a message to others in the court that nobody was safe.

Chapter 4

Murder

The death of Cleander was the beginning of the end for Commodus. He had devised a system of government that had been, in embryo, so to speak, available in the Roman Empire since Augustus, and had been attempted briefly earlier, but was almost fully realised by Commodus. But Commodus, perhaps inadvertently, perhaps through laziness – for it seems unlikely that he thought out the system rather than stumbled into it – had used it over a significant period of time. The system amounted to ignoring the Senate as a governmental institution, though he employed senators as administrators – governors, and so on. He employed his own slaves and freedmen and *equites* to exercise the governmental powers available to the emperor, using the praetorian prefect as his chief of staff, almost as a first minister. This enabled the emperor himself to withdraw from day-to-day administration, at least to a degree.

It was no more than a tentative system, in that there seemed to be nothing permanent about it, especially since the praetorian prefects varied a great deal in capability and longevity – one is said to have lasted in office for only five days. Yet there can be no doubt that the three men who lasted longest in the chief of staff role, Paternus, Perennis, and Cleander, had been able to run the administrative system without difficulty, and with little or no senatorial input. But it required the emperor to control the prefects, and this Commodus failed to do, at least by the last years of the reign. Throwing men to a baying crowd, which he had done twice, was not a sensible way of controlling their successors, even if it solved a momentary crisis.

Perhaps Commodus believed that the administrative machine would run itself, with only occasional decisions required of him, for after the killing of Cleander, and the associated murders, he did not settle on a new praetorian prefect for about two years, and it is clear that the next man, Q. Aemilius Laetus, who lasted in his office for some time, was able to appoint his own choice of governors. This had been what happened between Perennis and Cleander, but Cleander was more or less in charge in that gap, even if only as the *cubicularius*. And when Commodus did select a new prefect he chose a man who was clearly convinced that he occupied a precarious situation, was liable to be dismissed or killed, and so struck pre-emptively.

It thus took time for a capable successor for Cleander to emerge, an indication of Commodus' negligence. He had killed off Cleander, a useful and successful official, on the spur of the moment. He had been influenced by his mistress and a corrupt official and had been panicked by the sudden emergency he faced as the Roman crowd came closer (and the Guard failed to stop them). As a result, he had no suitable successor available. It seems that Cleander's colleague, L. Julius Vehilius Gratus Julianus, continued in office for a time, but was soon humiliated by the emperor and then killed,[1] as part of the purge of suspects and presumed opponents (listed by the *Historia Augusta* at this point).[2] During 190, two new prefects were appointed, Regillus and Motilenus, neither of any distinction (though they had presumably reached a fairly high rank among the *equites*). Both lasted only a fairly short time and were soon dead, Motilenus supposedly from poisoned figs presented by the emperor.[3] In 192 Laetus was appointed, and proved to be capable, both in the administrative role, and in his interaction with the emperor. He stayed in office for the rest of the year, apparently as the sole prefect.[4] He was capable of diverting Commodus from some of his more dangerous notions, so it appeared that the emperor had at last found a competent and agreeable replacement for Cleander.

At the same time, P. Helvius Pertinax emerged as a power in Rome. He had already had a long public career, beginning in the reign of Antoninus Pius with some *eques* posts, governed several provinces under Marcus, who adlected him to the Senate in praetorian rank, and commanded legions, armies, and navies. He governed Moesia Superior and Dacia while Marcus fought next door in Pannonia. He was governor of Syria in 179–182, being dismissed in the purge following the 182 conspiracy, when it became clear there had been a Syrian dimension to the plot; he then returned to his inherited estates in Liguria and devoted himself to increasing his possessions and his wealth. After Perennius' fall he was recalled to office by the emperor to quell the army problem in Britannia, which he did with some brutality, and then did something similar in Africa as governor.[5] In all this he had been assisted by several prominent patrons, notably including Ti. Claudius Pompeianus.[6] He had become the hard man of Commodus' government. In his career, he had served from end to end of the empire, from Britannia to Syria, and from Dacia to Africa, but he had not spent so much time in Rome. He had been a soldier since his adlection in 171, but he had been employed in provincial posts, or had been in retirement, most of the time since then. He had been consul in 175, but even that post had been held *in absentia*. His colleague in that office was his future successor, Didius Julianus.[7]

Pertinax' career, largely in provincial administration and army command, pursued mainly in the provinces, and having little to do with the Senate, must have impressed Commodus as a man after his own predilections. He was a member of the Senate who hardly ever attended that assembly, and a man fully willing to employ violence to accomplish his ends. On his return from Africa, probably in 189 or 190, Pertinax was appointed *praefectus urbi*, city prefect of Rome, in command of the city police force, and served as consul *ordinarius* with the emperor at the start of 192, his second consulship.[8] This was an extraordinary career, especially for the son of a freedman, but it relied on two aspects: first, he was helped along in the normal Roman way by more than one patron, but notably by Claudius Pompeianus, who was tainted by his wife's involvement in the conspiracy of 182, and had retired to his villa at Terracina. But Pertinax' main recommendation must have been his obvious ability. He was clearly seen as a Commodus loyalist, at least after his recall in 185, and a man in tune with Commodus' methods.

By the last two years of his reign (190–192) Commodus had developed into a playboy, who had been permitted (again, because Cleander in particular had taken over much of the emperor's work) to indulge himself in such recreations as pretended hunting in the circus, slaughtering animals by the hundred and acting as a gladiator, with guards attending to ensure that the emperor survived – hardly a fair fighter. Laetus and the *cubicularius* Eclectus were detailed at times as his guards in the arena.[9] He had moved away from the palace in the city to the Quintillian Villa on the outskirts.[10] He was there when the crowd bayed for Cleander's destruction, and was blissfully unaware of the events that had produced this crisis until the crowd was fairly close. This location made him even less accessible and more out of touch than before. He was well aware that he was popular amongst the plebs, with his gladiatorial displays and animal killing, and especially after giving Cleander to the crowd. Yet that episode had clearly constituted a danger to the emperor himself; such a crowd was quite unpredictable.

The final section of the reign, though of course no one realised it was approaching its end, was, however, to those close to power, a disaster obviously approaching. To people accustomed to see omens in natural disasters, an episode of plague constituted a warning, as did a large fire in the city.[11] Commodus was apparently obsessed with being a gladiator, emphasised his own divinity (perhaps this latter helped protect him from the dangers of the former), and dressed up in fancy clothes, all to entertain the plebs.[12] (Shades, clearly, of Nero and his musical performances.) The empire was under the rule of a man who had come to regard it as his playground. He also seems to have believed in his own divinity, and this was no doubt supposed to protect him. But he was clearly undergoing a separation from reality.

One result of Commodus' increasing political isolation was an increase in the enmity and contempt between emperor and Senate. Commodus' dislike and disdain for the Senate was reciprocated by the Senate's anger and fear. There was a steady stream of executions of obstreperous or awkward senators in the period after Cleander's fall in 190. The *Historia Augusta* lists about thirty names of those who were executed, many of them in the last year of his reign; many of the victims were of consular rank.[13] These are only the names of the principal victims, however, and since it was Roman practice to execute the family members of those condemned, in order to eliminate feuds continuing over several generations, the result was that each executee was accompanied in death by his family, wives and children, and so the number of known dead must be multiplied by a minimum of two, and most likely by up to six or seven, to account for the families and the total number of deaths. He had ordered the execution of his own concubines, by whom Cleander is said to have fathered children, and the children were also killed.[14] The names of the victims in the list are probably no more than a selection of the best-known victims. The probable author of this part of the *Historia*, Marius Maximus, was present in Rome at the time, so the list, so far as it goes, will probably be roughly accurate, if incomplete; some of those killed are only known of because they were in the *Historia*'s list.[15]

Thus Commodus, probably gripped increasingly by the paranoia he had displayed since the plot of 182, was relying on the popularity he believed he enjoyed with the plebs, but this was fickle and chancy, as the events that produced the fall of Cleander showed. By dispensing with a successor to Cleander, and then appointing Laetus as praetorian prefect, after several uncomfortable and brief choices, and moving out of the city, he had become separated from the court as well as from the Senate; by executing prominent senators, possibly on only minimal pretexts, and almost at random, he had scared the senators into outright opposition; and senators had access to him, unlike the plebs.

The three sources for the events at the end of 192 (Dio Cassius, Herodian, the *Historia Augusta*) vary in many details, but sufficient information is presented, when sieved to exclude propaganda and lies, to present a reasonably convincing story. It was a palace plot that led to the killing of the emperor, but the conspiracy was much wider than the palace staff themselves, most of whom, of course, were not involved; those actually involved are likely to have been tools of more powerful figures. Then there was the general atmosphere of anger and contempt among those of the court and the Senate, essential for the existence of the development of the conspiracy.

The people actually involved, that we know of, begin with the new praetorian prefect, Laetus, and Eclectus the *cubicularius*. The latter, an Egyptian by origin, was probably more than a *cubicularius* if, as we are told, he was able to stand alongside the gladiatorial emperor in the arena. He feared he was due to be killed; Laetus, an African from Theaenae, may have feared the same, having been in office for longer than several of his predecessors. The *Historia Augusta* makes the point that Commodus frequently changed his city prefects, and that he 'took pleasure in killing his *cubicularii*', and that none of his praetorian prefects completed a three-year term.[16] This would be enough to put fear into Pertinax, Laetus, and Eclectus.

There seems no doubt that Commodus, late in 192, had prepared yet another murder list, and that this included the two men who were to be installed as consuls on 1 January 193, C. Erucius Clarus Vibianus, whose family had been senatorial since Domitian's reign, and consular since Trajan's, and Q. Pompeius Sosius Falco, of an even longer aristocratic pedigree, going back to the triple consular Julius Frontinus. They were also brothers-in-law, Erucius having married Sosia, Falco's sister.[17] Commodus' purpose in proposing to have these two killed was to take their places as sole consul, and, having spent the night in the gladiators' barracks, to emerge to take up his office (and perhaps to take part in the games), dressed in the official robes. Quite apart from having no further justification for killing the two men, this display, even more extravagant and extraordinary than usual, was bound to offend many of the senators, especially those who could recall the dignity of Commodus' father – which, of course, may have been its purpose. It is not surprising that senators were involved in the plot to have the emperor killed.

There is a story that the list, on a wax tablet, was taken by a slave boy ('Philocommodus') from Commodus' bedroom while he was asleep, was then seized by Marcia, the emperor's current mistress/concubine and later Eclectus' wife. She showed it to Eclectus, who then gave it to Laetus – all three saw their names on it. This was supposed to have triggered the murder, though the whole sequence looks contrived, probably to cast the blame for the emperor's death on his inner circle; it has not escaped notice that the slave-boy motif had occurred in Suetonius' story of Domitian's murder. Those involved, but outside that group, could then claim innocence, if necessary. It is hardly likely that Laetus or Eclectus needed to see a purloined tablet of the emperor's to know what was planned. Their names were not necessarily on the tablet, but they were almost certainly in Commodus' mind as candidates for execution.

Laetus, as prefect, had extensive control over the placement of men in governors' posts. It is therefore striking, but not surprising, that there was a high proportion of governors in office in that year who were from Africa. Laetus himself was from Africa, and he promoted a whole series of other Africans to key governors' positions, that is, the provinces which were garrisoned by large armed forces.[18] Africa itself may be dismissed as a source of the plot, since it had only a single legion, and that stationed in the neighbouring province of Numidia, though there were quantities of *auxilia* there; but it is unlikely that one would wish to bring a large part of the African garrison to Italy when there were threatening nomads avid to raid into the settled lands.

A large garrison was not necessarily a threat outside a province, but a large garrison that could be moved quickly, and could be covered in the province by assistance from neighbouring forces, really was a clear threat. Nero's downfall and those of his successors were brought about by invasions of Italy from Spain, Germany, and the Balkans. The German provinces, with four legions, the Pannonias with five, and the Moesias with four, could collectively mount an invasion force of several legions and still keep the northern frontier safe. Then there was Syria, the source of Vespasian's successful usurpation over a century before; together with Cappadocia and Arabia there were seven or eight legions in the region – and it was next door to Egypt, with one legion – while Egypt was also the main source of imported grain for Rome. This source Vespasian had used to mount a threat to starve Rome, and it was to be used for that purpose later as well. (Africa had a similar, but lesser, power of threat of starvation.) The British legions, three of them, had recently displayed considerable hostility towards Commodus and his government, but they were clearly under threat from enemy raids from the north – the Maeatae had invaded twice in recent years – and they were a very long way from Rome.

These well-governed provinces were, surely by no coincidence, governed by the African Clodius Albinus (Britannia), the African Pescennius Niger (Syria), the African brothers P. Septimius Geta (Moesia Inferior) and L. Septimius Severus (Pannonia Superior), all of these men having been appointed in the last year or so, and at least partly through Laetus' influence.

This would suppose that Laetus (it is presumably he who did the work of selection and placing governors rather than the emperor) was deliberately placing potential political allies from Africa in the crucial posts. He had done this before any indication of a viable plot to remove the emperor had emerged; it was presumably simply to build up a powerful set of clients and potential supporters by providing them with lucrative and influential jobs, and possibly as an insurance against what the emperor now intended. This function was the normal Roman method. Cleander had done the same, for example by sending Pertinax to Britannia and then to Africa. And it is not necessarily only Africans who were in Laetus' debt.

Laetus himself had theoretical command of the Praetorian Guard at Rome, but he must have had doubts about his ability to use them. We do not know the details of his career, but it is unlikely he had any military experience that would fit him to command the Guard; also the Guard detachment had failed to control the Roman crowd in the crisis over Cleander's end, and had been separated from the crowd by a detachment of the *singulares*, the city police force, which was evidently more effective in the city. It had already driven off the Guard once, and was regarded with less hostility than was the well-paid and showy Guard; it was commanded by the *praefectus urbi*, the highly experienced and effective soldier Pertinax. The praetorian prefect would wish to be able to deploy both forces in a crisis, which had meant finding a new *praefectus urbi* who could be counted on. Laetus found this in Pertinax, who was brought over from Africa where he had put down some trouble using the same brutal methods as he had used in Britannia. During 191, Pertinax took up the post in Rome. He was also in favour with the emperor, his partner as consul *ordinarius* in 192, which would imply that he was safe from execution/dismissal for a time; and yet Commodus was addicted to dismissing and often executing his officials. Pertinax is said to have been 'mild and humane' as *praefectus urbi*, which suggests he did not face troubles that might rouse his anger, or that he was also being extremely careful not to annoy the plebs; he was perhaps being extra careful not to exercise his severity on those whom the emperor regarded as his supporters. This would suggest a very political temperament.[19]

Pertinax returned to Rome from Africa, to take up his second consulship – since it was *ordinarius*, he would need to be present at the start of the year in January. At that time there is no indication that there was a plot in existence, even amongst the palace staff, to kill the emperor. But during 192, Commodus' behaviour became steadily more eccentric and outrageous, and he could only be called mad. He staged an even greater display of animal killing, and in the midst of it he turned from killing ostriches – how brave of him! – to waggle an ostrich head he had just taken at the senators in their seats; he had insisted they should attend to watch him; he held his sword in the other hand. Dio Cassius, who was there, claims he and his fellows could scarcely refrain from bursting out laughing at the ludicrous display of non-bravery. But they are more likely to have reacted with fear, for the emperor was clearly threatening them.[20]

He cut off the head of the statue of Helios and had it replaced by his own image. He announced that he was Hercules. He renamed the twelve months of the year in an eccentric way. He announced that he would rename the city of Rome as Colonia Commodiana. And he threatened to burn the city to the ground.[21] Much of this was hardly original, and perhaps not serious, but the city had suffered a serious fire quite recently, and Nero was reported to have enjoyed an earlier fire. Madmen are not usually inventive. Commodus was recycling old ideas, going back as far as Hannibal's threats to the city. But the very variety of ideas and suggestions for exercising his powers suggests a mental imbalance.

That he was probably insane by this time, or at least verging on insanity, is not the point. He actually sounds desperate; if he could have abdicated he might have recovered – or gone finally insane. But he was the emperor, and his whims and jokes carried consequences far beyond the immediate event. He had played tricks on the prefect Julius Julianus, pitching him into the bath while fully clothed in his official uniform. This might be considered a practical joke, but not long afterwards Julianus was executed.[22] The jokes and the humiliation were stages in Julianus' condemnation. The ostrich head waved in one hand and the sword flourished in the other, and the imperial grin behind them, were clear threats to the watching senators, and they will have realised it after they got over their inappropriate mirth. Commodus was in a murderous mood, but at the same time, he was realising the extent of his power, not only over institutions like the Senate, but over individuals.

This brings obvious corroboration to the list of murder victims which Marcia is said to have intercepted in the hands of the little slave boy. That story is probably not true, being most likely invented after the event, but the threat of more killings was clearly present. Commodus had in the last year or so killed at least four praetorian prefects – the odds on Laetus surviving were shortening by the day; the emperor had ordered the deaths of a number of his concubines and their children – what were the odds on Marcia surviving? He had ordered killed other members of his household, including several *cubicularii* – what price the survival of Eclectus? Whether or not they saw their names on a wax tablet, written in the emperor's own hand – such a list cannot have existed, for he would scarcely have needed such a memorandum – they knew that to survive the next months they would need to strike first.

We may assume that Laetus, the senior member of the group, made the first move to construct a murderous plot. For the only solution to their difficulty was to kill the emperor before he killed them.

Laetus contacted Pertinax. This follows from Pertinax's powerful position; he had to be brought into the plot, if possible, before the attempt was made to kill the emperor. But Pertinax had clearly been an imperial favourite. He was city prefect, as noted, and had been in that office for a couple of years, but he had also been consul *ordinarius* at the beginning of 192 alongside the emperor, a signal of imperial favour. It is possible that he was on Commodus' list for killing, though this is not stated. (The report of that list is clearly edited, if not an invention.)

Whatever Pertinax' status with the emperor, he was the obvious person for the plotters to contact, and if possible recruit, being the senior official of the city. He was known to be ruthless and stern; to some his support would actually neutralise the city guard. Laetus and Pertinax certainly knew each other, for they must have come into contact fairly frequently in the course of their work and duties, and presumably as confidants of Commodus. They could well have discussed the emperor's mental condition between themselves, with possibly similar apprehensions of foreboding. Whether Pertinax was part of the murder conspiracy is not certain, but there are certain indications that he knew that such a conspiracy existed, and it would make sense that he was probably a part of it.

It is worth making the assumption that Pertinax was part of the plot; indeed it begins to look as though he may have been one of the organisers of the plot. Making such an assumption helps to organise the facts as we know them, bearing in mind that these facts are incomplete, and much of what we are told is either wrong, or distracting, or irrelevant. But if, instead of beginning with the palace staff, we begin with Laetus, praetorian prefect, and with Pertinax, double consular and city prefect, we begin with two major political figures, with Pertinax much more influential than the newly appointed praetorian prefect, the *cubicularius*, or the emperor's mistress, all of whom were thoroughly unpopular with the senators and so having little direct influence outside the palace.

Pertinax had hardly been in Rome since he entered the Senate. His career leads from schoolmastering into the army as a junior officer, into the status of an *eques*, but still only as an officer. Once adlected by Marcus he spent 176 to 182 as governor of four successive provinces, then in internal exile in Liguria, then from 185 to 189 governing provinces again. It was not until 191 that he settled in Rome on his appointment as *praefectus urbi*. He was not a practising senator until then. He was probably largely ignorant of senatorial procedure; he knew only a relatively few senators – though he had known Claudius Pompeianus, who had also absented himself from the city, this time on a plea of age and near blindness. The sentiment of the Senate was thus unknown to him until 191. And until 191 he had been beholden to the Emperor Marcus and his son for every post he had served in, including *praefectus urbi* in 191–192. Even his first consulship, 174, had been held *in absentia*. His knowledge of the empire was that of a provincial, and his knowledge of Rome was also that of a provincial.

So when he arrived in Rome for essentially the first lengthy stay he had ever made in the city, and served as consul and in the Senate, the contrast between his experience, governing provincial territories, and the situation in the city will have hit him hard. In the provinces, the army guarded the frontiers, and the population worked at producing the necessary goods and foods for life, and the emperor was distant but probably respected for his position. In the city, the population, a mix of several ethnic groups, demanded entertainment and food, free, and the emperor, to whom Pertinax was indebted for his employment and promotions, and for his two consulships, and as enabling his acquisition of wealth, played at being a hunter in the amphitheatre, killing bears and lions and ostriches, and fighting gladiators (under protection) to amuse the Roman plebs. The contrast was stark and hurtful.

The culture shock was powerful and disquieting, and it would not be surprising if Pertinax was not thoroughly disgusted by what he now saw. Yet he also knew that the imperial government was ever suspicious and vindictive, so he would no doubt express himself quietly, and only to carefully selected men: Claudius Pompeianus, no doubt, who was his patron and was living out of the city, also perhaps Acilius Glabrio, and at some point Laetus, unless Laetus spoke first. The plot that eventuated, therefore, involved Pertinax recruiting senators who could keep silent, and Laetus appointing sympathetic governors and army commanders who could be trusted to support the coup when it took place. And Laetus had to organise the murder, since he had access to the court, where senators were regarded with suspicion.

The only thing missing would seem to be the date of the deed, so when Laetus and his palace conspirators actually killed the emperor on the night of 31 December 192, Pertinax, and no doubt other co-conspirators, was surprised. Laetus turned up at his house with an escort of guardsmen, which would have unnerved anyone, hence his nervousness and his surprise. But he rallied, and his part of the plot went into action. That Pompeianus was close enough to Rome – he lived normally at Terracina, 100 kilometres away, say, three days' travel – to attend the Senate next day implies that Pertinax' surprise was less at the deed than at the date.

None of this can be proved, but putting Pertinax in as the head of the plot is rather more sensible than having the praetorian prefect in that role. It was clearly necessary that the imperial replacement be selected in advance and be part of the plot – that was the lesson of Domitian's murder and the instant installation of Nerva as emperor. And the post-murder actions of the murderers imply that this reconstruction is probable.

First, Pertinax was the first man to whom Laetus reported when the emperor was dead.[23] This might have been the obvious thing to do, given Pertinax' office as *praefectus urbi*, but it seems clear that Pertinax expressed only momentary surprise, which could have been due to the unexpectedly early success of the plot and the appearance of the guardsmen. (The alternative would have been to report to Commodus' relatives, perhaps his eldest sister, but the family was not in the plot.) Second, next day, when Pertinax presented himself as the new emperor to the Senate, he was supported by two distinguished double consulars, Pompeianus, his former patron, and Glabrio.[24]

Pompeianus was one of Marcus Aurelius' sons-in-law; his wife had been Lucilla, killed in exile because of her participation in the plot in 182; he had survived the purge that followed because he had been estranged from his wife, and he had since been in self-exile, claiming age and poor eyesight as his excuse – but the killing of his wife was surely a cause of resentment, at least, or perhaps insult. He lived at Terracina (Anxur) on the Italian coast, well away from Rome, but close enough to be in touch with events. Yet there he was, in the city, the day after Commodus' killing, and, as Dio Cassius comments, his eyesight was now fine. It is clear that he knew in advance that the killing was intended, and that he had been brought into the plot; Pertinax, not anyone in the palace, was the obvious person to have recruited him. (It may well have been dangerous for him to go to the palace while Commodus was still alive.)

His fellow supporter of Pertinax in the Senate, Glabrio, was, in aristocratic terms, perhaps the most distinguished man in the Senate. The descendant of a family whose members had been consular every generation since about 200 BC, and himself consul for the second time in 186, his very presence at Pertinax' side would impress the Senate. But how did he know to be present in such a role in the Senate within only a few hours of the killing? Advance knowledge of the plot is clearly again indicated; another recruit by, probably, Pertinax, but one now living in Rome.

The choice of Pertinax to be the new emperor should give pause. He was the son of a freedman – that is, a man who had been a slave. He was from a family no one had heard of. He had been, as noted elsewhere, largely absent from the Senate and from Rome for all his adult life. He was, it would seem, the most unlikely candidate to be emperor. But perhaps this was the point. He was almost the direct opposite from Commodus, being strict, stern, an accomplished governor, with a knowledge of most of the empire outside Rome – qualities in which Commodus was deficient. And he was an Italian, from Liguria, the first emperor of such origin since Nerva and the Flavians. He was so different from Commodus that the Senate could choose him as their man automatically.

Commodus' plans for his performance in the amphitheatre on 1 January 193, to kill the designated consuls and engage in gladiatorial combat in consular costume, and the other intended killings, were not known by anyone, except perhaps those in the palace. In the Senate, one of those designated to die, Sosius Falco, one of the consuls designate, objected to the killing of the emperor, and the elevation of Pertinax. He clearly did not know he was on Commodus' killing list, written or mental, nor was he in on the plot. So Commodus' plans were only for the killing; the others involved, from Pertinax outwards, were in ignorance of Commodus' intentions until they were revealed after he was dead, possibly several days later – unless, of course, the planned killings were invented by the plotters as justification. The details of the plot are so murky that one is compelled to assume that such interpretations are possible, even likely.

There are other hints in the three accounts of events that we have, which suggest that others were also involved. Herodian comments that the three murder-plotters in the court, Laetus, Marcia, and Eclectus, were accompanied by 'others' when Laetus went to see Pertinax.[25] They are never named, but given the geographical situation of events, they can only have been other members of the palace staff, and Laetus' guard of soldiers, who had been part of the plot, no doubt carefully selected by Laetus. The first murder attempt failed, but the plotters were able to call up a strong athlete, Narcissus, to assist. In the middle of the night, Narcissus was brought in quickly. The timescale implies that he was present and nearby. It is thus likely that he was also part of the plot, perhaps stationed on guard outside the bedroom to deter any interferences, and be available if his strength was necessary. The emperor himself was a powerful man and would no doubt resist.

It is difficult to go further in attempting to identify more plotters, but there is one other item worth noticing. A successful assassination, to be successful, has to take place in a society in which an atmosphere of hostility towards the victim had developed beforehand. If he has widespread support, the assassination plot would all too easily be betrayed, or if successful, there was likely to be an angry demonstration and the rapid murder of the assassins. That did not happen, and in fact when it was announced in the Senate that Commodus was dead, the senators burst into applause, and began chanting a mock chorus based on those which they had had to chant for Commodus in appreciation of his gladiatorial feats.[26] And if the Senate was pleased, even overjoyed, and the Guard had been squared after the killing, as had happened,[27] the plebs who liked Commodus could be ignored or crushed if they objected. The political atmosphere had thus been favourable for the development and implementation of this assassination plot.

What actually happened in Commodus' bedroom is only superficially known. The story is that (ignoring the slave boy), having indicated his plans for killing the incoming consuls, and taking their places as sole consul and displaying himself in the gladiator's costume as the consul, Commodus fell asleep for his afternoon siesta, possibly drunk. Laetus, Eclectus, and Marcia, probably in fear of their own lives, conferred and resolved to kill the emperor with poison. (How this could be administered to a sleeping man is unclear, also how they could find the poison so easily.) Marcia mixed the poison with wine, and persuaded Commodus to drink it. The poison did not work – he vomited up the dose – though it may have weakened the emperor, who then fell asleep again. He is said not to have realised that poison had been administered; presumably vomiting up disagreeable foods was a common problem. (The poison story is less than convincing – poison is often suggested when someone who is disliked dies suddenly, but such deaths were much more likely to have been natural, by a heart attack, or a stroke; the poisoning of Commodus must be reckoned as only a possible event.)

The three then called in the powerful athlete Narcissus, who strangled the emperor, taking advantage of his weakened condition. Narcissus is a key figure. The emperor was physically a powerful man and very fit, as his exploits in the amphitheatre had shown, and someone considerably stronger than he was (as well as willing) was required. Since poison, if it had been administered, was always a chancy means of murder, Narcissus must have been available from the start, and in on the plot.[28]

The story told of the slave boy, the poisoning, Narcissus, and so on is riddled with problems, and was generally unbelievable as a sequence of events. The fact that the sources are in general agreement over what happened may only be the sign of a successful story spread afterwards. Some of the plotters have been pointed out in the last two paragraphs – the poison and the slave boy – but the timing is the basic problem. The events are supposed to be essentially spontaneous, a sudden decision by the three courtiers, as the direct result of the discovery and reading of the wax tablet. Yet they had poison available, Narcissus was quickly found, and this all went on in the course of a single afternoon and evening. Commodus had been asleep in his siesta when the palace three found the tablet. They had to be gathered together, and then discuss what to do, then came the poisoning, the poison having been found, the vomiting, and the summoning of Narcissus. Since it was 31 December, it must be assumed that it was dark by the time all this had been accomplished and the emperor was dead. As a spontaneous series of events, this cannot be accepted, since there were too many items that had to have been prepared in advance. So, either it was a spontaneous murder whose details are unknowable, or it was planned in advance and this curious story was invented later in explanation. The first story put about was that Commodus had died of an apoplexy, but no doubt the signs of strangulation were all too obvious, and so this elaborate story was concocted, but only sometime later. The apoplexy story had thus been the original explanation, when his death by poisoning was expected to be successful. The way Pertinax reacted, the unexpected presence of Acilius right away, and above all the appearance in the Senate of Pompeianus next morning, for the first time in a decade, all imply strongly that complete spontaneity is not to be accepted, and if so the details of the story of the murder are also to be taken as invented. One may also note that the story cast the blame for the murder of an emperor on slaves and freedman; senators might be considered to have been absolved.

So the murder story must be rejected. Yet the murder did take place, and was clearly planned, though it was probably plotted over quite some time, rather than spontaneously done in an unexpected emergency. Pertinax, Acilius, and

Pompeianus were all involved in the planning, but their roles were to take over once the murder had been accomplished. The murder was necessarily committed by members of the palace staff, who alone had access to the victim. Since it was night when the killing finally succeeded, it was a time when there were fewer people moving about the palace. None of the senators, nor the city prefect, would be there, just as the palace staff had to stay out of sight next day, when Pertinax and his fellows took centre stage. The actual death of the emperor was certainly accomplished, but it will have been some time before the details emerged into public knowledge, and therefore those involved had plenty of time to invent this unlikely story.

Despite the holes in the story as recorded, it has to be said that the assassination was competently done. The emperor was taken by surprise, and competently murdered (even if the poison part is a nonsense); the agent in the killing was presumably Narcissus, who is conveniently absent from the story from then on until killed by order of Severus.[29] And the follow-up, the actual seizure of power, which was the crucial part of the plot, was well prepared and well executed. Pertinax acted surprised, but at once checked to see that Commodus was really dead – and if not, no doubt he would have congratulated him on his survival. Then he headed for the Guard's camp with Laetus to secure the soldiers' support, or acquiescence.[30] Then to the Senate to celebrate, and have his titles and offices voted. This was the traditional sequence, pursued by Claudius and followed by Domitian.

This is how any Roman *coup d'état* takes place. There was no room in the events for the citizens and the plebs. The only elements to consider are to ensure that the emperor was dead, then go to the Guard and the Senate for the ratification of having seized power. By comparison with earlier assassinations – Caligula, Nero, Domitian – it was very efficiently done, and this was, no doubt, the result of checking on these earlier coups. After Caligula's murder, which does seem to have been almost spontaneous, it took some time before Claudius emerged as the new emperor, and there was a certain conflict, inevitably, between the Guard and the Senate, which could have been disastrous if it had lasted much longer than it did. Nero's death, whether it was suicide or assassination (say, forced suicide), happened without any preparation and degenerated into a dangerous civil war, in which repeated coups took place, always violently and murderously, leading to the deaths of the three emperors and many soldiers and civilians. This was not a model to be emulated. The killing of Domitian – slave boy, palace coup, soldiers involved, a plot involving a group of senators, a new emperor selected in advance, at least one praetorian prefect involved, and the *cubicularius* supervising the killing – went off most satisfactorily, but the senators who then took power – by a vote in a purged Senate – were careless.[31]

They had omitted to bring the army onside, though they included two or three guardsmen and a prefect, but then compounded this carelessness by failing to have the courtesy to inform the army commanders – and this with an army of ten legions concentrated on the Danube frontier and known to be loyal to Domitian. Their time in power lasted only until the army command organised itself to put in place an acceptable candidate of its own. The lesson was to commit an efficient murder and then swiftly bring both the Senate and the army to support the new regime – and, above all, to prepare all this in advance; improvisation would probably mean disaster.

It would seem obvious that the plotters of 193 had taken due notice of the methods and failings of previous Roman coups. A palace murder in secret, a group of prominent senators onside, the guard quickly convinced (and bribed with a handsome donative), and with the praetorian prefect involved, the instant production of an acceptable successor – Pertinax was a successful commander – and the main army commanders squared beforehand. It was a model for later coup leaders to copy, a distillation of the successes, and an avoidance of the failings, of earlier coups.

Such a pity it failed. Such a pity it led to a civil war. Such a pity that the Senate, which expected to revive in power once Commodus had gone, found itself soon even further excluded from power, and subject to even more senators being executed even than under the hated Commodus.

It is clear that Commodus had gone beyond the acceptable range of behaviour of Roman society. Supposedly playing to the plebs, there were surely considerable numbers of his so-called supporters among them who were aghast at his doings. The ludicrous plans for the games on 1 January 193 – if they were not invented as justification afterwards – would have angered any senatorial supporters he had left. Yet his method of government was effective, despite sidelining the Senate, many of whose members were kept happy by the rewards of office, consulships and governorships. Had he been less of a showman, he could well have continued applying his governmental method for years to come, but the combination of play and reform was eventually unacceptable. It must be said that he brought his death on himself.

Chapter 5

Contenders

There were two conflicts in motion in the six months following the accession of Pertinax to the imperial throne. One was the obvious one in which at least six men grasped for that throne; the other is a more profound and important contest, between whoever was emperor, and the Senate.

Commodus' reign, at least from 182, had been disastrous for the Senate. It had been ignored, humiliated, packed, and deprived of its usual influence on events, as Commodus relied on his freedmen and praetorian prefects to govern the empire, a group of men who were even more unaccountable than the emperor himself. The Senate's basic problem in such a situation was, of course, that it did not have, nor ever did have, any executive power. Even at its most powerful, in the old Republic, as in the third and second centuries BC, its constitutional role had always been to oversee the elections of the executive officers – consuls, praetors, and so on – and to assign them defined areas of responsibility, mainly geographical. It had, therefore, influence, and was generally successful in promoting men of ability into these roles, but always found it difficult to control them once in power. The basic method of doing so was term limits, or in flagrant cases by trials after leaving office. The civil wars that ended the Republic then delivered executive power to a succession of warlords and emperors; from Augustus onwards these formed a quasi-dynasty (the 'Julio-Claudians'), whose basis of authority was command of the armed forces.

The Senate retained influence in the Augustan system, if less so than before, and was capable at times of producing men brave enough to criticise the executive. Its members were appointed as governors and to other administrative posts, but as a collective body it had sunk to a legal body. The emperors tended to be impatient with criticism, and resorted all too readily to killing their critics. But in the third imperial dynasty, that curious sequence of successive adoptions from Nerva to Marcus Aurelius, the so-called Antonines, the Senate's influence continued, if somewhat more muted than before. It appeared that a new balance between emperor and Senate had been struck. Antoninus Pius and Marcus Aurelius rarely felt the need to resort to senatorial executions, and the Senate mainly avoided any outright criticism of the emperors. But the balance was delicate.

Commodus upset it. In his reign, the Senate was pushed decisively to one side. Commodus was impatient with criticism even more than most emperors, and his reign saw a steadily increasing number of senatorial executions. The exact number of those killed is not known, but at least thirty can be named, and there were certainly many more. He also appointed, or oversaw, the practice of making unsuitable men senators, those who had bought their way in, so it was said, by bribery of *cubicularii* or prefects – or of the emperor. Those men thus became senators without going through the sequence of offices referred to as the *cursus*.

The anger of the Senate as a collective body at Commodus' conduct, and his dealings with senators, emerged on 1 January 193 when it met to install the new consuls. Instead, the senators found that one of their members, Pertinax, had been proclaimed as the new emperor by the praetorian prefect Laetus and the Guard. They, like Pertinax during the previous night, had to ensure that Commodus was really dead before celebrating, so fearful of his wrath were they, but then they voted every possible honour and office to Pertinax, and burst into cheers, and into a mock mass chant which ridiculed the dead man's gladiatorial antics.[1]

So far Dio's version of events. Herodian claims that it was the soldiers at the praetorian camp who acclaimed Pertinax as Augustus, which is likely correct, and that in the Senate House Pertinax tried to persuade Acilius Glabrio to take the throne itself instead of him, but Glabrio refused.[2] Dio was in fact in Rome at the time, but was not a witness to much of this, until the scene in the Senate. Herodian, so far as is known, relied on later testimony. The *Historia Augusta*'s essay on Pertinax is taken to be acceptably accurate, based on an account by Marius Maximus (though this was written years later, and from a pro-Severus standpoint). It largely corroborates Dio's account, if with more detail of minor importance.[3] The *Historia* reports that, while waiting for the Senate building to be opened (it was apparently still dark) he was visited by Claudius Pompeianus, and offered him the throne, just as later he offered it to Glabrio – Pompeianus also refused.[4] These offers may be the products of Pertinax' modesty, or fear (which would be later justified), or it may be an indication that all three of them were part of the plot to eliminate Commodus: Pertinax and Pompeianus certainly seem to have been. Presumably, they had not finally settled on who was to seize power in this plot, and Pertinax was selected by Laetus, possibly because he was the easiest to reach on the night of the murder.

These suggested offers, however, came after the Guard proclaimed Pertinax as Augustus, so it was too late, at the Senate, even before the doors were opened, to offer the imperial title to others. The Guard would scarcely be pleased if it was now expected to proclaim someone else. Possibly Pertinax was assailed with doubt, which is surely possible. Maybe this tale is another invention, along the lines of explaining the reluctance of a man to accept such a promotion, which was the usual performance put on at new accessions. If so, it was even less persuasive than such gestures usually were, coming after the Guard's proclamation. And neither Pompeianus nor Glabrio had ever, so far as we know, shown any ambition for the throne. It is another detail that may have been invented to enhance the reputation of Pertinax – his low birth would be something of an insult in the Senate.

All three were certainly Senate men, even if Pertinax had little experience there. Pompeianus had been in retirement for ten years, and their collective reluctance to exercise imperial power may derive from a likely expectation of trouble. When Pertinax appeared before the Senate he was accompanied by Laetus and Marcia, and was challenged by the new consul, Sosius Falco, who pointed out that by relying on those two, he was being supported by damaged goods, enemies whom the Senate had long feared and hated. Pertinax claimed they had acted by Commodus' orders, only in obedience to the orders of a superior, with the implication that he would be doing things differently.[5]

This turned out to be very difficult to accomplish. Within only a few days some of the soldiers had second thoughts about supporting him. Their donative had to be paid, and this meant an auction of Commodus' gear, clothes, ornaments, gladiator's tools, concubines, slaves, and so on, which were found in the palace and elsewhere.[6] Pertinax tried to rescind some of Commodus' measures, only to find that those who had benefited from them objected. One measure he took was to decree that those who were deemed to have jumped the queue to reach the position of praetor were to be made junior to those who had gone through the *cursus* (and so delay any possibility of further offices), but there were so many of them (probably this is evidence of the extent of bribery and other nefarious means of promotion) that he had to abandon the plan. It had to go through the Senate, where opposition was strong, notably, of course, from those members who would themselves be adversely affected.[7] This was not the only measure that had to be abandoned.

The whole story of these early attempts to rescind Commodus' erratic measures is one where Pertinax' inexperience of the Senate was all too obvious. It is odd, however, that his opponents did not apparently intervene to rescue him from this error.

The method by which Pertinax had become emperor, nominated in effect by Laetus and the conspirators, and carried through in a rush at the Guard's camp, made his position very precarious. Acceptance by the Senate was not seen as sufficient, a clear result of Commodus' treatment of it. When he announced in the Senate that he had paid the same donative as Marcus twenty years before, some soldiers who were present objected that he had paid 12,000 sesterces, Marcus 20,000;[8] in his first nights there was a mix-up over the watchword, and the soldiers either saw this as an insult, or incompetence, or an evil omen.[9]

Normally such matters could be easily corrected, but the soldiers were clearly in a refractory mood. They had been bounced into a surprise acclamation of a new emperor without any preparation, and Pertinax was an old man,[10] as they perceived it (he was sixty-seven), though why they should have objected to him on these grounds is not altogether clear. Perhaps they simply looked for things to object to. This is a curious development. Pertinax was an experienced soldier, and should have been able to deal with these soldierly complaints. There was clearly something else at work.

Pertinax' age in fact is probably the clue both to the opposition to him that was developing, and to the difficulties he experienced in ruling. He really was an old man by contemporary standards, where the average lifespan for men was about forty years (less for women). Only two earlier emperors were older, and both of them (Augustus and Tiberius) had ruled for years before reaching his age, and were well established in power, unlike Pertinax.[11]

The nearest comparison is actually with Nerva, who was about the same age as Pertinax on becoming emperor, and failed almost as quickly. He did so in part because he was expected to survive only a short time, being in poor health at his accession, and so therefore there was an almost constant competition to become his successor, and as early as possible. He faced at least three hostile plots and a Guard insurrection in his first year, and was only rescued by the army officers' coup, which placed Trajan in position as his protector/successor.[12] Pertinax was no doubt also expected to die from old age fairly soon. This may be the cause of the complexity and hurry of his attempts at legislation – an old man in a hurry – but it is also at the root of the political problems he soon encountered. Like Nerva, he needed to select a successor quickly, as a move in stabilising his own rule – but once he did so, he was in danger of being removed by that successor. This was obviously one reason why Commodus had never made a choice.

He attended the Senate regularly, according to the *Historia Augusta*.[13] He brought Pompeianus and Glabrio to sit next to him,[14] presumably as an indication of his regard for them, and perhaps for advice on Senate procedure, though if they had been plotting together this may have been part of the agreement beforehand, and it may have seemed a recognition of their plotting history to the other senators. The more one looks at Pertinax' time as emperor, his actions and his friends, the more his term of office as emperor looks like a purely temporary arrangement, and that he was expected to give way relatively soon to a younger man.

Pertinax sent his son and daughter away from the palace to live with their grandfather, Ti. Flavius Claudius Suspicianus, and divided his possessions between the two children. He refused the title of Caesar for his son, which would have implied that his son was his designated successor. By this decision, he was opening the way to finding a successor elsewhere than in his own family. Sulpicianus was appointed city prefect in his own place.[15]

Further, Pertinax rarely left the city during this time. He did have responsibilities elsewhere, or assumed them; at one point he went to Ostia in connection with the grain supply[16] – Dionysius, the *praefectus annonae*, had been dismissed and executed by Commodus after his role in the fall of Cleander became clear; his successor is not known, but the arrival of the grain ships from Egypt and Africa was crucial to civil peace in Rome, and well merited the emperor's attention.

It was thus not the Senate as a collective entity that was his problem. Quite probably, his very attendance at the House was enough to reassure the senators that they were once again valued. He had even in these early months been attending to the appointment of magistrates for the next year (194); Dio Cassius was to be praetor, and this would mean that the other magistrates were being nominated also.[17] So far as is known, no governors had resigned or been dismissed on Commodus' fall, but some would certainly need to be replaced as their terms of office expired; Pertinax had settled on 21 April 193 as the date for announcing the new appointments. All was work for the emperor to do.

So the Senate and the provinces were controlled and quiet – though it must be recalled that Pertinax' reign only lasted three months, hardly time for the provinces or the governors to react. The changes in Rome did not occasion any barbarian invasions across the frontiers, though it was winter, not the best time for invasions to take place, and it usually took open civil war within the empire for such a reaction to develop. Pertinax' problem lay with the army, specifically with the Guard in Rome, and with some individual senators; in the background, scarcely mentioned but surely in everybody's minds, was the issue of the succession.

The problem of the Guard's restlessness had in fact manifested itself within a few days of the new emperor's accession. A group of guardsmen, seemingly more discontented at events than others of their fellows, or perhaps merely more opportunistic, seized hold of the Senator Triarius Maternus and attempted to pull him into the barracks with the aim of proclaiming him emperor. Triarius struggled and escaped, losing his clothes in process, and ran naked to the Senate (or the palace) and fell at Pertinax' feet, babbling that it was not his fault and apologising.[18]

This episode is only noted in the *Historia Augusta*, and is ignored by both Dio and Herodian. It is possible they did not know of it, or regarded it as unimportant, though a senator running naked through the streets was surely noteworthy. There had been, in fact, no real danger of Triarius being successfully made emperor, assuming that he was actually implicated; his tears and apology afterwards could be because he had failed; the soldiers clearly thought that Pertinax was vulnerable and Triarius was capable of becoming emperor – *capax imperii* was the phrase. Triarius was awarded the derisive cognomen Lascivius ('wanton') in the *Historia Augusta* as a result of the escapade, or escape, or plot; sensibly, he retired to his estates.

This was farcical, but Pertinax had very quickly been put on notice within three days of his accession, and it may have been this that persuaded him to protect his children by refusing his son the title of Caesar and putting them in the care of their grandfather, who was also the *praefectus urbi* and so had control of a protecting force.[19] But it was evident that the garrison of Rome was lacking discipline, which is not surprising after Commodus' time. It was also not long before new challenges emerged from the same direction. It was clear from the start that his tenure of the throne was precarious, but also that, at least in the short term, any challenge would emerge from the Senate or from the Guard, and possibly from senators who had not been part of the original plot.

The likely challengers may thus be noted; they were reasonably numerous, so guaranteeing conflict. Triarius Maternus himself is something of a mystery. Several attempts have been made to work out his ancestry, with contradictory results. He was the first of his family to have reached the consulship (in 185). His wife was called Procula, but there is a dispute as to whether she was Junia Procula, the daughter of Junius Rufinus (cos 153) or Egnatia Procula, the daughter of a member of the Egnatius family. Either way, Triarius was clearly well connected with prominent senatorial families, but he was hardly a prominent figure himself. His career is almost entirely unknown, except for his consulship, held, of course, under Commodus.[20]

T. Flavius Sulpicianus was Pertinax' father-in-law, the man who became the protector of his children. He was born an *eques*, and came from Hierapytna in Crete, son of T. Flavius Titianus, who was governor of Egypt in the 120s (an *eques* post). Whether this means he was of Greek ancestry, or his father was a Roman citizen who had settled in Crete, or was in Crete in an office, is not known; but he again might well have been an object of Roman contempt (just as Pertinax' origin as the son of a freedman made him automatically unsuitable in some senators' eyes for membership of the Senate, never mind being emperor). His mother was presumably a Sulpicia, and he had a second *nomen*, Claudius, perhaps from an earlier ancestor. As the son of a wealthy man (governors of Egypt notoriously emerged from their term of office rich), he would have had no difficulty in ascending the senatorial *cursus*, and became suffect consul about 170, and proconsul of Asia, usually the final post of a career, about 186. This was a distinguished career in view of his origin, though the stages and the offices he held are not known. He must have been in his sixties if he had been consul about 170, and so he was about the same age as Pertinax.[21]

Ti. Claudius Pompeianus, Pertinax' sponsor and mentor, was a member of a prominent family from Antioch in Syria, which had reached the Senate in his or his father's generation. He had distinguished himself in Marcus' Marcomanni wars as a military commander, and became consul in 162 and then for the second time in 173, which was when he was married to Lucilla, Marcus' daughter, and Lucius Verus' widow; she had been one of the instigators of the plot to kill her brother in 182. He was not apparently involved in that plot, which was a clear mark of his loyalty to the emperor, but afterwards he returned to his villa at Terracina on a plea of ill health, emerging again on the night of Commodus' murder. Dio remarks that it seemed that his eyesight had suddenly recovered and his ill health vanished when he returned to the Senate on 1 January – but both conditions quickly returned after Pertinax' death. He was by now about Pertinax' age, and had already refused the throne once. His eminence and royal connections nevertheless put him in the group who were clearly *capax imperii*.[22]

M'. Acilius Glabrio was the senator with the longest consular ancestry list, back to a colleague of Scipio Africanus (and even before that to two mythical goddesses). Once again, the details of his political and administrative offices, if any, are not known, but he had been consul twice, and, like Pompeianus, he had refused the throne; he was also clearly regarded as *capax imperii*.[23]

These three men were all almost as old as Pertinax, and one is reminded of the group of aged senators who plotted with Nerva in 96 to kill Domitian (twenty years younger than them) and install Nerva in his place, and who then awarded them a series of second consulships at his gift; they surrounded him in his enjoyment of the throne as his *consilium*, and it may be that Pertinax, like Nerva, became the dupe, or tool, of these other men.

The two men who took office as ordinary consuls on the same day as Pertinax was installed as emperor are also to be included in this list of contenders. Even if they did not make a move to claim the throne, they would have been seen as available. Both were descendants of several generations of consulars, and as noted earlier, they were brothers-in-law. C. Julius Erucius Clarus Vibianus was a descendant of a family that had produced consuls for the last three generations at least. It is possible that he was related to Triarius Maternus,[24] and thus he may have been an instigator of Triarius' curious attempt at a coup.[25] Ti. Pompeius Sosius Falco was again descended from several consular generations. His sister Sosia was Clarus' wife, which implies a political alliance between the two men. He himself was married to Sulpicia Agrippina, the daughter of C. Sulpicius Pollio, a senator from a major family in Lycia in Asia Minor; in this sense we may be quite certain that Pollio was Lycian by ancestry, and so also was Agrippina.[26]

For none of these men is any detail known about their senatorial careers, except for Sulpicianus' single year as governor of Asia, and Pompeianus' governorship of Germania Inferior during the Marcomannic Wars. It may be assumed therefore that such well-known men had not participated in the government of the empire except as members of the Senate, and that they became consuls by right of descent, wealth, and age. They were mainly patricians and so were entitled to take up the office at the age of thirty-five. If this interpretation is correct we may go further and suggest that by failing, or refusing, to take up official posts they were exhibiting a certain distaste, even opposition, towards Commodus, but in such a way as not to arouse the enmity of the emperor too decisively. One wonders if the other curiosity of this group had something to do with this absence of political activity, for three of these men had strong eastern connections – Sosius Falco was the husband of the daughter of a prominent Lycian, with an even longer aristocratic pedigree than most Roman senators; Pompeianus was a prominent Antiochene, and Sulpicianus had been born in Crete. The Greeks of the empire had been slow to take an active part in the government at the senatorial and aristocratic level, though they had been prominent in the lower administrative ranks since Domitian's time; the exception were the descendants of Italian colonists in Asia Minor. Both Sulpicianus and Sulpicia Agrippina may be in this group, but most such colonial descendants were inhabitants of the *coloniae* in Central Asia Minor.

It seems likely that the explanation for the new prominence of Greeks from the east was due to the Parthian War of Lucius Verus, who had lived in the east, specifically at Antioch, for several years – the first emperor to do so since Trajan's Parthian war. Verus was followed as governor of the entire eastern provinces by Avidius Cassius, also Greek (and like Sulpicianus, he was the son of a *praefectus Aegypti*). He held the governorship of the east for ten years or so until his failed insurrection. The presence over a long period (163–175) of these powerful men would certainly stimulate interest among the prominent men of the east. This was, therefore, a Greek group rising to imperial power at the same time as Laetus had been ensuring that many Africans held high positions.

Socius Falco was the only one of these men (apart from the visibly reluctant Triarius) to make any active move towards displacing Pertinax from his throne. This was a plot involving a series of interests. Sosius Falco himself was clearly aiming for the throne as an ambition for himself. He was supported by Laetus, still praetorian prefect, who had clearly become disillusioned by the man he had actually hoisted to the empire, but we have no real idea of why;[27] it is likely to have been a combination of thwarted personal ambition (perhaps he was seeking promotion to the Senate), and resentment at being criticised by the new emperor.

Laetus was able to collect a group from the Guard in support of his enterprise of promoting Sosius Falco as their candidate. They chose the day when Pertinax was out of the city visiting Ostia. Perhaps Pertinax knew of the possible attempt in advance, and he must have been suspicious of Laetus anyway, for a man who organised the assassination of one emperor and hoisted another to the throne, and commanded the Guard, was clearly dangerous. So he was out of the city when he heard of the attempt, possibly deliberately, and probably having had men available to reach him quickly in an emergency. He returned to Rome speedily and somehow (the details are absent) blocked Laetus' move. Sosius Falco was not punished, but neither was Laetus, who was plainly the actual guilty party; his status as commander of the Guard clearly protected him, as it had Paternus ten years before. Sosius Falco's criticism of Pertinax in the Senate on his accession may have been what suggested him as candidate to Laetus.[28] It may be, indeed, that Falco was as involuntary a candidate as Triarius.

Pertinax was trapped by his professed honesty and his policy of forgiveness. It worked with Triarius, and with Falco, who, according to Dio, also retired from the city to his estates and kept his head down; but Laetus was clearly a continuing present danger, and obviously should have been removed and/or punished after the failed coup. The two senators escaped punishment (and if Falco was let off, so should Laetus be, if justice was the issue), but Pertinax, a stern soldier in his earlier life, certainly appears to have ordered the execution of the soldiers involved – hardly fair, and resented by the other soldiers.

After this, it was not long before a more serious and effective attempt was made to remove the emperor. At the end of March, a group of men of the Guard approached Pertinax in the palace. They were once again instigated by Laetus, so Dio says,[29] who blamed Pertinax for executing those guilty of the earlier threat; Herodian, however, claims that it was annoyance at the emperor's imposition of stricter discipline.[30] This was the same problem Pertinax had faced in Britain, and so possibly this was Herodian's own assumption; it seems very probable also that the Guard had become uncontrollable, except by Laetus. The *Historia Augusta* also blames Laetus, who had already been disillusioned with Pertinax, but it seems that the palace staff had also begun to loathe the new emperor, again for his reimposition of discipline.[31]

Dio explains in detail that the palace was overflowing with possible defenders of the emperor, none of whom intervened when the group of guardsmen arrived.[32] Herodian includes a speech by the emperor, which seems unlikely in the circumstances, and claims that he almost persuaded them to go back to barracks; Dio claims he hoped to persuade them by his very presence, which, since he was the emperor, was a reasonable expectation.[33] The *Historia Augusta* says that one soldier, a Tungrian called Tausius, presumably enraged even more than the rest, threw his javelin at Pertinax, who was wounded but not killed. He was defended by just one man, the Egyptian *cubicularius* Eclectus, but the soldiers were too many, and when Pertinax was down, they joined in with their swords.[34]

That Pertinax did not make any attempt to defend himself – other than by words – or summon assistance from the many sources available in the palace, is certainly curious. Dio points out that he had 'the night guard and the cavalry' available, that 'many other people' were in the palace at the time, and he could simply have hidden himself away. (The *Historia Augusta* reports that some claimed that he had actually tried to flee and was killed in his bedroom; this may well be yet another item copied from the killing of Domitian.)[35] He did not summon help, nor did he try to hide. Possibly, it was assumed that the men were coming to present a petition, but even so, he clearly should have had a guard with him. (It is said that the men adopted a military formation, as though attacking the palace, as they approached, but that may not necessarily have been seen as threatening.)

Perhaps, by making his speech, which, if he did, would have been rather briefer than that which Herodian suggests, he hoped to calm the guardsmen, and thus the situation in the city beyond them; perhaps he wanted simply to cease to be emperor, and could see no other way out, abdication not being possible; 'assisted suicide' possibly, the Guard providing the assistance. Perhaps he was in such a tangle of obligations to his supporters that this was a way to leave the choice of his successor to them. This is a mystery, as the successive use of 'perhaps' implies, but his assassination by a group of the Guard was hardly a surprise. The earlier attempts, involving Triarius and Sosius Falco, and Pertinax' reimposition of discipline on the Guard and in the palace, had shown clearly that there were plenty of men and institutions discontented with him after only three months. His basic fault, if it can be called that, was clearly not to resort to punishments – Triarius, Laetus, Sosius Falco, and the soldiers associated with them, were clearly committing treason, even if involuntarily, and, in the Roman system, merited execution. The officers were not punished, but the soldiers were. This was a grave error of judgment; it should have been the other way around.

The question of Pertinax' successor had not been decided, which was hardly surprisingly in view of his brief reign. He had presumably removed his son from consideration by refusing him the title of Caesar, and despatching him to a rural estate. This opened up the succession to other candidates, or, as it happened, to a free-for-all. He had also blocked a proposal to award his wife the title of Augusta, which might have given her some authority, and could have been used to make her regent for their son. He did not realise, of course, that his reign would be so short, but he must have understood that, at his age, his early death was very possible, and not to organise the succession was a derogation of his imperial duty.

Sulpicianus, his father-in-law, who was acting as guardian for the boy, was also the city prefect. He therefore had considerable authority over some elements in the armed forces in the city, such as the *vigiles*. He was, at the moment that Pertinax was murdered, in the camp of the Guard, the only part of the armed forces in the city he did not control. This put him in a prime position to claim the succession, either for himself, or possibly on behalf of the younger Pertinax. But the boy was only fourteen years old; no one will have wanted another teenager as emperor after Commodus.

Pompeianus' son, with the same name, was also available, and moreover was the grandson of the Emperor Marcus. But again, he was young, being the son of Pompeianus' marriage to Lucilla, which had taken place in 173, so the boy was no more than twenty years old – the age of Commodus at his accession, an ominous precedent. No senator will have considered boys of that age suitable for the throne after the experience of the last decade.

Since he was at the camp when the news arrived of Pertinax' murder, Sulpicianus was in theory in a good situation to persuade the Guard to proclaim him. And yet some of the Guard had been responsible for Pertinax' death; they would fear punishment at the hands of Sulpicianus, and there must have been some hesitation on both sides. The Guard had resented the action of Pertinax in executing those of its members who had taken part in the attempted coup on behalf of Sosius Falco, and had no doubt seen the injustice of punishing the men while letting the principals go free. This perception hardly helped Sulpicianus, whose claim to the throne was based on his relationship with the dead emperor, plus his age, and his administrative competence. On the other hand, the Guard must also have been aware that it was thoroughly unpopular with the Roman population. This was used by the authorities, such as the city prefect, as a riot controller, and came out of its camp fully armed and armoured, and did its duty in a most violent and brutal fashion. Pertinax and Sulpicianus had both been city prefects. Sulpicianus controlled the alternative riot controllers, the urban militia, who had successfully dealt with the anti-Cleander riot when the Guard's tactics had merely made things worse. In their invasion of the palace to kill Pertinax, the small group of guardsmen – 200 or 300 of them – had organised themselves into attack formation, as though assaulting an enemy city; no wonder few had stood up to them.[36]

Into this fraught stand-off came M. Didius Julianus, who was a distinguished senator of the same generation as Pertinax and Sulpicianus. He had heard of the emperor's killing and had gone to the Senate House, which he found locked, but was there met by two military tribunes of the Guard, who directed him to the

Guard's camp, with the suggestion he could become emperor.[37] He was known to be both rich and ambitious, which made him normal for a Roman senator, and had a long experience of command and government, which was less than usual by this time. He could not get into the camp when he got there, the gates being locked, but shouted that he was a better candidate to be emperor than anyone else. It is not clear that he knew of Sulpicianus' presence, but no doubt he was soon informed of it. The scene has been elaborated by hostile interpretations into a shouting match between the two, with the guardsmen egging each of the men to bid higher and higher donatives for the men's support.[38] The money they were promising was not, of course, their own, for the donatives would come from the imperial treasury; Julianus is said to have promised to pay the money to the soldiers out of his own resources, and straight away.[39] This could be one of Herodian's elaborations, or possibly a cunning move, and it was surely known that the imperial treasury was in bad shape – Pertinax had been selling Commodus' treasures to raise money for his own donative to the soldiers.

Julianus had the advantage of not being the city prefect, of course. His followers – every senator went about with a group of attendants – wrote placards promising various things, such as to honour the memory of Commodus, whom the Guard was known to have favoured, and another promising no punishments for the murderers.[40] Julianus was allowed to go into the camp, and it was at this point that the negotiations took place, which have been described as an auction, with the two men positioned at opposite points in the parade ground, and emissaries moving back and forth between them. Julianus won the bidding contest with an offer of 25,000 sesterces per man.[41] Other details were agreed, in a sort of treaty between Julianus and the Guard, including that Sulpicianus be allowed to leave unharmed and to be able to live out his life in peace; no vengeance on Pertinax' killers was to be undertaken. There followed an assembly of the guardsmen present, and Julianus' proclamation as the new emperor.[42]

The whole process left a nasty taste in the mouths of those who heard what had happened – and of its later exaggeration and distortion – but it was distaste at the idea of the two candidates being incited to bid against each other, as though the empire was a house for sale, not at the process itself, which was essentially no different from Pertinax' proclamation, or that of other usurpers back to Claudius in AD 41. The next stage, however, really was different. Julianus was escorted by some of the soldiers to the Senate House, now open and thronged with senators, and no doubt awash with rumours. The soldiers were present in 'vast numbers', according to Dio, with standards 'as if prepared for action'.[43] This was a similar, if larger, array as the group who had murdered Pertinax. It is evident that the Guard saw the Senate as an enemy. They took Julianus into the Senate and with them around him, armed and threatening, he reported his proclamation by the Guard. With little choice, the Senate voted him the necessary authority. He said in a speech that he would respect the Senate, an ironic statement while he was in the Senate House surrounded by the soldiers.[44]

There could be no doubt that Julianus was emperor. He had gone through the necessary processes, proclamation by the Guard, acceptance by the Senate, which had voted him the usual authority and titles. He was not even an usurper, as Pertinax had been, not having been involved in the previous emperor's murder. Even the auction, if that was really what it was, was not all that different from the usual donative promises. Sulpicianus had been in the process of making such an offer when he was interrupted by the arrival of Julianus. The difference is that two men were making rival offers, a situation that would have produced a result at some point so long as the Guard had the final say and required a donative. Julianus was as qualified to be emperor as any senator was, and more so than most. His career had been long and he had wide experience of government. He was born the son of a consular, and he had climbed through the *cursus* stage by stage, which is more than many other senators had done. He was brought up in the household of the Domitia Lucilla, the mother of Marcus Aurelius,[45] which certainly gave him a good start, but he then served successively as military tribune in a legion, quaestor, aedile, and praetor. In that rank, he served as legate to the governors of Achaia and Africa. He had commanded Legio XXII Primigenia in the 160s in the Marcomannic Wars, stationed usually at Mogontiacum. He governed Belgica in the early 170s, and was consul in 175 (which would put his birth in the 130s). He then governed Dalmatia in 176–177, and was *praefectus alimenta* about 180. This was an exemplary career of public service, with only the usual occasional breaks, and although he was given support from Marcus Aurelius in the early stages, none of those stages was omitted. But in the 180s he fell foul of Commodus, who ordered him into internal exile at his home city of Mediolanum (Milan) in northern Italy. This, however, was only temporary, and he was soon rehabilitated and made governor of Pontus-and-Bithynia in 186–187. His last post has been as governor of Africa in 189–190, usually the final post before retirement.[46] He had a reputation for greed, both for money and for full rich food, but also for heavy spending.[47] This reputation may be his enemies' denigration, of course.

There are several parallels with the career of Pertinax here. Julianus was several years younger, and had been brought up in an imperial household, whereas Pertinax was the son of a freedman; but their homelands were geographically close – Julianus' in Mediolanum, Pertinax' in Liguria. And in their careers there were strong similarities. They both served in Marcus' war in Germany, and they had been consuls in the same year, 175; both had been *praefectus alimenta*, and Pertinax succeeded Julianus as governor of Africa. They appear to have indulged in a friendly rivalry accompanied by raillery.[48] Pertinax had perhaps seen more of the empire, in service in Britannia and the east, but then he had begun his career as a schoolmaster, a lowly social position, not in the household of the mother of the emperor, and had had to work hard to reach higher. Otherwise, their careers were strikingly parallel, and, of course, in the end they converged in the imperial palace, but successively.

Julianus had had a notable career, therefore, though it was generally typical of those senators who pursued the traditional cursus. He had experience of war, of the administration of a state institution (the *alimenta*) and he had governed several provinces in many parts of the empire. It was probably one of greater experience and usefulness to the empire than that of Sulpicianus, and infinitely more useful to the empire than the antics of the wastrel playboy Commodus.

The only trouble was that he was unpopular, and perhaps he was seen as a joke. His greed made him an easy target for mirth. Mainly, however, his fellow senators were distinctly annoyed at the fear he had put them in because of the method of his enlargement, and particularly because he had required an armed guard to threaten them at his first appearance as emperor in the Senate, even though it had probably been the guardsmen's idea. Then he was unpopular with the populace of Rome, because of his open alliance with, and reliance on, the Guard, whose brutality reflected back on him.

This general unpopularity with everyone but the Guard was decisive for the shortness of his reign. The popular attitude was shown almost at once. At his earliest appearance in the city in the forum he went to sacrifice, and the crowd which gathered cursed him; he attempted to reach the capitol for the same purpose, and was blocked and stoned by the crowd; he set the Guard on the crowd, and the resulting riots lasted all day.[49]

Julianus' rule had begun very badly. He soon made it worse.

Chapter 6

Civil War

The events in Rome between January and March of 193 had little immediate impact outside the city, and for a time, there was no obvious reaction, though no doubt full notice was taken of the murders of two emperors and the unexpected and controversial accession of a third. The end of Commodus may well have been welcomed, but since his activities had been largely confined to Rome, the impact of his death was probably limited elsewhere. Some governors, when messengers reached them with the news of Commodus' death, imprisoned the messengers, at first assuming that it was one of Commodus' tricks to test their loyalty.[1] It seems that the accession of Pertinax, well known in many parts of the empire, and to the Roman governors, was generally welcomed. It was his killing and the accession of Julianus on 28 March that alerted the rest of the empire to the size of the problem in Rome, and, for many officials, to the opportunities that were thereby being presented to them.

Julianus fed these reactions by his actions and behaviour, or so it seems. It was later claimed that he sent a man, a centurion, to assassinate the most prominent governors, those with large armies, as a precaution against rebellion, but, since these were identified as those governors who later rebelled against him, this is clearly a later allegation;[2] he certainly tried to compass Severus' assassination later, and the story was then simply shifted and expanded. His behaviour, rather taking after Commodus by apparently neglecting his duties, may have been of greater significance than mythical assassination attempts.[3]

However, one of those governors, L. Septimius Severus, almost at once began preparations to overthrow Julianus. Pertinax' death took place on 28 March, and by 9 April, Severus had made sufficient preparations to confidently have himself proclaimed emperor by his army.[4] The timing would suggest he had been making some preparations even before Julianus' accession, possibly when it became clear, with the attempted coup by Falco, if not the earlier one of Triarius, that Pertinax' tenure was unsteady.[5] It was possible, also, that his original intention was to prepare to march in support of Pertinax, rather than replace him. The preparations he made included sounding the sentiments of his forces, probably through the junior officers – tribunes and centurions – who were in closer contact with the soldiers than he was. When he began to consider an attempt himself, he had to contact his neighbouring governors, who could easily have stopped his move if they had wished to. Since one of these was his elder brother, C. Septimius Geta, governor of Moesia Inferior, he was already partway there even before he began negotiations with his other neighbours. The governor of Pannonia Inferior, C. Valerius Pudens[6] (situated as he was between the two brothers) provided early support; the governor of Moesia Superior will also have been contacted, and Noricum, Raetia and Germania Inferior were within easy reach.

He also needed rapid and up-to-date news from Rome, and it seems he may have moved from his Carnuntum headquarters to the south-western part of his province, which would put him 240 kilometres closer to Rome; most certainly he received the news very quickly, perhaps from family members and old friends living in the city.[7] But he was at Carnuntum again on 9 April for his own proclamation. The news he received was no doubt both of Pertinax' killing and Julianus' accession, and yet it was very quick work, and a rapid decision, to make his proclamation within twelve days of those events.

This was very efficiently organised, and to any Severan observer, it was perhaps a surprise. His career had been less than exciting so far. His brother had moved steadily along the *cursus*, whereas Lucius had normally been sent to quiet provinces. His appointment to Pannonia Superior, a major military province housing three legions and a large force of *auxilia*, is usually interpreted as having been engineered by Laetus partly because Severus had never displayed any initiative, and partly because, as one of the Africans whom Laetus was busy promoting, he was reckoned to be dull but reliable. It was, in fact, a dangerous promotion, from the imperial point of view. Severus had certainly commanded a legion for a time, perhaps a year, in the past, but that was his whole military experience – he had skipped his year as military tribune. Had he faced a major barbarian invasion of Pannonia the empire probably would have been in trouble.

If there was one thing he had learned, however, in the governing of several minor provinces – Baetica and Sardinia, when he was quaestor, and Lugdunensis and Sicilia – it was how to organise and administer. In Lugdunensis he had co-ordinated the difficult campaign by three governors in the Deserters' War, the rebellion led by the inventive Maternus. Yet there is no indication that Severus had commanded troops during that campaign; at Lugdunum he had command of only 500 soldiers in the urban cohort.[8] And at his first post as quaestor in Baetica he was switched to Sardinia, apparently because the south of Spain was subject to raids from Mauretania, and so Baetica needed a soldier, and Severus was not thought to be adequate.[9]

He was never a great commander, but like any good administrator, he could identify men who had the abilities he himself lacked. He was rather excessively devoted to religion, indeed, he was clearly more superstitious than most Romans, and he claimed to be guided at crucial periods in his career by his dreams, some of which he recorded in his autobiography. In his pre-imperial career he had become as familiar with the empire as Julianus or Pertinax – he had governed all those minor provinces, commanded a legion in Syria (IV *Scythica* at Seleukeia Zeugma on the Parthian frontier) as well as organising the campaign against the Deserters in Gaul.

He may have been seen as a second-rater, but his career clearly, on closer examination, suggested otherwise. He came from a wealthy family of Lepcis Magna in Tripolitania, and this family had produced three other consuls in the last fifty years. Severus became the fourth, when he was one of the twenty-five consuls who were installed in the controversial promotion of 190. And, most unusual of all, after the death of his wife, Paccia Marciana, who was also from Lepcis, he married Julia Domna, from Emesa in Syria, a member of the defunct royal family of that city, a woman with wide connections throughout Syria; she was also an intellectual, so she complemented Severus' religiosity rather neatly.[10]

This marriage was one of the events that was part of the process that brought the Syrian aristocracy into the empire.[11] The process had begun with the success of Avidius Cassius' participation in the Parthian War in the 160s. He was a spectacular warrior and the governor of the whole east after Lucius Verus returned to Rome and under Marcus Aurelius, and continued with the rise of Ti. Claudius Pompeianus' family from Antioch under Marcus. Julia Domna was the secular and aristocratic equivalent of the contemporary spread of Syrian religions through the lands of the empire – the worship of Jupiter Dolichenus, of Jupiter Heliopolitanus, of Mithras, and including the sun god El of her home city, Emesa.

If the reason for posting Severus to Pannonia was his presumed reliability (to Commodus, and to Laetus), or his presumed lack of ambition, or his dull competence, it did not take into account what the prospect of a new and sudden larger opportunity opened up for him with the development of the crisis in Rome. He was governor of a province with a large garrison, which was in the most useful strategic position for intervention in Italy. One might add that the marriage to an aristocratic lady, probably of royal descent, could be a further spur to his ambition, along with anger at the killing of Pertinax, whom he had known for years. For it seems that he had been a Pertinax loyalist – or, at least after the emperor's death he said he was, even going so far as to add the name Pertinax to his own as an extra *cognomen*.[12]

But then, in all this we need to take account of the fact that Severus was a proven liar, a deceitful diplomat, and something of a propaganda genius.[13] He deployed all these qualities all through his campaign to make himself emperor, and then all through his reign. He was also even more vengeful and brutal than Commodus, or indeed than any earlier emperor, quite possibly because of an internal feeling of inadequacy, which had been developed by the general disdain for him earlier. At the end of his life his advice to his sons was 'stand together, enrich the soldiers, despite all others',[14] which was a pretty fair summary of his own methods.

The proclamation of him as emperor on 9 April was a response to the killing of Pertinax and the accession of Julianus. He already had alliances with his brother, with Pudens, and probably with other governors of the frontier provinces along the Rhine and Danube. Some of these men adopted a carefully neutral posture, the reaction that most men who knew Severus would have expected him to adopt. Yet none of them made any attempt to stop him or to hinder him in any way. But neutrality from such men was encouraging. He understood he did not need a large force for the expedition, and neutrality from political supporters was effectively support. He selected a force of legionaries and auxiliaries amounting to between 15,000 and 20,000 men, and set off on the march towards Rome.[15] It was a small army to seize an empire.

His wife and two sons were in the city, a practice originating with Commodus, who had compelled governors to leave their families behind as potential hostages. But there was already a party of supporters of Severus in the city who were conscious of the danger to his family and their cause if Julianus realised their presence. Severus' brother-in-law, probably called L. Flavius, husband of his sister Octavilla, was also in the city, as was his cousin C. Fulvius Plautianus. The children were quickly taken out of the city for safety, probably on the initiative of Fabius Cilo, who had authority in the city.[16] And it was at this point, when he understood that Severus' family had been taken away, before he could seize them as hostages, Julianus finally realised how dangerous his situation now was.

Until then it had seemed that the real danger came from the Pescennius Niger, the governor of Syria. He had somehow become popular with the Roman crowd and it was his name they had chanted while stoning Julianus at the capitol.[17] At some point in April, like Severus, he had had himself proclaimed emperor, and had gathered support, again like Severus, from the neighbouring governors in the rest of Syria, the Cappadocian frontier, Egypt and eventually the province of Asia.[18] This helpfully (for Severus) directed Julianus' attention towards the east. (He is alleged to have sent assassins against Niger as well as against Severus.) But Niger was a long way off, and Severus, with wide support from his fellow governors on the European frontier, was close by; his march from Pannonia to Rome was about 1,000 kilometres, and would take several weeks before he was actually approaching Rome; Niger, marching from Syria, would take months, not weeks to reach the city.

Severus employed diplomacy to smooth his path. On the one hand he marched his army from Pannonia into Italy fast enough to seize the Istrian passes before Julianus could block them, or even perhaps think of blocking them. He secured support from the governor of Illyricum, which might protect his rearward flank against any move Niger made.[19] He contacted the governor of Britannia, D. Clodius Albinus, and persuaded him not to intervene.[20] Had Clodius gathered his forces and crossed to the Continent he would have outnumbered any force west of Pannonia, though he would probably have found his province invaded behind him from the north for the third time in a decade. Severus suggested adopting Albinus as his son, and making him Caesar, a title Albinus used from then on, but Severus never carried through this promise in formal, legal terms; it is probable that he was insincere in his original offer, but he thus secured Albinus' support: he ignored Niger, who was, with his extensive support from his neighbours, too strong to be tackled – yet. And always the main target of any usurper in the Roman Empire had to be Rome before anything else. Neither Niger nor Albinus had any real hope of beating Severus to the city; their only chance was if Severus was held up or defeated, but in the result, he was too well organised for either of them – or indeed Julianus. Severus also gathered support from the single legions in Spain and Africa, not that this was of much military use, but the more governors and legions who came out in his support the more it seemed that he really had the empire behind him.

Julianus finally realised that Severus was approaching to remove him when he discovered that the Severan family had been evacuated swiftly and suddenly from the city by Fulvius Plautianus, and, then at last, he began actively preparing to resist. He gathered together the available forces he commanded in central Italy – the praetorians, marines from the fleet, the Roman police (*vigiles, singulares*) – and put together an army of over 10,000 men. But it was as heterogeneous in its abilities as in its composition. The marines had no training at battle drill, and in a battle they would need to be tough and well disciplined; the elephants from the elephant park at Larentum were not trained for war, and threw off their howdahs (and presumably their mahouts); the praetorians were almost as weak at discipline as the marines after the slackness and indulgence of Commodus' time, and resented strongly being made to dig ditches and build fortifications, some even paying civilians to do the work for them. In addition, they had not been in a serious fight for over a decade, except in Roman riots and imperial assassinations. Help from the Roman population was strictly limited, since the praetorians were deeply unpopular. All this provoked a good deal of laughter from spectators, who included Dio Cassius.[21]

Severus' force made reasonably good speed on the march south along the road from Aquileia to Ravenna, then south to Ariminum and on through the

Apennines along the Via Flaminia. (Thirty-four days at 32 kilometres a day is suggested, but armies do not march every day, so at least forty days for the march is a more realistic estimate.)[22] Along the Via Flaminia, the local forces of Umbria joined him.[23] All the way, he was able to keep up a barrage of messages to Rome, and he was able to infiltrate agents into the city. Julianus became steadily more desperate as Severus' forces came closer. He called a meeting of the Senate and asked for support, but received none; after the way he had compelled their recognition at sword point he could hardly expect their support. He appointed new praetorian prefects, choosing men who he thought might be acceptable to Severus – hardly men likely to be effective in support of Julianus; he suggested that he and Severus might share the rule of the empire. And all the time Severus came closer.

Julianus sent a centurion, M. Aquilius Felix, to assassinate his enemy; he not only failed to carry out his task but joined Severus instead and probably explained what he was expected to do.[24] A squad of senators was sent out, presumably to negotiate; Severus bribed them to join him.[25] Julianus tried to send a group of priests and Vestal Virgins to intervene; the Senate rejected the proposal.[26] He sent the then praetorian prefect, Tullius Crispinus, to convey his suggestion of joint rule; Crispinus, who had failed to defend Ravenna, was executed.[27] Julianus ordered Laetus and Marcia to be executed, believing that they favoured Severus; Laetus' career of attempting to select emperors thus ended; but a man who had encompassed the deaths of two emperors could hardly be expected to survive for very long.[28]

By this time, such was the loss of authority by Julianus, Severus' agents in the city were openly putting up notices announcing his policies and promises. Julianus convoked the Senate yet again, and asked for advice. None came. He appealed to old Claudius Pompeianus, summoned from his villa at Terracina, asking that he should join him in shared rule, but Pompeianus' old complaint of poor eyesight and old age had revived and he refused.[29] (This was a man who had twice, perhaps three times, refused the throne.)

Severus ordered the praetorians to put Pertinax' murderers in arrest, and was obeyed.[30] Messages to the praetorians in their camp near the city persuaded them collectively to indicate that they would join the pretender, and Severus sent a soft encouraging answer, requiring that they arrest Pertinax' killers. Thus was Julianus' last hope of support sabotaged.[31] Another meeting of the Senate, convoked this time by the consul Silius Messala, condemned Julianus to death, and Severus was proclaimed emperor.[32] Julianus was killed in the palace by a soldier.[33] Severus' camp had been by this time located at Interamna, 130 kilometres from the city,[34] where his army was encamped. He had orchestrated all this activity in the city from a distance; he had not had to fight anyone along his route of march, and the city fell to him without any resistance from Julianus' army.

The virtues of speed were demonstrated, not only by the gradually increasing terror exhibited by Julianus, which paralysed him into indecision, but by the fact that, as Severus at a distance secured control of the praetorians, the Senate, and the city, messages were arriving from Niger addressed to the Senate and proclamations addressed to the people. The messengers were intercepted, and Niger's children and those of Asellius Aemilianus, governor of Asia, were secured.[35]

Severus marched his army to the city. He had evidently worked out a programme of celebration that would please the spectacle-greedy Romans, but before reaching Rome he gave them a present. The praetorians, who had stood by Julianus, controlling the city, putting down riots, digging defences, but never actually fighting, and had finally deserted Julianus abjectly, were summoned to meet the new emperor in their camp outside the city, unarmed. They paraded in their best armour, but found that they were surrounded by men from the legions Septimius had brought with him from the northern frontier, men who had long been jealous of the better pay and conditions enjoyed by the praetorians, and were tough and much more militarily expert than the Guard. After a bitter speech from Severus, they were dismissed, and ordered to take off their fancy uniforms and jewelled daggers. They were then banished to beyond the hundredth milestone from the city. It is a mark of the demoralisation of the corps that many complied on the spot; in a gesture of maximum humiliation, those who did not do so at once had their armour ripped off.[36]

This was the force that had put down Roman riots with maximum brutality, and for two centuries had regularly intervened in the issue of the imperial succession, and more than once in this particular year of crisis. But an emperor could not do without his personal guard. Severus had surrounded himself on the march from Carnuntum with a group of 600 men, who no doubt took turns in guarding him, and who remained in their armour all the time. He sent a group quietly to take control of the Guard's camp; no doubt, these men now became the nucleus of his own imperial guard. He also reinforced the *vigiles* and the urban cohorts in compensation for the *praefectus urbi*'s loss of the use of the Guard in its riot control role.[37]

The Romans were no doubt vastly gratified at this event and relieved when Severus, ever the sensitive politician, dismounted and disarmed at his entry to the city – but his soldiers came with him, and were armed. The Romans turned out in good numbers, dressed in their best, to witness the entry of the new emperor who had in a sense liberated them, at least for a moment. The procession was a great spectacle, celebrated by Dio Cassius as the 'most brilliant' he had ever seen.[38] Then, a few days afterwards, another ceremony took place, proclaiming the deification of Pertinax, emphasising the supposed continuity of the new reign with that of the emperor.[39]

So far the propaganda exercise, faithfully retailed by Dio, a Severan partisan. Having gone to the capitol to sacrifice (which is where Julianus discovered his unpopularity) and then to the palace, followed by soldiers from his own forces, glorying in their defeat of the Guard, he went the next day to the Senate. Like Julianus, he was accompanied and guarded by his soldiers, even in the House, though Dio claims he left them outside the Senate House, where they were a clear menace, but not actually surrounding him.[40] He spoke to the senators, suggesting that he had campaigned against Julianus for two reasons: to avenge Pertinax, and because Julianus had sent assassins against him. He made the traditional promises, such as not to kill any senators (though Dio points out that he broke this promise, which had not been taken seriously by the senators – within a few days).[41] Here he was beginning the process of rewriting history, which culminated in his tendentious autobiography. He had begun his march, in fact, and had actually invaded Italy, before Julianus reacted, and the assassins were legal instruments employed by the emperor in accordance with the senatorial decree that condemned Severus for rebellion.

While this was going on, the soldiers outside the Senate began agitating for a donative – 10,000 *sesterces* per man was suggested – and Severus had to go out to calm them, and arranged for the sum of 1,000 sesterces per man to be distributed at once.[42] But the soldiers were also as badly behaved in the city as the Praetorian Guard had been; they were scattered throughout the city and quartered wherever there was room, and proceeded to help themselves to whatever they wanted. To the Romans, it was like being in a city under enemy occupation, a reasonable conclusion given that many of the men were recruited from frontier provinces or from barbarians.[43]

Severus, despite these military problems, had clearly accomplished his central goal, which was to establish his domination over the city of Rome, and over the Senate, and to extinguish the influence of the Guard. And all without a fight.[44] But he had still to deal with Pescennius Niger in the east, and then to solve the problem he had created for himself with Clodius Albinus in Britannia as his successor. And both of these issues would require armed force.

Clodius Albinus and his three legions in Britannia and been neutralised by the award of the title Caesar and the implied promise of the succession, though the successful rescue of Severus' two sons from potential harm in Rome should have warned him that the succession was hardly guaranteed to him. For the moment, however, Severus was satisfied. Albinus was to be consul along with Severus in 194, another detail to keep him onside.[45]

While Severus was eliminating Julianus, cowing the Senate and the city, and holding off Albinus with specious promises, Pescennius Niger had secured control of all the east from Cyrenaica round to Thrace. He had, however, made only one move to extend his territories. A force had crossed the Bosporos and had defeated an army commanded by Fabius Cilo, who had been dispatched very quickly by Severus, charged with the defence of Thrace.[46] Niger had kept control of Byzantion, a well-fortified city, and so blocked the Bosporos crossing but had advanced scarcely at all beyond it. He had eight legions under his control, but could use only a part of this force, for the Egyptian legion and those facing the Parthians along the frontier could not be thinned out too much – in this he had the same problem as Severus, but the latter had much more in the way of military resources, and a territory accustomed to providing new recruits. If he advanced beyond Byzantion, however, Niger had not only to face Cilo's surviving forces, but the legions along the Danube – two in each of the Moesian provinces, and whatever force Severus had left in Pannonia. The lack of enterprise by both Albinus and Niger contrasts strongly with Severus' busy activity. One wonders what other messages and distractions and promises were sent to Severus' enemies to make them stand still in the way that they did.

Severus had an army of up to 20,000 men with him in Italy, equivalent to two legions-plus-auxiliaries, and most of them probably marched with him to the east in July. Most of the Danube garrisons had remained in place, even if reduced, or had returned from Rome. Niger's hope was that the support he believed he had in Rome would preoccupy Severus, but that had faded away. He could therefore do nothing but wait to be attacked – at least he certainly did nothing – which is not an encouraging position to be in during a civil war. He had at least six legions at his disposal, and could have fielded a larger army than Severus – but probably Severus would have then called up more in that case.

Severus was in his organising element. Apart from conciliating Albinus, he made extensive arrangements in Rome and Africa. To the latter he is said to have sent 'a legion' or 'legions' to expand the African garrison of *legio* III *Augusta* and a large force of *auxilia*. He apparently feared an attack from Egypt, possibly aimed at his home town of Lepcis, whose loss would have an unpleasant effect on his prestige, and from there the enemy would reach the grain-growing African province, one of Rome's sources of food. The term 'a legion' is in fact inexact, even more so 'legions', so precisely what force was sent is not known – it may even have been no more than a rumour floated to deter any attempt by Niger, and it seems that no force was ever actually sent out.[47]

The city of Rome had shown itself distinctly restless and liable to riot in the past six months, and he put in place a series of tough officers aimed at maintaining control of the city. He made C. Domitius Dexter, his old commanding officer in

Syria, praetorian prefect. The professional assassin C. Aquilius Felix is decribed as a specialist in assassinating senators, so the *Historia Augusta* says,[48] a curious mark of distinction, perhaps public executioner is the real meaning; he was made the head of a group of officers which collectively gave him authority in all sorts of areas, notably in surveillance and intelligence. This suggests strongly that Severus trusted him, but trusted no one else. Severus' wife's brother-in-law, Julius Avitus Alexianus, retained his former position as procurator in Ostia, supervising the grain port. A portion of the new guard was left to garrison and overawe the city.[49]

The dismissal of the old guard had led to a new guard being formed out of men from many legions, and in particular from men originally from the provinces rather than from Italy, as had been the previous practice. It was thus necessary to recruit the old legions up to strength, but Severus, intent on conquest and facing two civil wars, decreed the recruitment of three new legions, to be denominated I, II, and III Parthica, which took place while he was campaigning against Niger. This would require enlisting perhaps 25,000 more men for the legions – 5,000 for each new legion, and the Guard's 10,000 (though it was recruited up to 20,000 later); in addition, as many more were added to the existing legions to bring them up to full strength.[50] The names given to the new legions were an indication of his military ambitions. He was intent on portraying himself as a successful soldier, distinct from his earlier reputation.

Severus set off for the eastern provinces at the end of June, having stayed only a month or so in Rome.[51] The expedition was officially entitled 'to set eastern affairs in order', which was a term designed to cover all sorts of possibilities; his first aim was to suppress Niger's 'rebellion',[52] but then he intended to attack Parthia, which would validate his seizure of the empire. New emperors traditionally made war somewhere in order to expand the empire, and claim a recognition as a warrior; Severus' lack of serious military experience or expertise made this all the more necessary; Severus was determined to emulate his more combative predecessors.

He had a number of competent commanders with him, so there was no need for his lack of expertise in warfare to be exposed. Fabius Cilo had held his ground in Thrace, after his initial defeat, he had been reinforced with a legion from Italy;[53] Ti. Claudius Candidus commanded the field army, and Cornelius Anullinus was later appointed to command the advance through Asia. Candidus ignored the fact that Niger held Byzantion and ferried his army into Asia across the Hellespont, the ships having been sent by Severus from the fleets stationed in Italy[54] – the marines mobilised by Julianus were thus able to fight for the new man. Then he drew Niger out of Byzantion and defeated him at Nikaia in a bravura display of command by leading from the front. Niger himself had been in command of his own army, and this defeat was crucial to his eventual complete failure.[55] The governor of Egypt, Mantennius Sabinus, withdrew his support (and his legion), and submitted to Severus;[56] Asellius Aemilianus, the governor of Asia, was captured in the fighting in Bithynia and was executed;[57] Anullinus drove Niger's army all through Asia Minor as far as the Taurus Mountains.[58] In one battle, Severus' generals had confined Niger to Syria alone, and even there his support was crumbling.

Once again, it is noticeable that Niger was curiously inept once he had gathered his support throughout the east. If Severus could ferry a force from Italy to Greece, Niger could have ferried troops the other way, say from Asia Minor to Italy. Yet once he had Byzantion, he apparently did no more. It was the same once he had been beaten at Nikaia; he defended his position only. Presumably, he was expecting support elsewhere; it never came.

Niger's army resisted competently in the mountains and fortified the Taurus passes; Anullinus' advance was held up throughout the winter of 193/194. He succeeded in forcing his way through in the spring, but Niger's army then held the Amanus passes as well. Nevertheless, Niger's support was falling away section by section, as his eventual defeat became the more likely. The governor of Arabia defected, as did the legion in garrison in Palestine (VI *Ferrata*); he had to punish the cities of Laodikeia and Tyre for seeming disaffected at his rule;[59] presumably Emesa, Julia Domna's home town, also defected in a timely fashion; she was certainly welcomed there exuberantly later.

The final fight was at Issos, below the Amanus, near to the former victory ground of Alexander the Great; again, the army from the west won. It was helped by a thunderstorm blowing into the faces of Niger's men and by a cavalry manoeuvre that brought the Severan cavalry to attack Niger's men in the rear. Much of Niger's army died in the fighting or were captured. Niger himself was captured at Antioch and executed.[60] The superstitious Severus seized on the intervention of the storm to liken his victory to the 'rain miracle', which had aided Marcus in the Marcomannic Wars.

Punishments and rewards were handed out, with Syria inevitably the principal victim. Antioch, where Niger had ruled and made his last stand, was reduced to the political status of a village.[61] An excuse was found to campaign east into Mesopotamia. Some Arab principalities had attacked Nisibis and explained that they had been fighting against Niger's forces in that city; they made it clear that they did not wish to see Roman soldiers in the area again, so Severus rejected this explanation; he also noted that some of Niger's soldiers had retreated into Mesopotamia.[62] These two excuses for a new war sufficed for him; they seem spurious, probably because he had always intended to efface the memory of a Roman civil war with a successful Parthian War. A campaign of sorts followed, with three of his generals commanding three wings of the army in a sweep as far east as the Tigris River. The resistance was minimal. A new province was added as Osrhoene (around Edessa), a second east of Osrhoene called Mesopotamia; he had defeated the Adiabeni beyond the Tigris, but apparently did not annex that kingdom.[63] No answer to this came from the Parthians, where the king was facing a rebellion in Media,[64] but the annexed area had been a Parthian sub-kingdom and it was unlikely that King Vologaeses would ignore the Roman incursion for long.

One constraint on further war in the area was the continuing siege of Byzantion, which was being conducted by Marius Maximus, commanding the *legio* I *Italica*. Possibly, he did not have a large enough force to make a serious effort, but the city, with a garrison of Niger's soldiers, and an active citizenry, held out for two years. Only when it was captured, late in 195 or at the beginning of 196, did Severus turn back to the west, first having destroyed Byzantion and enslaved its surviving population.[65] He had himself proclaimed *Imperator* in celebration; this was his eighth such acclamation; this was very good for a man who never took direct command of his forces.

He had left a major problem in the east, with the Parthian king seriously annoyed, and now he provoked another one in the west, for he had proclaimed his son Caracalla as Caesar, and so as his successor,[66] which was the title and position he had agreed Albinus should have; he also adopted himself, retrospectively, into the family of Marcus Aurelius. There could be no doubt that he would favour his son; Albinus was thus challenged, and of course, he reacted. Severus had provoked a new civil war. The people of Rome were angry; the senators remained silent, but obediently declared Albinus a public enemy.[67]

Severus undoubtedly knew what he was doing by, in effect, challenging Albinus, and Albinus was not surprised by the challenge. There may have been already an attempt on his life by Severus' messengers,[68] and Severus had ceased to use the title Caesar for Albinus.[69] At one point, late in 195, while Severus was still moving west through the Balkans, Albinus had himself proclaimed Augustus, that is, emperor.[70] This may have happened before Caracalla – now 'M. Aurelius Antoninus' – was declared Caesar, though Albinus had left it rather late. It must have been clear that he would be Severus' next target when Niger was defeated and killed, and then again when Byzantion was captured.

Albinus was, of course, in a difficult position. He could, like his later emulator Carausius, simply stay on guard in Britannia behind the sea barrier. He certainly had contacts and supporters in the rest of the empire, and he could have waited until they were organised to come out openly to his support. That support included the governor in Hispania Tarraconnensis, L. Novius Rufus, and there were supporters of his in Noricum, though this may not have included the governor: Severus' general, Claudius Candidus, campaigned against them on his way to Gaul.[71] Severus later established that sixty or more senators had written to Albinus offering their support,[72] and there were no doubt others who waited to see what resulted, but would support Albinus if he were victorious, just as there were governors who did not openly join him, but probably would if he won. The savagery Severus had occasionally displayed in the earlier campaign in the east – the execution of Niger's family, for example, or the sack of Byzantion – had been to a degree counter-productive because it firmed up opposition to him; the legion in garrison in Arabia (*legio* III *Cyrenaica*) rebelled in support of Albinus during the war, though this is attested only in the *Historia Augusta* biography of Severus and seems very doubtful; if the legion did rebel, its action did not last long.[73] Severus later conducted purging campaigns through all Spain and into Mauretania.

Albinus was therefore in with a chance, if he could get his supporters to take action. Most, notably the senators, did nothing; they were essentially powerless in Rome, with the city under Severus' strict control. Apart from such men as Aquilius Felix in strategic offices, Severus had appointed his cousin T. Fulvius Plautianus, who had removed his children, as head of the *vigiles* by 193, and promoted him to praetorian prefect by late 195. He had also accompanied the emperor in his expeditions. He is a sinister figure, even more so than the professional assassin Felix, exactly the sort of man whose appointment would instil fear into senators, especially any who were wavering in their allegiance.[74]

Severus returned to Rome late in 196 from the east, but stayed only briefly. He will have known of the demonstrations against his new war, and no doubt saw no need to stay in the city, riddled with opponents and with many Albinus supporters. He took no action against them, but certainly stored up resentment against these men for later use. He travelled to Pannonia to organise his new expedition. Troops had already been sent to block the Alpine passes under Julius Pacatianus,[75] and his field army was assembled in Pannonia from the garrison there and the expedition force which had won the war in the east. With the Alpine passes blocked, he was able to march directly westwards through Noricum and Raetia and so into Germany and Gaul, arriving in southern Germany, a strategic march which, along with the Guard in the Alps, compelled Albinus to fight in Gaul. (This was where Claudius Candidus was campaigning in advance of the emperor, and ferretting out opponents in Noricum.)

Albinus had moved his forces into Gaul and established his headquarters in Lugdunum, where he had to expel the governor, who supported Septimius. (There is no sign that his enemies in Britannia, Roman or barbarian, took advantage of his absence.) He probably did not know where Severus' attack would come from, since the emperor was first reported in Rome and had then moved to Pannonia – the blocked Alpine routes, manned by one of the new legions, might have been the signal, or to disguise, his choice of approach – presumably both leaders received regular reports of the movements of the other. Albinus had sent a force into Germania Superior, where the governor was hostile, and a small victory there over the governor Virius Lupus blocked any interference from that direction – until Severus arrived that way, of course.[76] Albinus' forces besieged Trier, which was defended by the *legio* XXII *Primigenia* from Mogontiacum.[77] He secured the support of the governor of Tarraconnensis to his south, Novius Rufus, but the legion in that province, VII *Claudia*, eventually supported Severus, changing sides in time to receive a reward from the emperor rather than punishment – Rufus later died, of course. The supporters of Albinus in Noricum will have provided him with information when Severus made his move westwards.

The clash between the armies took place near Lugdunum.[78] As in so many ancient battles, one wing was victorious but then settled into plundering the captured enemy camp, while the fight on the other wing was almost lost. Severus' right wing was victorious, but the left blundered into an Albinian trap; it was rescued, as at Issos, by a cavalry attack on the Albinian flank, launched by Julius Laetus, whom Herodian claims was wavering in his support. Severus himself, in the thick of the fight for once, was wounded and reported killed.[79] This was probably the largest battle, in terms of numbers of soldiers involved, since the Republican civil wars, and casualties were very severe on both sides; the result was made worse when Severus gave his men licence to sack Lugdunum. But the results of the action were very clear. Severus was now the undoubted and victorious emperor, a position he had achieved by brute force.

Chapter 7

Severus, the Severans, and the Senate

Commodus clearly despised the Senate, and had no qualms about executing a considerable number of senators, nor in replacing them with men whom the rest of the Senate regarded as unsuitable. Pertinax had proclaimed in his initial speech to the Senate house on 1 January 193 that he was an emperor who wished for the Senate's support; he took the ancient and almost disused title of *princeps senatus*, and attended the Senate when it was in session and he was in Rome. Julianus made similar gestures, but he was clearly unpopular after using the Guard to compel the Senate to accept him as emperor and will have known that. He was clearly on an even more unstable throne than Pertinax; in the end, the Senate deliberately declared him a public enemy, and this made him vulnerable. He was soon afterwards killed, though that was at the behest of the new pretender, Septimius Severus.

This brief period, from the death of Commodus at the end of December 192 to late May 193 and the arrival of Severus, saw a short revival of senatorial authority. True, this came about as a result of a decision by Pertinax, an emperor, and the revival was cut short, first by the ineptitude of Julianus, and later by the will of Severus. This conflict, between emperor and Senate, set the scene for the next period of internal Roman history, the period known as the Severan (193–235, or perhaps 238), but it was one in which the empire was ruled by a series of less than competent emperors, or by emperors who permitted a powerful family member to rule for them. Their conflict had, however, been in evidence under Commodus, whose example was followed by Severus.

The legacy of Commodus was thus, first, that he left the throne to yet another family that attempted to form an imperial dynasty of birth. Dynastic rule in imperial Rome had been a constant aim and yet a repeated failure, covered over by a thin figleaf of adoptions. Historians describe the genetic legacy of Augustus as the Julio-Claudian dynasty, but in fact, it was not a joint enterprise of two families, but an amalgam of members of four families – Julian, Claudian, Domitian, and Vipsanian. The only true dynasty to rule before Commodus inherited from his father was the Flavian, when Vespasian was succeeded by his two sons, but the first lasted only two years, and the second was sufficiently unpopular to be an accessible assassination victim – a total of two generations – twenty-seven years. Even if Domitian had lived on it is likely that he would not have been succeeded by a family member. Then a trio of homosexuals, Nerva, Trajan and Hadrian, then two men, only one of whom survived his children (Pius), and they ruled until Commodus succeeded Marcus. Marcus himself was hardly a healthy man, and most of his sons were dead before him. Commodus, the only son of his left when he died, succeeded at the age of nineteen, and this was the basic problem of his reign, since he was given too much power too soon. He also had, so far as can be seen, no children of his own. Genetically, every emperor was clearly a failure.

From Nerva to Marcus, the succession had been thus determined by adoption, but if adoption really had been the master institution of the Roman imperial system, as some modern historians have evidently believed, it ceased as soon as an emperor left a son. It was actually never more than an expedient resorted to in the absence of genetic successors, and Commodus' succession was both a reversion to what had been intended all along, and a sad mistake. His succession was inevitable given the Roman affection for family inheritance, which rivals that of western European royal families. Had adoption been the master institution, Commodus was a prime example of one who should have been set aside in favour of a more suitable candidate. There was in fact no true dynasty that ruled the Roman Empire for more than two generations until the family of Constantius I.

The adoption 'system' was resorted to only because none of the emperors from Nerva onwards – indeed from Titus onwards – left any living descendants. The next century and more saw repeated attempts by emperors to establish a dynasty, and all failed until Constantine. This is an extraordinary sequence, much in need of an explanation – the repeated assassination of emperors is part of it, of course.

In 193, the accession of Severus launched the empire on another experiment in dynastic rule, in this case a fairly wild ride. Over the next forty-two years, the succession in the Severan 'family' went to two sons (Caracalla and Geta), one of which was rapidly murdered by the other, to the grandson of the sister of the wife of Severus (Elagabalus), to the son of the sister of that wife (omitting Macrinus, no relation in any of this). This was a new version of the adoption system – which Severus himself had revived by his retrospective adoption of himself into the family of Marcus. Furthermore, all four of these emperors were children or teenagers, and all were murdered. It is thus a surprise that the 'dynasty' lasted as long as it did. This was a mess, and was no way to provide for the government of an empire. It was also one of the prime causes of the political collapse that shook the empire in the mid-third century. The basic fault was Septimius', his method of seizing power, and his methods of rule.

Back in Rome after his victory at Lugdunum, Severus met the Senate. The senators and the general population had laid on the usual celebrations for a victory,[1] but Severus was not in any way mollified. He made a fierce speech to the Senate, in which at last he revealed his intentions towards it. By announcing that he was the son of Marcus, he pointed out that he also became the 'brother' of Commodus. This was a faux-legitimation of his emperorship, though it might have seemed to some a desperate eventuality by a man of limited social skills who was conscious of his outsider status in Roman society. For Severus, however, it had a major political purpose, for by calling Commodus his brother he necessarily favoured his conduct and his reign, and he expressed this in the speech, by praising Commodus and his reign and his habits, or at least some of them (rewriting history in his usual way). He also praised the Republican commanders who had won battles against senatorial opposition – Sulla, Marius, and Augustus. They had followed their victories by extensive purges of their senatorial opponents (the process called 'proscription'). He then condemned the failure of Pompey and Caesar to do the same, when they forgot who their enemies were – and by attending to the Senate, attempted reconciliation.[2] Clearly, Severus had no intention of being attentive to senatorial power and authority.

This was clear enough, and he had under arrest over sixty senators. Half of these were released, the rest – twenty-nine men – were executed.[3] This is probably not the total of those senators he killed, and he did not hesitate in the rest of his reign to execute more. He seems to have made a special effort to eliminate any senator who was involved in the *coup d'état* of 193. T. Flavius Sulpicianus was one who died, theoretically because he supported Albinus, actually because of his near-valid claim to the throne; Erucius Clarus was killed after, so it was said, refusing to betray others, but also because he had supported Albinus, and so no doubt because of his role in 193 as well. Two who survived were the two men who had steadfastly and repeatedly refused the throne, Sosius Falco and Claudius Pompeianus. Their repeated refusals must have carried conviction, and, of course, rendered them unlikely to be asked again. The assassins – not senators, of course – were also sought out: Narcissus was killed by wild beasts in the arena; Laetus and Marcia had been killed by Julianus, Eclectus in defending Pertinax; and the praetorians involved in killing Pertinax were sought out and punished early in Septimius' conquest of Italy. No ruler was going to tolerate an assassin going free; it might have become a habit; and a free assassin could be an inspiration to others. And yet he employed and promoted the professional assassin Aquilius Felix.

Like Commodus, Severus could then appoint new senators, who were therefore his own supporters. More to the point, those who were killed, as well as those who were released, had their properties confiscated; Herodian explains the executions and confiscations as a product of Severus' obsession with money.[4] In the western provinces, procurators were even then scouring the local communities to find

1 & 2. Two views of the emperor: the formal portrait, a stern ruler, if too extravagantly hairy; and the overgrown adolescent who played games and dressed up as his mythical hero. It was his fate that the second version overtook the first.

Following the murder of Commodus, Pertinax took the throne, with senatorial approval, but was soon murdered by the Guard; Didius Julianus bribed the Guard to proclaim him, but failed to establish his authority in the face of Septimius' inexorable military advance.

3. PERTINAX, emperor 193 (murdered).

4. DIDIUS Julianus, emperor 193 (murdered).

Severus projected an image of a serene family life, as suggested by the tondo found in Egypt. But the scratching out of the second son Geta, after the father's death, shows up the fraternal tensions. Soon after Geta's murder, by Caracalla, their mother, Julia Domna, committed suicide.

5. The family, Geta's image destroyed.

6. SEPTIMIUS SEVERUS, emperor 193–211.

7. CARACALLA, emperor 211–217 (murdered). (*Marie-Lan Nguyen/ https:// creativecommons.org/licenses/by/2.5/deed.en*)

TWO PRETENDERS

Two men claimed the right to become emperors in competition with Septimius Severus. Pescennius Niger, governor of Syria, lasted only a year, though Clodius Albinus, governor of Britannia, lasted four. Niger did make a serious attempt to reach Italy, but was defeated in two battles. Albinus sat out that war, then was defeated in battle separately at Lugdunum. Albinus and Severus both came from Africa.

8. PESCENNIUS NIGER, pretender 193–194 (executed 194). (*Numismatica Ars Classica NAC AG, https://creativecommons.org/licenses/by-sa/3.0/ch/deed.en*)

9. CLODIUS ALBINUS, Caesar 193–197 (died in battle or by suicide, 197). (*Carole Raddato, https://creativecommons.org/ licenses/by-sa/2.0/deed.en*)

THE LATER SEVERAN FAMILY

The later Severan family was an unusual construct, of emperors only distantly related to the founder and of very assertive women. Furthermore, the two emperors were both boys when they took office – hence, of course, the assertive women. The sequence of the dynasty was interrupted by the brief reign of Macrinus, an even more exotic ruler, a Moor and an eques.

10. ELAGABALUS, emperor 218–222 (murdered). (© *José Luiz Bernardes Ribeiro/ CC BY-SA 4.0*)

11. MACRINUS, emperor 217–218 (murdered). (© *José Luiz Bernardes Ribeiro/CC BY-SA 4.0*)

12. ALEXANDER SEVERUS, emperor 222–235 (murdered).

13. JULIA DOMNA, wife of Septimius (committed suicide).

14. JULIA MAESA, sister of Julia Domna, grandmother and promoter of Elagabalus (murdered). (*CNG Coins/CC BY-SA 2.5*)

15. JULIA MAMAEA, mother of Alexander Severus (murdered). (*Wikipedia/Shakko/ CC BY 3.0*)

THE EMPERORS OF 238, THE YEAR OF SIX EMPERORS. The year of revolution, 238, began with Maximinus, who never visited Rome as emperor, campaigning to restore the empire's boundaries and strength. He was challenged by the usurpation of the two Gordians in Africa, an episode lasting only three weeks. It did, however, inspire further usurpations, and Balbinus and Pupienus seized power in Italy. They succeeded in defying Maximinus, no doubt to general surprise, but quarrelled and then were assassinated. The survivor of the year was Gordian III, a child, so the empire had eliminated five adult and capable emperors, and ended with another boy ruler.

16. MAXIMINUS, emperor 235–238 (murdered).

17. GORDIAN II, usurper 238 (murdered); (no reliable portrait of Gordian I exists).

18. BALBINUS, joint emperor 238 (murdered). (*George Shuklin/CC BY 2.5*)

19. PUPIENUS, joint emperor 238 (murdered).

20. GORDIAN III, emperor 238–244 (probably died of battle wounds). (© *Marie-Lan Nguyen/Wikimedia Commons/ CC-BY 2.5*)

21. PHILIP the Arab, emperor 244–249 (killed in battle). The tumult of the year of revolution was followed by a difficult war with Sassanid Persia, in which Gordian III died. Philip the Arab was chosen by his military peers on the battlefield as the new emperor, with no reference to the Senate, though Philip did cooperate with the senators, and presided over a great celebration of the city of Rome's millennium. (*Rabax63/CC BY-SA 4.0*)

Philip was overthrown by Decius, who disdained cooperation with the Senate, despite being an active senator. He had been almost the last supporter of Maximinus, and inherited his policies. He died in battle, and the army chose Trebonianus Gallus as his successor. Trebonianus, however, was killed in battle against the usurper Aemilian, who in turn was killed in battle against Valerian, who sought revenge for the death of Trebonianus.

22. DECIUS, emperor 249–251 (killed in battle). (© *José Luiz Bernardes Ribeiro/CC BY-SA 4.0*)

23. TREBONIANUS GALLUS, emperor 251–253 (killed in battle). (*Katie Chao and Ben Muessig/CC BY-SA 2.0*)

24. AEMILIAN, emperor 253 (killed in battle). (*Rasiel Suarez/ CC BY-SA 3.0*)

25. VALERIAN, emperor 253–260 (died a prisoner of the Persians). Valerian was a superficially successful emperor, busy and campaigning throughout the empire. He was a junior colleague of the Gordians in Africa, and a supporter of the Senate's authority.

27. GALLIENUS, emperor 260–267 (murdered). Valerian's son Gallienus had been joint emperor with his father since 253. But the capture of Valerian destroyed the imperial authority, and parts of the empire seceded, and other parts were conquered. The solution was increased militarisation, centralisation of power in the hands of the emperor, and a final blow to the Senate's authority. Gallienus was the first of the autocratic emperors.

26. Valerian went to war with the Sassanid Empire. Defeated in battle, he was kept a prisoner by the Sassanid emperor and displayed to the Persian people as such. The Persian victory was celebrated in this sculpture at Naqsh-i-Rustam. (*Adobe Stock*)

those who had supported Albinus, and their properties went to fill the imperial treasury, even if they were allowed to live. There can be no doubt that this had been part of his purpose in his proscription regime all along. For a start, three new legions, and the new Praetorian Guard, were expensive.

The same happened in the east, where the procurator Claudius Xenophon had operated after the defeat of the army of Asellius near Nikaia; he then went to Africa with the same intention. In Gaul, there are signs that the killing of proprietors of the pottery kilns producing Samian pottery led to the destruction of much of the industry.[5] Since the emperor also claimed censorial authority, no doubt any opponents who were not killed off but had lost their property could easily be expelled from the Senate for falling below the required wealth threshold. This was the opposite of Augustus' policy, who had given gifts to hard-up senators who found themselves in financial straits – but this had the same effect of making those senators his creatures. The purge of the Senate was thus accompanied by a clear threat of sudden condemnation and financial destruction for any or all senators.

Clerks in Rome were kept busy recording the property now acquired by the imperial government in all parts of the empire. Severus had also devalued the currency by reducing the silver content of the coins minted in his name; this was hardly a new measure, and his son did the same; it is not certain that it was noticed by the general population, though hoards have been found in many areas, many of them consisting of older coins with a higher silver content; this suggests that people saved up the old 'good' coinage, and spent the new 'bad' coins as quickly as they received them.[6]

So Severus had plenty of money from rents and products and taxes from his new and very extensive imperial possessions, and from the confiscations, plus the ability to mint many more coins from the same supply of silver. He was also in the habit of apparently spontaneously handing out money gifts to those he wished to have as his supporters, such as the population of Rome.[7] His new riches also enabled him to increase the pay of the soldiers. This may have seemed generous, an overdue pay rise for the first time in a century, but it was perhaps more a consequence of the currency devaluation he had instituted. The soldiers' pay, in value terms, remained much the same.[8] (And there were now so many deductions from the soldiers' pay, for food, clothing, savings, and so on, as well as taxes to be paid, that each soldier received very little cash in hand.)[9] But it pleased the troops and cemented their loyalty to him and to his family, which was no doubt the real object of the pay rise. He was even more lavish with the public funds than the competitive senators in 193.

The same process of purging, execution, and confiscation that had hit the senatorial class was applied to the *equites*. Sixty of them were punished for having fought with Albinus in Gaul,[10] and no doubt this policy was applied also in the east. The local elites in the cities of Asia Minor and Syria and the local aristocracies had supported the governors of these areas – Niger and Asellius, and were thus vulnerable. They had, of course, no choice of whom to support any more than the Samian pottery manufacturers but Severus in his revenge took full advantage.[11]

This process represented a true revolution. The events of the first half of 193 had been *coups d'état* in which little actually changed except the person of the emperor – Pertinax for Commodus, Julianus for Pertinax, Septimius for Julianus; little more than the city and the Senate had been directly affected, and few executions had taken place. But with the arrival of Septimius Severus in power, the next years, 193 to 198, saw such a constant and extensive alteration in the personnel in government, imperially and locally, that it is clear that Severus was intent on altering the constitution of the imperial ruling class decisively. The extensive killings changed the balance of power between emperor and Senate, reducing the latter to the same subservience it had had to show towards Commodus, and down to the individual city councils.[12] Severus therefore confirmed the policy of Commodus, only rather more systematically and even more brutally. The even more extensive confiscations shifted the balance of economic power away from the localities to the centre, with the *res privata*, the 'Privy Purse', which had been first established by Marcus, now decisively expanded, and so made more important. It was not long before the cities were in trouble financially, and the central government had of the empire to devise ever more detailed and rigid rules to compel men to take up public offices which carried extensive financial obligations. It was obviously one of the consequences of Severus' policy of murder and confiscation, by transferring many resources from the localities to the centre.

It is unlikely that Severus or perhaps anyone else gave a thought to these implications – seeing into the future is not a human facility. (The author of the Severus essay in the *Historia Augusta*, however, comes close when he pointed out that 'he left an inheritance from the proscriptions greater than any of the emperors had left'.)[13] What he did aim to do, and succeeded in for a time, was to establish his family as the ruling imperial dynasty. Of course, it disintegrated into the oddest 'dynasty' that ever ruled an empire, even stranger than the Julio-Claudians, but his effect on government had been sufficiently thorough that opposition to the dynasty, as opposed to the individual incompetent and hapless emperors, was never effective until the dynasty itself committed genetic suicide by reducing itself to a single vulnerable life. Only when that life was extinguished in the murder of Alexander Severus in 235 did another dynastic change become possible.

One of the unintended consequences of the Severan revolution in 193 and after was that power then resided ever more centrally in the emperor himself. Perhaps the change should be called the 'Commodus-Severus Revolution', for his policy was a continuation of Commodus'. They had cowed the Senate with executions, and Severus continued to kill senators through the rest of his reign, a practice that continued with his son Caracalla. He had bribed the soldiers with pay rises, bringing them into a firm support for the dynasty, and this continued too. He had expanded the *res privata*, which was, by its very name, out of reach of any senatorial supervision. He had even taken over the posting system,[14] no doubt in part with the aim of having access to private letters, though the author of the *Historia Augusta* claims it was to 'make himself popular'. This was a series of centralising measures, which, along with the purges in all parts of the empire, was intended to enforce dynastic control.

Septimius Severus died at Eburacum (York) on 4 February 211.[15] Within a year, his eldest son, Caracalla, killed his younger brother Geta, pacified elements of the army who objected – more lavish handouts, and the concession that permitted soldiers to marry – and set about instituting a purge of all those who had favoured Geta in any way throughout the empire, but especially in Rome and in the Senate.[16] There cannot have been all that many, but Geta had been well liked, and Caracalla was certainly determined. He had learned the lesson from his father, of course, whose murderous reaction to opposition he had observed ever since childhood. This display of unnecessary savagery effortlessly crushed any complaints or opposition – for the moment.

Then the (sole) emperor set off to the east to wage war against Parthia. He did not return to Rome, and was murdered in Syria in April 217. His assassin was immediately killed; and that killer was then also killed; it has also the implication of a carefully laid-out plot, for the sequence of killings effectively prevented any investigation, though it is presented as a spontaneous murder.[17]

The Senate stirred, at times. In the reign of Caracalla, as in the later part of that of Severus, the emperor's long absences from Rome left the Senate without influence. In formal terms, it might be informed of imperial accomplishments, and compelled to register imperial achievements, but was not expected to do anything, other than act as a law court. After the purges and proscriptions this is not surprising, but they made a clear marginalisation of the Senate's remaining authority, which continued from Commodus' early reign to the end of Caracalla's, with only the first half of 193 as a break in the humiliation. So there was some rejoicing when the news came that Caracalla had been killed – and by one of his soldiers, one of the men he had so conspicuously favoured and rewarded.[18]

So far so good, but Caracalla was succeeded by M. Opellius Macrinus, Caracalla's praetorian prefect who had accompanied the dead emperor on his planned eastern campaign (he had not actually begun it when he died). Macrinus was, in all likelihood, the organiser of the assassination, certainly Dio Cassius and Herodian thought so. He was, of course, an *eques*, but a high flyer, an efficient administrator, and an intelligent man. He was also a Berber from Mauretania. It was, therefore, a surprise to the Senate to learn, first that Caracalla was dead, and then that Macrinus had imposed himself as his imperial successor, after a formal election by elements of the army.[19] This was the process that Severus had gone through at Carnuntum in 193. This time it happened on the eastern boundary of the empire, perhaps two months' journey away from the Senate, and the Senate could do nothing to affect or change things at such a distance. As Tacitus had remarked in his book on the civil war of 68–69, an emperor could be made elsewhere than at Rome.

The senators were actually so pleased to be rid of Caracalla that scarcely a murmur of complaint at the succession by a Mauretanian *eques* to the imperial throne on the border of the empire was made, at least at first. Macrinus wrote to the Senate, explaining that he had been made emperor by the army. The Senate, as usual, acquiesced, but grumbled about the new emperor's political appointments.[20]

Macrinus is accused, by both Dio Cassius and Herodian, of being the instigator of the plot that killed Caracalla.[21] Since Caracalla was popular in the army this would explain the killings of the assassin and then of the assassin's killer, properly muddying the waters for any investigation. (It looks as though Macrinus, or whoever organised the coup, had studied earlier assassinations – that of Domitian was a prime exemple.)

In the following year, the new emperor was killed. He had not left Syria, and the army there selected a new ruler, almost casually. He was claimed to be an illegitimate son of Caracalla, and he came equipped with a formidable grandmother, Julia Maesa, the sister of Caracalla's mother.[22] Since the new emperor was only fourteen years of age, she acted as his regent; his mother, Julia Soaemias, came too, though she was overshadowed by Maesa. (For the record, Caracalla was only twenty-nine when he died, so fathering the new emperor was scarcely probable, but the soldiers ignored this improbability.) At first, only a single legion, III *Gallica* at Emesa, supported the boy's pretensions; Macrinus failed in an attempt to get support from II *Parthica* at Apamaea, and then fled to Antioch. He gathered his forces and met III *Gallica* at Immae near Antioch, but in the end, he commanded only the Praetorian Guard and some auxiliaries, for he had lost a large part of his army in a lost battle against the Parthians. He mismanaged this fight as well and then again fled the scene.[23]

The new Emperor Antoninus (usually now referred to as 'Elagabalus', a name derived from the god El worshipped in his home city of Emesa) apart from being a teenager, was also a religious devotee and the priest of El.[24] The coup conducted to propel him to the position of emperor was slow and violent, and totally ignored the Senate. His initial base, apart from his mother and the people of Emesa, was a single legion, III *Gallica*, stationed nearby, whose soldiers knew of him from his performances as priest. When Macrinus' support disintegrated, he was left as an acclaimed emperor, but only in northern Syria (the province of Syria Coele). It is not surprising that Macrinus had thought he could snuff out the challenge with just his guard.

The deaths of Macrinus and his son were followed by those of the governors of Syria Coele, Arabia, Cyprus, Cappadocia, and Egypt, and several high-ranking members of Macrinus' court. It was a cull of the most senior officials in the east. All of these men were seen as supporters of the dead Macrinus, and unwilling to accept a boy priest as emperor. This ensured that the eastern provinces quickly came under the new emperor's authority when replacements were appointed. This replacement policy was what Macrinus himself had done, though in a rather more limited fashion.

In Rome, the city prefect, Marius Maximus, was a Severan loyalist, and organised the killing of a number of opponents of the new ruler.[25] Since he later condemned Elagabalus, it may be assumed that he, and therefore all Rome, had no idea who he was other perhaps than that he was a descendant of Septimius Severus.

The selective but geographically extensive killing spree was followed by the appointment of successors to those executed, who were often soldiers promoted to senators, in some cases from the rank of centurion, and appointed as governors or legionary legates, probably because there was no senator available and willing to be appointed. Marius Maximus disapproved, as did Dio Cassius, together representing the conservative group of senators[26] – which were probably all senators. Nevertheless, the new regime succeeded in becoming established, partly by its slow passage from Syria to Rome, which must have seemed menacing, but was probably slow as the new emperor's people tried to persuade him to be less flagrantly Syrian and adolescent in dress, worship, and behaviour.

The battle at Immae was in June 218. Elagabalus did not reach Rome until September of the next year.[27] The new emperor was, of course, almost unknown in the city, but as a Severan, he could be accepted by a court that had been purged of anti-Severans. As the soldiers in Syria had seen, he bore an obvious remembrance to Caracalla as a child – not surprising, given their ancestry from sisters. Perhaps the Senate believed that the child could be guided by the senators' wise old heads – the method Marcus had devised to control Commodus; perhaps they were as relieved to be rid of Macrinus as they had been of Severus and Caracalla. Most likely, they feared for their lives – the new regime was as homicidal as those of Severus and Caracalla. Some observers must have understood that to go from an experienced emperor to a homicidal emperor to jumped-up bureaucrat and then to an impressionable teenaged religious zealot was a catastrophic downward slope, and that the actions of the dynasty were damaging the Roman Empire generally.

Inevitably, the Senate was ignored by Elagabalus' regime. There is virtually no place for it in the surviving inventions and fictions that pass for an account of Elagabalus' reign, apart from a story in the *Historia Augusta* that he ordered the senators to leave Rome on one occasion.[28]

Elagabalus, however, in many of his more comprehensible actions, exhibits a clear wish to become accepted in the city and the empire. He introduced the worship of his god, having a huge classical type temple built for it.[29] It was not the first eastern god to be imported: the Senate itself had brought a similar god from Asia Minor, the Magna Mater; in the Second Punic War, Egyptian Isis and Serapis were well known; Jupiter Dolichenus and Mithras came from further east, and their worship had spread widely in the previous century; while Christianity was spreading in Italy and elsewhere. Elagabalus himself married a series of aristocratic Roman women, which was surely aimed at linking him with the Roman aristocracy; one of these was a Vestal Virgin, where clearly the aim was to link him with the old Roman religion, and that with his new god.[30]

All of this is, of course, the rationalisation of the antics of a deluded teenager, who was experimenting in all directions, social, sexual, and religious, in a personal situation where no bounds had been set to his conduct – reminiscent of Commodus. But his wild ways meant that it is not surprising that he had little support in the Senate. The populace of Rome was amused by his antics, as they had been by Commodus in the arena; but the religious amongst the Romans were shocked by the importation of an alien god, or at least they claimed to be shocked, no matter how well intentioned the experiment was. The treatment of Vesta, one of the most revered goddesses of the city, was, for some, profoundly disturbing.[31]

In June 221, the emperor was induced to adopt his cousin Alexianus as his heir, and give him the title of Caesar, and the name Marcus Aurelius Alexander. This was technically an act of the Senate, which obediently did as it was told, but Elagabalus claimed that it was an instruction from his god, which came to him in a dream.[32] No doubt older senators will have recognised the technique, which was one exploited by Septimius. But now both the emperor and his opponents must have come to understand that Elagabalus, by acquiring and appointing an heir, had made himself vulnerable, for a replacement was thus immediately available, and the elimination of Elagabalus was now clearly possible without serious political disruption.

Elagabalus retained the support of the praetorian prefects for some time. These were able to control the Guard, but more than one mutiny by the Guard demonstrated the precariousness of his position. He was also beginning to have doubts about the instructions he claimed to have received from his god – a sign that he was wavering over the adoption of his cousin.[33] His grandmother Julia Maesa had actually been the engine for the adoption, and it was her influence that helped swing the Guard towards supporting Alexander. His new name, composed of memories of the Emperor Marcus and of Alexander the Great, was a clever composition, appealing to the soldiers. The imperial court was clearly divided on the issue, and Elagabalus made an attempt to remove Alexander's supporters. By the end of 221, the division between the boys was becoming public, and a display of mutual affection between the two of them only stayed the disaffection briefly.[34]

In March 222, the praetorians broke loose. They murdered the emperor, his mother, the two praetorian prefects, the *praefectus urbi* (not Marius Maximus any longer) and some others – a murder spree very like that conducted at Elagabalus' proclamation.[35] Then Alexander was conducted to the palace and installed as emperor. The accounts we have of these events vary in important details, above all in why Elagabalus went to the Guard camp where he was in effect kidnapped and then murdered. The net result, however, was that Alexander was proclaimed emperor by the Guard, to which the Senate acquiesced, probably once more with relief at the removal of an embarrassing emperor, which is what the Senate had done for Septimius in 193.

One must feel sorry for Elagabalus, plucked from a comfortable life in Emesa and dumped in Rome, where he clearly believed as emperor that he could do anything he wished – as other emperors had acted. His reputation has been traduced by the ancient historians, whose inventiveness is only exceeded by their inaccuracy – in this followed by modern historians – and the truth about the boy himself is virtually impossible to find. What stands out quite clearly is that the Senate and the senators had virtually no influence on events. They registered such things as the adoption of the heir to the empire, and the installation of three emperors in five years (Macrinus, Elagabalus, and Alexander), none of whom were suitable for the position, at least in the Senate's eyes. And yet the senators made little or no protest at being so cavalierly taken for granted – the reaction being one in fear of their lives, in all probability.

The new emperor, Marcus Aurelius Alexander Severus, was about thirteen years old when he was so abruptly propelled onto the throne of the emperors, though, since he had been Caesar for several months, it cannot have been all that surprising. He reigned for as long again, dying – being killed – in 235 at the age of about twenty-six. He was, of course, like his four predecessors, murdered by the soldiers. And this time there was no member of the family, or even of his court, to take over when he was killed. He was the end of what can only be considered a failed dynasty, and a notably divisive one.

It is difficult to characterise Elagabalus as 'ruling' the empire. At first, he was too young and inexperienced, both at ruling and with regard to the Roman system and society; later his only recorded actions are personal to him. Accordingly, the empire was clearly being governed, out of the palace, by such people as his mother and other appointed officials. The consuls were still appointed, governors were sent out, and so on, but the emperor was scarcely involved, except perhaps to sign whatever documents were placed before him. That is, his governing methods were those of Commodus, though in this case it was not the emperor's choice but his youth and ignorance that was the source. The re-emergence of such a regime so easily was a mark of the Senate's impotence as much as of the competence of the emperor's court.

Throughout his reign the new emperor's mother, Julia Mammaea, and for a time his grandmother, Julia Maesa, acted as regents for him; Maesa died soon, probably in 223,[36] but Mammaea continued to dominate the emperor for the rest of his life, and was killed along with him. It used to be thought that the man who was promoted to be praetorian prefect in Alexander's first year, Domitius Ulpianus (Ulpian, noted for his legal expertise), was also influential, but he was killed in riots in Rome in 223, and his deeds now seem to be less judicious than self-seeking, even murderous.[37] The early removal of Julia Maesa and Ulpian, both strong and politically experienced characters, also removed useful props from the Severan throne.

Another interpretation has been that the reign of Alexander Severus saw a return to the cosy relations of Senate and emperor, as had existed, it was believed, in Marcus Aurelius' time, and that the murder of the emperor and the accession of Maximinus Thrax shattered that partnership. The problem here is that this is an exercise in nostalgia, not fact. There is indeed very little evidence of any relationship between the emperor and his senators except that he continued to employ senators in governing posts, just as did every other emperor, but perhaps more so than with his cousin Elagabalus, whose regents had favoured appointing *equites* to such posts.

For it is, as with other Severans, the case that the sources for the reign of Alexander are, not to put too strong a point on it, dire, even more so than with the other Severan biographies. There are only fragments of Dio Cassius, and none after about 228; the *Historia Augusta* life of the emperor is very largely fiction, with just occasional nuggets of fact in it (though it is still being relied on by modern biographers in the absence of anything else), but sorting out fact from fiction is laborious and unsatisfying; Herodian has what purports to be a continuous narrative, but he is even more woolly and averse to engaging with the facts than usual; rhetorically, and perhaps when it was recited, his account would sound impressive, yet on a closer inspection it is distinctly lacking in hard and verifiable fact.[38]

So, to say that the emperor and the Senate got along well is to make an optimistic assumption, as airy as any Herodianic persiflage; it may have been so, but we have little or no evidence for such a conclusion about their relationship; if anything, it seems also that the main influence on the emperor was his mother. This interpretation may be wholly misleading; yet there is also just as little evidence of conflict between them. Senators were employed, gained consulships, and appear to have exercised their opinions without the danger of immediate execution, which made a change, but this only means that the Senate remained as cowed in the face of imperial power as it had been ever since Severus' scythe cut down so many of its members, and Caracalla continued that role – a quarter of a century of oppression and killing. It would take more than the rule of a pleasant youth and his mother to allow the senators to raise their vulnerable heads too distinctly above the parapet.

It is therefore necessary to put aside any theories regarding the Senate's attitude to the reign of Alexander. Instead, the only items to be noted are, where Alexander went, where he lived, his court, and his actual activities; though needless to say, given the inadequate sources, much of this is invisible as well. For here what stands out are the tribulations of the first years of his reign, and his virtually continuous absence from the city throughout his last years.

The emperor spent a large part of his reign either too young to rule, or outside Rome. He was probably about thirteen when he was made emperor in 222, so he could scarcely be expected to rule before the late 220s; he left the city in spring 233 for the Persian War, and when that war was abandoned he went at once to Germany with only a short stay in Rome in between. He can therefore only have been in a position to exercise authority in Rome for a few years. Throughout his reign, even in his adulthood, he, like his cousin, had people ruling for him – and the Senate, even if its members were no longer subject to sudden execution, had as little influence on events and affairs as earlier.

The soldiers in Rome were uncontrollable for a time at the start of the reign, perhaps intoxicated by the success of the killing of Elagabalus and the others. In a riot in 223, they deliberately targeted Ulpian, killing him in the palace before the eyes of Mammaea and Alexander.[39] (Shades once more of the killing of Domitian's murderers by the Guard, despite Nerva's explicit protection for them.) The instigator was Aurelius Epagathus, a freedman who was *praefectus annonae*; he had provoked a group of soldiers to kill their commander, the praetorian prefect (Ulpian), which may not have been a difficult task – either success in provocation or in killing – the lack of military experience of the prefects made their command of the Guard increasingly theoretical. The deed actually emphasised the early lack of authority of the emperor, but Mammaea (probably) had read her history; Epagathus was promoted to be *praefectus Aegypti*, and then extracted to Crete and executed – just as Paternus had been shifted out of his position as praetorian prefect by being made a senator, and then, out of reach of the protection of the Guard, killed at Commodus' order; in their new positions neither man had any protection.

Such deft moves suggest that the new regime's regents had useful political skills (except Ulpian, of course), together with the capability to gain control of the imperial governmental machine, and eventually the troops in the city. The senators who were promoted and who are recorded in the sources, tended to be men who had last held office in Severus' reign.[40] Caracalla and Elagabalus had tended to promote *equites* to high positions (as had Macrinus, an *eques* himself, of course) adlecting them to the Senate where necessary. They thus tended to ignore the experience of the senators, an apparent dislike that was fully reciprocated by the Senate. But now men such as Dio Cassius and Marius Maximus who had been sidelined for the last ten years, and in Dio's case had been away from Rome during that time, were back in favour. Second consulships became available again, and the prefectures and governorships went to senators.[41] It must have seemed like a return to the old days, at least to the old methods. *Equites* were not ignored, but they were expected to work their way along the *cursus* in the old way. The restoration of the old procedures was no doubt a relief to those senators who benefited from it, and perhaps to senators as a whole. This is one of the sources of the later nostalgia for Alexander's reign, though the Senate itself, as opposed to individual senators, had no useful role.

The result of the hostility towards the Senate of the previous emperors from Commodus onwards could not be overturned by a few years of rewards for a few selected senators, though it might keep the rest quiet in hopes of future benefits, precisely the attitude which had kept the Senate quiet under Commodus and Severus. The Severans had put their faith in the support of the army, and had ignored or denigrated the Senate, but under Elagabalus and then Alexander this military reliance began to fail. Caracalla could continue his father's methods, of rewarding some and executing internal dissidents, but Macrinus, Elagabalus, and Alexander were not soldiers. The killing of Elagabalus was army work, as was the killing of Ulpian. Then from 230 the empire came under attack, first in the east, where a new dynasty had taken power in Persia (the Sasanids) and then in the west, from the Alamanni, another new factor.

The twenty-two-year-old Alexander travelled east to take command in 230.[42] (Before he left he 'went to the Senate and announced his departure to them in terms similar to what he had said to the soldiers' – note the priority of the army over the Senate.)[43] This journey was no doubt a mistake, since he was as lacking in military training and skills as his cousin, and the Severan name assumed that the emperor possessed both, even though Septimius and Caracalla had none to speak of; it might have been better to emulate Septimius and put experienced soldiers in command, but his very inexperience required him to be seen to be in command, and Septimius could avoid direct command by his administrative expertise. The campaign against the Persians in 231–232 was relatively successful nevertheless, but costly in casualties, and it included at least one severe defeat on the battlefield.[44]

The problem with reliance on the army for support is that it might – literally – become a spike to pierce the hand that held it. While Alexander was in the east, and probably not by coincidence, the Alamanni in Germany launched an attack on the Rhine frontier, directed at the region called the *agri decumanes*, which had been captured a century and a half before by Domitian. The Alamanni in attacking the Rhine frontier were replicating the attacks of the Marcomanni and Quadi against the Danubian frontier in Marcus' time; in both cases, the reduction of the forces on the German frontier by removing contingents to fight in the east left the western defences vulnerable to attack, and their enemies took advantage. The Alamanni were a new and formidable threat, a federation of German tribes that could deploy greater strength than its constituent members could individually. Another federation of the same sort, the Franks, soon began to threaten the frontier on the lower Rhine.[45] So the unmilitary youth who ruled the empire and was unpopular with the army had to face the simultaneous threats in Germany and the east, which were the most potent problems the empire had faced for two centuries.

Septimius had confiscated large numbers of rich estates as well as personally owned treasure, so that he disposed of large quantities of money, the source of a reputation for generosity and spontaneous gifts. Much of this acquired wealth had been used to expand the army, which enabled him and his son to conduct several expensive military campaigns. This resource had evidently now expired – the dynasty was particularly extravagant – and the army was now once more short of men. Hence the military diffidence of Alexander's reign, which was clearly not entirely due to his youth and inexperience.

Alexander had become unpopular with the army because he was not really an Alexander. The two rulers were of the same age when they took command to fight their wars, and both commanded skilled fighting armies; the difference between them was partly the difference in the skills that these similarly named boys had learned, but also in their speed of action, and their mothers – Alexander the Great's mother was left at home, and was kept under control by regular letters.

The army in which the commander's mother was present, as was Mammaea with Alexander, and dominated him, would hardly earn the army's respect; and, as for speed, he had travelled slowly through the Balkans collecting his forces, and after fighting against the Persians ended he returned to Rome, where he celebrated a triumph, and spent some time in the city.[46] The contrast was not only with Alexander the Great but also with Septimius Severus, whose name he also bore; both of these commanders were noted for their speed of travel and their decisiveness.

It was thus not until 234 that the emperor was able to travel to Germany to engage against the Alamanni.[47] The invaders were successfully driven out of Roman territory, and a large force was gathered at Mogontiacum for a reverse-invasion next year. This army was partly composed of men who had been part of the less-than-successful war against the Persians, and men whose homes and/or camps on the German frontier had been destroyed by the Alamannic invasion. They were very unhappy, so much so that a prominent soldier laid a plot to remove the emperor (and his mother) in the name of more vigorous military campaigning. Alexander had, as in the Persian war, decided that it would be best to buy peace, not a pleasing prospect for the soldiers, who wished to go on campaign; those whose homes had been burnt down sought revenge, others looked to collect loot, and more simply wanted a fight, while all needed a victory for their military pride. Alexander's reputation sank still lower. When the coup came, those who did not support it also did not oppose it. In the winter of 235 (late in February or early in March), the coup succeeded, emperor and mother were killed, and the leader of the plot, C. Julius Verus Maximinus, was proclaimed emperor by the soldiers.[48]

This marked almost the end of the Severan system. It ended with the reign of Maximinus Thrax, which was a purely military regime. He never went to Rome, wholly disdained the Senate, which, in his determination to rescue the empire, repair its frontiers, and defeat its barbarian enemies, had no place. It was not just the end of Septimius' system, but also the culmination of it. The dominance of the army had been evident in the reigns of Septimius from the beginning, when he distributed his treasure to solicit popular support and use his confiscated wealth to enlarge the army. It had also, of course, been implicit in the Augustan system as well, but Augustus carefully retained a role for the Senate. The Senate now saw its role eliminated, while it continued in existence with little to do. The military regime was perfectly viable, of course, but it would not be acceptable in the long run, either to the plebs, to whom most emperors played up, or to the senatorial aristocracy, who had reserves of political and military strength which turned out to be surprising.

Chapter 8

The Revolution of 238

Revolutions come in various guises. Some are mild, others violent; some are brief and quickly over, others long drawn out; some happen so fast that we call them by a special name, *coups d'état*. Modern European history, at least since the Reformation, has provided a series of examples. The archetypes are the French (from 1789) and Russian (from 1917) revolutions, violent and lengthy; the Dutch (from 1572) was fairly quick, but led to a long defensive series of wars; the English (from 1641) was slow and violent; the Scottish (from 1637) was carried through with speed, but led on to years of warfare.

Some revolutions produce deep changes in their societies – the French, Russian and German are examples – others in effect achieve much less, at least in the short term, but can have much longer consequences. The English revolution is of that type, with slow changes over a decade, then a 'restoration' which restored only the monarchy, but left the original purpose of the revolutionaries, the establishment of a permanent parliamentary regime, intact; this was followed by a long tail over the next fifty years, including the 'Glorious Revolution' – leading again to war, and the unification of the British islands. The American Revolution, which produced the United States, superficially changed very little in the short term, and even among the rulers in the United States there was little change between the personnel before and after, but it could be argued that subsequent changes continued developing through the society until after the American Civil War, which is sometimes called the Second American Revolution. And these revolutions can be dated to a particular year, at least at their beginnings, but no one would suggest that they had not been long in preparation; all had been brewing for years, decades, before the outbreak.

The point is that revolutions vary, and though they might seem to be quick and sudden, they had long origins and long consequences. The Romans went through a violent and lengthy series of changes in the last century BC, beginning even as far back as the 130s BC, but the final episode is usually reckoned to be from about 60 to 30 BC, with a long tail of subsequent changes under Augustus' experimentations.

There then followed violent changes of rulers in AD 68–69, AD 96–99, AD 193–197, and in 238; there were others later. These were all concentrated on the person of the emperor, and by comparison with the European and American revolutions, none of these would really count as true revolutions, except the first, because the rest of society was not usually much affected. But each episode after the first was also violent and confusing, if not necessarily lengthy. These events, of course, are characteristic of revolutions, and, in another characteristic, they all ended in highly unexpected ways. In 68, no one would have predicted Emperor Vespasian; in 96, Trajan was on no one's list of pretenders; Septimius Severus was just as unexpected in 193.

In so far as Roman society was a stable construct, with accepted and recognisable layers of classes, no revolution involving the person of the emperor was going to affect more than the topmost social layer, though each revolution was lethal within that group in varying degrees, and when it developed into civil war, the lower classes might suffer in various ways, from local massacres to military conscription to extortion. And yet society as a whole did not change in any fundamental sense, nor was any revolution achieving any such change. What did alter was the composition of the ruling group, partly society aimed at achieving any such change because many of that group died, and partly because those who survived had to keep their heads down under the new regime.

The Roman revolutions of the imperial period were therefore not really up to the violent and disruptive revolutionary standards set by the French and Russian events (few revolutions are), though the late Republican revolution of 60–30 BC certainly was in terms of violence and death. What distinguishes all of the Roman ones, however, is their violence, and the restricted range of effects, which are mainly confined to the personnel of the ruling class (or caste). It is a truism in revolutionary studies that most revolutions change little, in the sense that politically the result is usually the replacement of one ruling class (French monarchic aristocrats, Tsarist bureaucrats, Charles I) by a similar set of people (Napoleonists, Stalinists, Oliver Cromwell – the return of the Bourbons, the end of the Soviet Union, but still a dictatorship, the Restoration) whose government regime is little different from the regime preceding the revolution – the autocracy of Napoleon replacing that of Louis XVI, for example. In this reckoning, the Roman imperial revolutions certainly measure up to the norm, with the obligatory violence included.

The archetypal Roman revolution, that which replaced the senatorial regime of 60 BC with the Augustan autocracy of 30 BC, replaced only part of the old regime, and considerable parts of the senatorial system and personnel survived. This happened also in 68–69, and 193–197 (though not so much in 96–99). But the casualty rate among the supporters of the replaced regime was usually heavy. The deaths among the actual participants must be added to those inflicted in the last years of the previous regime – those caused by Claudius and Nero may be added to those killed in the subsequent civil wars, and those killed in Commodus' reign may be added to those of the succeeding warfare. The events of 193–197 certainly changed the ruling group from the 'Antonines' to the 'Severans', with plenty of killings before, under Commodus, during, under Septimius, and after, under Elagabalus and Alexander's early regents, and it also degraded the power of the Senate drastically. The extent of the change certainly justified the appellation of 'revolution'.

Which, of course, brings us to the Roman Revolution of 238. The events of that year bring out another characteristic of revolutions. They often enter into the violent phase only after a preliminary period of slow change and relatively minor events and developments that was resisted by those who conducted the revolution. In England, King Charles I attempted to impose monarchical rule, disregarding the parliament, and the revolution came when he relaxed his grip and in desperation summoned a disobedient parliament, which he hoped to control and swiftly dismiss; this was in its effect similar in the French Revolution, the changes triggered by the summoning of the estate general. In the American colonies, the British attempt to impose tighter control on those colonies was resisted for ten years, but was broken at the first violent revolutionary outbreak, the siege of Boston, which resulted in driving out the British forces, after which British control was never reimposed, except temporarily here and there. The Roman revolution of 238 came about when the Emperor Maximinus reimposed a much stricter regime with increased taxes, total neglect of the Senate, increased pay for the army than had existed under the later Severans, and it broke out when he was defied in a minor riot in a distant province. This then set in train the long period of violence and confusion of the next half-century, a consequence that strongly suggests that the preparation for the revolution was long and originating deep in the past. The revolutionary period thus can be said to have begun in 235 with Maximinus' *coup d'état*, but building on long discontents. The end result, after half a century of turbulence, was the imposition of a much more rigorous imperial dictatorship – the Roman version of Bonapartism or Stalinism – under Diocletian and his colleagues, something hinted at under Commodus and the Severans, and briefly reached with Maximinus.

Emperor Maximinus,[1] who seized power in March 235 by murdering the existing emperor, Alexander Severus (and his mother), has been the subject of more than usual sets of lies and distortions which has come to be expected of the historians of the time, notably the *Historia Augusta*. All these authors may be described as of the senatorial persuasion – for the Senate was the institution at which Maximinus directed his main measures of control, and perhaps his enmity. He did not only neglect it but also failed to honour it, which was clearly painful.[2] Whatever the truth of the nostalgic remembrance of a supposedly

Senate-friendly regime under Alexander Severus – and there is probably little in it – there is no doubt that Maximinus imposed seriously restrictive and unpleasant measures, particularly on the senators, who were also the men most likely and able to make loud complaints, and have an effect.

He had taken power above all for military reasons, because the regime of Alexander was seen as failing to defend the empire adequately.[3] He was therefore required to exert and increase his military forces, and that meant he needed more money to pay his soldiers. He had specialised in training recruits, and, like Severus, whom he much resembled in his policies, he was generous with praise and rewards even then.[4]

The troops had changed as a community since the days of Marcus Aurelius. The men were now permitted to marry (a decision of Septimius'), and married men required higher pay and housing outside the camp. They were also more likely to be recruited from the frontier regions rather than Italy, as had been the main practice before Severus; the Italian recruits had been Roman citizens, at least those in the legions and the Guard, and were from property-owning families, whereas those recruited from the frontier lands were quite probably landless, going into the army as a means of acquiring economic support. Maximinus' requirement for money was clear from the start in his appeal to the soldiers that he led in the coup: he promised them double pay, plus the usual imperial donative.[5] This, when he was in power, necessarily required increased taxation.

The treasury he inherited was seriously run down from the recent fighting in the east and Germany. To raise the money for his promised pay and donative he resorted to extraordinary measures. He reduced the money allocated to the dole at Rome – grain and oil notably, but also occasionally meat – and imposed taxation on the senatorial class.[6] The details of this last are unclear, but the pain was such that wild tales of murder and the theft of temple treasures appear in the sources.[7] Herodian in fact includes the standard accusations usually levelled against oppressive emperors, though without being actually specific to Maximinus' reign.[8] These are probably in many cases invented for propaganda purposes; what they actually indicate is the reaction of the senatorial class, being taxed for the first time. They were, of course, rich, which is not to say that they could afford what was being taken.

Maximinus used the money gathered to pay his soldiers. The money came in slowly, and only those army units under his direct command were paid at first at the increased rates. Since he was personally in command on the Rhine, the legions and regiments on the Rhine frontier, the area most seriously threatened, were paid first and then campaigned successfully. The Danubian forces went into battle later, and had also probably received the new pay scales by then. The eastern legions did not come out to support him when opposition developed;

possibly he had not yet paid them the new rates, but since there was Persian trouble on the eastern frontier, no doubt he intended to pay them when he got round to dealing with the eastern problems.[9]

Maximinus had thereby pleased parts of the army, having presumably made promises to the rest, but found it difficult to fulfil those promises – and the soldiers will have heard all this before. He had in the process, however, also alienated the Roman mob by reducing the dole, as well as the Senate, and neither of whom could be convinced of the imperial necessity for their sacrifices (though neither of these groups were directly involved in the exercise of power). Increased taxation on the wealthy, of course, spread out to other social groups, as the rich landowners increased the rents they took from their tenants, who were generally peasants. Peasants were unlikely to blame the emperor for the increases in rent charges, but certainly, they would complain to their landlords and bailiffs, and peasants were not usually reticent in complaining vocally and physically.

The new emperor's life and experiences are heavily obscured by the distortions of the propaganda-laden accounts that we have. It seems he was neither of peasant origin nor a Thracian but, from his name at least, he was a Roman citizen and probably from Moesia. This was certainly one of the frontier provinces, and like many of his soldiers, his ancestry was probably among the Italian colonists who had been established with a small estate in many of the frontier provinces.[10] He was also probably of the *eques* class, and so he will have been possessed of some considerable personal or family wealth. He had risen to the equivalent of high rank in the army. He was clearly a capable soldier, and, in March 235, he carried through a well-planned coup. He was not a nonentity, nor a buffoon.

He had experience as a soldier almost exclusively (so far as we can see) and had little or no experience of either politics (other than the army kind) or of diplomacy. He probably thought that having made himself emperor, the rest of the empire would obey him automatically, as soldiers usually expect. He clearly understood the military requirements on the frontier, and was a successful commander against the German tribes and along the Danubian frontier.[11]

It would have been interesting to see how he coped with the different fighting in the eastern lands. It is quite likely that he had experience there already, and he evidently knew the capabilities of the Osrhoenian archers and of Persian cavalry. He was the archetype of the 'soldier-emperor', but, as usual with such men, he was probably baffled by the politics of the empire, which are less amenable to barked commands, and he reacted quickly with force when opposed.

The situation, therefore, was that the supposed easy regime of Alexander Severus was discarded, and a much tougher regime was imposed, for a more aggressive military policy. This internal change alienated some important classes of the population, notably the Senate and the wealthy. Whatever consideration

Alexander had shown towards the Senate – and there had not been much – ended, and taxation of the wealthy, including the senators, was imposed. This produced an approximation to a pre-revolutionary situation. The apparent gradual relaxation of the severity of the early Severan emperors which had been pursued under Alexander, perhaps inadvertently given his youth, and his mother as regent, was being reversed, and the Severan severity was being restored, to the detriment and annoyance of those who had previously benefited and been relieved by the relaxation. No consultation with the Senate existed. The reason for the increased severity and the new austerity was not understood, perhaps, and it was never explained, nor were the reasons well publicised by Maximinus, who probably thought it was not necessary given the situation on the frontiers, with which he was very familiar, but which may not have been well understood in Rome.

The reaction was fairly slow in coming. Maximinus' coup took place in spring 235, but it was not until 238 that any serious opposition emerged. There had been a couple of plots against him in those three years, in the names of men described as senators – 'Magnus' and 'Quartinus' – which did not go anywhere, though Quartinus' revolt was mainly a mutiny by the regiment of Osrhoenian archers, who had been brought west by Alexander and 'bitterly regretted Alexander's death'.[12] Perhaps the failures of these plots deterred other senators from taking action for a time, but it did not quieten their resentment or appease their growing anger.

The German campaign, which Maximinus undertook almost as soon as he had made himself emperor, is difficult to describe. The only specific indication of what took place is that the army is said to have advanced 48 or 80 kilometres, presumably against the Alamanni, and then fought a battle in marshy country, where the emperor's own skill and bravery contributed much to the victory – he was *Imperator II* and *Germanicus Maximus* before the end of 235, according to his coins, no doubt as a result of this victory, and this would thus confirm the campaign.[13] Further precision is impossible given Herodian's vagueness and the *Historia Augusta*'s fiction. (This has not prevented elaborate modern accounts of an extensive campaign which had taken the army as far as the Elbe River and even further.)[14]

He caused 'huge pictures' of his triumphant campaign to be displayed before the Senate House in Rome, which may be the source of Herodian's descriptions.[15] This was something that is likely to have appealed to the people of Rome rather than the senators, who will have taken a fairly cynical view of the accuracy of the portrayal. By placing the pictures before the Senate House, also, the senators may well have felt that they were being insulted.

The physical evidence of his activity consists of repairs and rebuilding at several of the forts along the Rhine frontier in the salient of the Taunus Hills around the Wetterau; other indications of his presence are in inscriptions at several forts and camps. It would seem that the campaign went only a limited distance into 'free' Germany, but that it was generally regarded as successful.[16]

The army he used was that which Alexander Severus had collected for the same purpose, and included troops he had brought with him from the eastern campaign – a regiment of Osrhoenian archers, some Parthians and Armenians, who had been recruited. These units were usually formed of deserters from their original armies; there were also units brought in from Britannia (*numeri Brittonum*) and Mauretania (also *numeri*). Even the bridge of boats across the Rhine (though Herodian only calls it 'a river') had been built at Alexander's orders. So the difference between the two commanders was that Alexander would have used his gathered forces as a threat, to extract a negotiated peace from the Alamanni, which could be enforced by a payment of gold; Maximinus, by contrast, used the army to punish the Alamanni, but also perhaps to cement its loyalty to him. The object in both cases was a durable peace. Maximinus' policy worked, in the sense that the frontier line was quiet for the next two decades. He also recruited German mercenaries; the prospect of peace in the area would only make well-paid military service attractive.[17]

This campaign occupied 235, and was over by the winter. Maximinus then moved his headquarters to Sirmium, in Pannonia, and 236 was spent in campaigning north of the Danube. Even less information is provided about this campaign than about that against the Alamanni. (Herodian omits it.) It has been supposed that fighting took place against the Iazyges, in Moesia Inferior, and in Dacia – these latter two areas of conflict would suggest that the empire had been invaded. Whatever precisely happened, the emperor collected two more acclamations as *Imperator*, and then another in the first part of 237, which implies a good deal of fighting; he also took the titles of *Dacicus Maximus* and *Sarmaticus Maximus*, which marks them out clearly as his enemies.[18] But he had not finished campaigning in the area, and was preparing another army at Sirmium for the campaign of 238.

The consequences of the campaigns, of Maximinus' activities, and of his achievements, has encouraged more speculation but few persuasive conclusions. By staying at Sirmium for the winter of 237–238 it seems probable that another trans-Danubian campaign was in prospect, no doubt to finish the work already started. Then there was the problem of the east, not yet dealt with, but surely on the list of tasks to be accomplished – Alexander Severus' campaign there had been less than successful. So it would seem that he intended to drive his armies to repel invaders, but there is no sign that he aimed to extend the empire by occupying new territory. It has been suggested that his campaigning for three years on the northern frontier may have indicated an ambition to expand the empire, completing Marcus Aurelius' work.[19] It is perhaps more likely that he was like almost all the other imperial campaigners from Tiberius onwards – waging war in order to hold on to imperial territory, but not normally to extend it. The conquests of Britannia and Dacia had been relatively expensive in manpower, not just in the campaigns but in the subsequent garrisons they required – each of these provinces was held by three legions plus *auxilia*, and both were regularly invaded even so. (And Trajan's eastern campaign was a lesson in what not to do there, while Septimius' conquests had been abandoned.) Maximinus was a conservative strategist, if innovative in his internal policies.

The political constitution of certain groups in the empire had thus become volatile, and trouble could emerge from almost any quarter or person, just as in 68 when it came unexpectedly from Spain, or 193, unexpectedly from Pertinax (and in 235 from Maximinus). The proximate cause of the outbreak of the rebellion against Maximinus in 238 was a minor incident in or near the city of Thysdrus in the province of Africa Consularis, when a gang of young men of the region turned on an oppressive and greedy procurator. This was no more than a local reaction against Maximinus' policy of increased taxation. The procurator, who is never named, aimed at squeezing maximum taxes out of the large estates; he delivered sentences – presumably in response to accusations such as failures to pay due taxes – of confiscation, or at least heavy fines. But the estate owners resisted, and one of the means at their disposal were the groups of young men who were organised into a local militia, which was normally used to suppress peasant and urban disorder, protect trading caravans, and so on. Africa was a senatorial province, and although there was an urban cohort to control the city of Carthage, and the governor had a personal bodyguard, possibly much the same men, it was thus these militias who enforced order in the countryside. Since the landowners controlled them – the young men in the militias were often their sons, and so the militia was recruited from the wealthiest class in the province – they could be used for private purposes as well as public.[20]

The procurator arrived at Thysdrus at the height of the oil harvest. His task was to collect the state's share of the product, which was to be used as the *annona* at Rome. He was reputed corrupt, greedy, and oppressive, and he fined some of the young men of the militia for some unstated reason. Annoyed, his victims asked for three days to collect the money, to which the procurator agreed. (If his sentence was just, he was acting reasonably.) They went off, gathered their colleagues, their tenants, and a group of local peasant farmers (*coloni*), who were presumably also annoyed at the procurator's aggressive assessments (which may have been exaggerated for his personal profits, but may have originated from

Maximinus' order). The whole group came back to Thysdrus on the appointed day, where they mingled with the crowd that had gathered, presumably because of the assessment and perhaps because of the town market. The procurator had a guard with him, probably a detachment from the urban cohort of Carthage where he himself was normally based, but the crowd seems to have come between the Guard and their chief; no doubt, trouble was not expected. The young militiamen (but not it seems the *coloni*, some of whom were armed) were, of course, able to get up close to the procurator because he was expecting them to arrive with their payment. Instead, they drew daggers and killed him. The Guards attempted to wreak revenge on the attackers, but the *coloni*, wielding clubs and axes, intervened and protected the young militiamen.[21] The whole event was clearly well organised.

Carried along so far by their consciousness of injustice and oppression, the killers now realised that they had to go further, or disappear into hiding in the countryside and see their families punished. Quite possibly, at least some of them had been recognised by the Guards – they were the sons in many cases of prominent local men and were hardly anonymous – so that fleeing would have meant cutting themselves off from their families, and possibly putting those families in danger. The alternative they came up with was to seek out the governor of Africa, who had a house in the city, and was apparently present, perhaps for the same reason that the procurator was there, to supervise the harvest. There was certainly a large crowd in the city, and some disorder, or a drunken riot, may have been anticipated, so guards for both governor and procurator were also present. The young men found the governor at his house. Their purpose was perhaps uncertain at first, but protection against the procurator's men would be their first consideration. The governor does not seem to have had the chance to investigate or to discuss any demands they made. With an improvised purple robe, the militiamen and their followers proclaimed him emperor.[22]

The usurper thus unexpectedly proclaimed was M. Antonius Gordianus Sempronianus Romanus, who added the *cognomen* 'Africanus' to his name on being elevated in this way, as though he had won a victory in Africa. He was of Anatolian ancestry, probably Galatian in some degree – 'Gordianus' implies an origin from Gordion, of the knot fame. His *nomen* of Antonius might suggest a family that had acquired the Roman citizenship from Mark Antony, who was certainly active in the region in the first century BC. Vague theories of further origins and connections have been propounded but none is certain.[23] He had, as Herodian insists, governed other provinces, of which Britannia Inferior in 216 is the only one known, but Achaia and Syria Coele have been suggested, and of course, he was governor of Africa at the time of his elevation. This post, usually the last in a successful career, would imply that he had been consul fifteen or sixteen years before his governorship.[24] His consulship or consulships are not clearly dated but one would be about the time of his post in Britannia. He was about eighty years of age, and his career had clearly been very slow to advance, suggesting a problem with ambition, and also perhaps it had been interrupted by the changing imperial powers over the previous fifty years – but he had evidently been appointed to Britannia Inferior, a praetorian command, by Caracalla (in 216), and to Africa by the Senate during Maximinus' reign; he might be considered a Severan loyalist after this series of appointments. This in turn might mean he was actually a supporter of Maximinus, whose policies were essentially Severan; there is a suggestion, however, that he had fallen out with Septimius, which had delayed his consulship until after the British governorship.[25]

He was accompanied in Africa by his son, with the same name, as his legate. The son had also been consul at some time, fairly recently, and if the father really was eighty years old, as Herodian says,[26] the son was probably in his fifties. The father insisted on making the son joint emperor, perhaps because he himself could not move about so easily, but also for dynastic reasons; he would hardly expect to live much longer, and a swift nomination of his heir would be sensible.[27] The two new emperors took up residence in the gubernatorial palace at Carthage; they knew they had a major problem of survival to face.

Gordian I (the father) sent a messenger, P. Licinius Valerianus[28] (also of senatorial rank – and a future emperor) to notify the Senate of his elevation, and presumably to ask for the Senate's approbation and support.

The emergence of an emperor-usurper from the unmilitarised province of Africa was undoubtedly a surprise, as was the person of the new emperor. An eighty-year-old man, a less than successful senator, mainly known for his dabbling in philosophy – he had been one of Julia Domna's discussion group for a time, and was known to Philostratos[29] – was certainly unexpected. In addition, he was from an obscure eastern province. None of this amounted to good omens. These aspects – the province of origin and the age of the usurper – are the best indications that the whole set of events was unplanned. And yet there are certain indications, at least at Rome, that something of the sort was not entirely unanticipated.

Gordian communicated what had happened to the Senate as soon as he could. He had been at Thysdrus – 'at home', which suggests he owned property in the region – when he was proclaimed emperor, and this was several days' journey from Carthage (200 kilometres, in a straight line). Arrived at Carthage, he then spent several days going through the necessary procedures of becoming emperor – enrobement, promises of donations, acclamation by the plebs, and so on – before sending his formal message to the Senate.[30] It seems unlikely, however, that the imperial letter was the first news of events in Africa that the

Senate heard. We must allow at least a week, perhaps more, for all the events at Thysdrus and Carthage before Gordian sent off his formal letter, carried by Valerian. Three or four days must be allowed for Valerian's journey, so there must have been a good ten days to a fortnight, at least, between the proclamation at Thysdrus and the reception of Valerian at the Senate. This is only one of the many problems of dating in this particular year. The chronology of the various events during the year 238 has occupied much puzzled conjecture. The fact is that few precise dates are recorded, and it is necessary to make estimates based on travel times and other factors.[31]

For the dates of events – which are few, and none precise – we are reliant on records kept at a distance from the events in Africa – papyri in Egypt, specifically from Oxyrhynchos in the Fayum (several days' journey upriver), records at Rome, an inscription in Syria – and then there must be back calculations, allowing for the lengths of journeys from Africa to various destinations, vagaries of weather, delays in recording the events, and all the problems of physical journeys by horse, foot, and sailing ship. The one secure date seems to be 10 May 238 in Rome, by which time events in Africa had run their course, and the scene of decisive events had shifted to Rome, where a new set of emperors had been installed. This means that the Senate had successfully seized control of events by then, at least for a time. That is, for the events between Thysdrus and the proclamation at Rome of the new emperors we must simply relate the events in the several regions separately, and attempt to correlate them without the benefit of precise dates.

In Africa, the several days taken on the journey between Thysdrus and Carthage and carrying the message to Rome also saw the news spread out from Thysdrus and Carthage in all directions. This was helped by Gordian, who wrote to his friends in Rome, and probably to other regions as well. He clearly understood that for any hope of success, indeed survival, he had to enlist help from elsewhere. The news was certainly in Egypt by mid-June, according to the papyri, and probably earlier, since it was only then that it was written down. And it also spread through North Africa westwards, first to the neighbouring province of Numidia and its governing centre at the legionary base at Lambaesis. The distance from Carthage to Lambaesis is, in a straight line, 500 kilometres, and it was somewhat longer in actual marching distance. From Thysdrus to Carthage the 200 kilometres was perhaps seven days' travelling without a break; Thysdrus to Lambaesis would be thus about three weeks' travelling, though news of the imperial usurpation would probably travel much faster. At Lambaesis, presumably, the governor of Numidia was told the news. He had under his command the *legio* III *Augusta*, resident in the province for over two centuries, and numerous auxiliary regiments.

The Numidian governor's name is given as Capelianus. Much effort has gone into attempting to identify this man more precisely, but to little avail.[32] To be governor of Numidia and commander of the *legio* III *Augusta* – the two offices were always linked – he must have been of praetorian rank, but records at that level are practically nil in the third century. His ancestry might involve a Capelianus known in the time of Marcus, or perhaps a man with the *cognomen* Capella in Severus' time, but this is only conjecture. Two items, however, seem certain, or at least very probable. He had been appointed to be governor of Numidia by Maximinus, and so, unlike Gordian, he was loyal to that emperor; second, he is noted by Herodian as being an enemy of Gordian as a result of a legal dispute much earlier.[33] No more details of this are known; it might be an assumption by Herodian, or even a back-projection of their hostile relationship in 238. What did result, however, was rapid action by the Numidian governor.

He mobilised his legion, which, since it was still March, had probably been in winter quarters for several months. He was able to bring the legion direct to Carthage (no *auxilia* are noted as being mustered – and some of these had been withdrawn by Alexander and Maximinus to reinforce the forces in Germany, or on the Danube). The journey of 500 kilometres will have taken, for a marching force, up to three weeks, and Capelianus had therefore to calculate the response first – Herodian claims that he was later to canvass his troops in case the time came when he might make his own bid for imperial power. He cannot have received the news from Thysdrus in less than a week, assuming an efficient pony express system to carry messages, or privately delivered letters, so quite probably he was organising his legion for the march while Gordian was entering Carthage and celebrating his elevation. The timing of all this is obviously difficult to sort out, and extremely conjectural, but Capelianus and his legion were certainly quick off the mark.

Gordian I's reign lasted either twenty or twenty-two days, depending on the only sources to suggest a figure,[34] neither of which can be assumed to be accurate. This is probably, in fact, the length of time it took for the legion to march from Lambaesis to Carthage. It was met outside the city by an assorted force of citizens, *coloni*, militiamen, and others commanded by the younger Gordian (II). Not surprisingly, this heterogeneous untrained force was scattered at first contact, and the younger emperor (and his entourage) died in the fight.[35] Gordian I must have expected this result, and one wonders why he bothered to make any gesture of apparent resistance. Possibly, he hoped that such a display of an essentially civilian force in support of an emperor might give both Capelianus and the legion pause, and so provide time for negotiation. He may have hoped that the troops might accept him and so overthrow their governor. (He should, of course, have attempted to suborn the legionaries away from their commander, but perhaps Capelianus and his forces arrived unexpectedly.) Whatever his hopes and plans, the legion, perhaps determined to prove its loyalty, performed efficiently. Gordian II having been killed in the fight, in Carthage Gordian I committed suicide rather than face the public execution he will have expected at the hands of Capelianus. He could expect no mercy from his personal enemy.[36]

Capelianus, in true Severan-Maximinus fashion, then set about rooting out and killing anyone accused of giving support to the usurpers. The casualties in the fight had, according to Herodian, been heavy, both in the fight itself and in the subsequent pursuit. But Capelianus then set about a systematic purge. He could assume that almost any prominent person in the province had accepted the Gordians, and had given him their support, and he let his soldiers loot extensively. The purge spread into the countryside – after all, it was doubtless known that it was there that the attempted coup had begun. Precision of wording in Herodian is never to be expected, and he is here in full rhetorical mode, but the killing and looting was probably not restricted to Thysdrus and the palace at Carthage.[37]

Gordian I, however, had not simply sat in Carthage waiting for the enemy to arrive. He had, as noted, written letters to many senators and to others seeking support. He had sent Valerian to Rome, but he had also sent some soldiers there as well, who moved more quickly. Their target was P. Aelius Vitalianus, the praetorian prefect.[38] He had been the equestrian procurator in Mauretania Caesariensis – that is, the province to the west of Numidia – until appointed praetorian prefect by Maximinus in about 236. This made him a Maximinus loyalist. Most of the Guard were with the emperor on the northern frontier, as was the other prefect; Vitalianus was in Rome with the remaining fraction of the Guard, and so, along with the *praefectus urbi*, a man called Sabinus, he was the ranking authority in the city with the power to enforce control. He was also the senior military commander in the empire, second only to the emperor and therefore he would have responsibility for dealing with the Gordians' usurpation.

The soldiers who were sent by Gordian are not specified, but they were evidently both Gordian supporters and competent at their clandestine task, which was to murder Vitalianus. Succeeding in this, they reported to the Senate, according to Herodian, presenting there the news of the uprising in Africa, which is often attributed to Valerian.[39] This must mean that Valerian was one of the assassination squad, perhaps in charge of it, but that his participation was later suppressed when he became emperor; alternatively Valerian went publicly, and the soldiers secretly – they had to reach Rome before Valerian saw the Senate, and before their victim could be alerted. Valerian was of quaestorian rank at the time, and this would be a task for such a man, young, perhaps a little reckless, but clearly competent. A rumour was spread in the city at the same time that

Maximinus was also dead. This might well be another trick of the assassination squad, sowing useful confusion on top of the sudden elimination of the prefect.[40]

One would expect further emissaries to have been sent out by Gordian, as well as the letters he sent, or perhaps the letters went by his emissaries. He probably wrote to selected provincial officials whom he knew were antipathetic to Maximinus, though we cannot name any of them, neither emissaries nor contacts, not surprisingly. It is, however, the reaction of Rome and the Senate that was the most important, though despite the suggestion of speed implied by Herodian, the Senate did spend some time considering its options.

The rumour of the death of Maximinus excited the volatile Roman crowd. Already angered by the reduction in spending on the dole, the crowd was presumably as hostile to the emperor as was the Senate.[41] Rumours of his death therefore brought celebrations, perhaps more exuberant than usual – such celebrations took place whenever an emperor died – and this developed into a substantial riot, as these things often did. But it was a riot aimed at selectively removing evidence of Maximinus' rule, and in vociferous favour of the Gordians.

It was perhaps this demonstration, together with the elimination of Vitalianus, which convinced the Senate to go along with the Gordians. The remnant of the Guard had been left without a commander and was perhaps less dangerous than usual. It was also encouraging that the usurping emperors in Africa were formally asking for the Senate to support them. Gordian was also the first emperor since Septimius who had pursued a normal senatorial, if lengthy, administrative and gubernatorial career. This was not an emperor who had turned to the army to make him the empire's ruler. He was one of the most distinguished senators alive in 238. He had emerged from the population of an unmilitary province, with the support of its citizens and its landowners, even its peasants. His organised killing of the praetorian prefect was another indication that he was an emperor in the senatorial mode. The Senate therefore gracefully agreed to his accession, voted him the title of Augustus, and his son also, and the necessary offices and titles. Senators and delegations and letters were sent out to the provinces with the news, with the suggestion that the provinces should show their support.[42] Maximinus was voted to be a public enemy. This last detail was the signal for another Roman riot, with Maximinus' known vocal supporters now the target. One of the victims of the riot was the *praefectus urbi*, Sabinus.[43] He may or may not have been a Maximinus supporter, but he had certainly been appointed by that emperor, and during his time in office he had carried out whatever instructions he was given; it seemed most likely he was one of those targeted by the crowd, simply because he had been doing his job, whether or not he was a Maximinus supporter.

The sequence of events left the Senate in charge in the city. Of the rival emperors, two were in Africa, and the other two (Maximinus and his son the Caesar Maximinus) were on the Danube frontier. Neither the city prefect nor any praetorian prefect was left in the city. By default, authority over the city and its empire fell into the lap of the Senate. The usurpations, the killings, and the reaction of the Senate were, in terms of Roman politics, revolutionary. Having taken up the revolutionary baton, the Senate now had to run with it.

Chapter 9

The Senate's War

The reaction in Rome to the news of the sudden irruption in Africa was remarkable. Almost instantly – instant, that is, so far as a body of several hundred politicians is concerned, was no doubt several days – the Senate accepted the pretensions of the usurpers. The two Gordians were quickly voted the traditional titles and offices of emperor, including an unprecedented sharing of the position of *pontifex maximus*, and the Emperor Maximinus was condemned as a public enemy.

The speed of the Senate's reaction and acceptance suggests two possible explanations – that the plot had been well prepared and that much of the Senate was in on the event, or that feeling against Maximinus and his regime had developed to such an intensity that the merest incident of defiance was sufficient to set off a much wider reaction. On the whole, the second seems the more likely; the possibility of much of the Senate being involved without the secret leaking is vanishingly small. But the animosity towards Maximinus was obvious once it was allowed to come into the open, and, of course, given the history of Roman *coups d'état*, most knew how to proceed.

The future, however, suggested that there would be difficulties. The new emperors were in Africa, the senior one was elderly, they had little military experience that we know of (the elder Gordian had, if the count is correct, governed mainly civilian provinces – Achaia and Africa – but also Britannia Inferior, which was the northern half of the original province, and possibly Syria Coele, a well-garrisoned province;[1] the younger, though of consular rank, had no such experience on record). By contrast, the threatened Emperor Maximinus was in command of a large and loyal army, to which he had just granted double pay and a donative, and which he had recently led to several victories. Furthermore, that army was only a few days' marching distance from Italy. The preferred route had been shown by Septimius Severus half a century before, when he had arrived in Italy from the same region, making the journey in less than a month. (This route had been followed in 69 also.) Having accepted the authority of the two Gordian emperors, the Senate would now need to make urgent preparations for war.

The news of the death of the Gordians required a further election, of a replacement emperor. A closed session in the *cella* of the temple of Jupiter on the capitol first selected the twenty members of the executive committee, then a vote took place on selecting the new emperors. Out of a number (unspecified) of candidates, two were to hold the office simultaneously. Herodian's description implies that the whole assembly took part in the voting, and that 'many received votes', but all but the final two were eliminated. It sounds like a deliberate series of votes devoted to removing the least popular.[2]

The double-rulers system was also an innovation, in a way. It may have been a reflection of the dual nature of the brief regime of the Gordians – a sort of compliment – or possibly a reminiscence of the Republican system of dual office-holders of the consulship, which, of course, still operated, or perhaps they recalled the repeated dual emperorships which had happened in the last century (Marcus and Commodus, Marcus and Lucius, Septimius and Caracalla, even Vespasian and Titus, Augustus and Agrippa, were examples). It may also be a result of a tied vote.

The innovative element was thus not that there were two emperors, but that they were selected by the senators, that they took office simultaneously, with the implication that this was to be a permanent arrangement. Other double-emperorships had been the result of the existing emperor co-opting another man, usually his son. Here therefore was another part of the intended revolution. One might also point out that this suggests preceding thought, a political theory which had evolved in the light of the absence, whether physical or mental, of the recent rulers. It is also most likely to be a reflection of the difficulty of the job of emperor, especially in this time of disturbances, and more than one man was needed, perhaps, as in fact happened, with one emperor remaining in Rome, while the other was able to travel about to deal with more distant matters. And they did divide the tasks between them.

The two men chosen as emperors were D. Coelius Calvinus Balbinus[3] and M. Clodius Pupienus Maximus.[4] A joint biography of sorts is included in the *Historia Augusta*, but the details are thoroughly unreliable.[5] Pupienus is normally listed first when the two men are jointly referred to, but it seems unlikely that this implied any seniority on his part; in fact, he seems to have been the younger of the two – he was about fifty years of age, Balbinus ten or more years older – and would have been the junior if such a distinction was made. But Pupienus was certainly the more active of the two; in their coin portraits Balbinus is clearly fat and probably less active physically, which is perhaps the reason for Pupienus' activity. He also, so far as the record goes, was the more experienced, having been governor of one of the German provinces under Caracalla in the 210s, proconsul of Asia, and consul for the second time in 234 and then *praefectus urbi*, a post generally held along with the second consulship. Balbinus' career references are limited to a second consulship in 213, but no governorships are known.[6] Any posts he held were thus probably in non-military roles. As will be seen in the discussion of the other known members of the Committee of Twenty, experience and age appear to have been the criteria used to choose these men, so it seemed reasonable to suppose that Balbinus was as experienced (or, given his long career, even more so) as Pupienus, though it is unlikely.[7]

Both men were well connected in an imperial sense. Balbinus was descended from three generations of consuls, and was related to the Valerii Messallae, one of whom was another member of the Twenty. The family was from Spain, specifically Italica, it seems, which led to the claim that he was descended from, or perhaps related to, Trajan and the Republican Gracchi. His wife may have been Aquilia, of the family of Pompeius Falco,[8] and ultimately descended from Julius Frontinus; they seem to have had no children. Pupienus was from a Tuscan family from Volaterrae, an *eques* adlected to senatorial rank, probably by Septimius. He and both of his two sons were of consular rank by 238. The eldest was married to Tineia, of a consular family, and their descendants were prominent for the next two centuries; Pupienus' sister was married to a member of a Greek family from Hypata in central Greece.[9] The connections of the two new emperors thus spread from Greece to Spain, which may have been a point in their joint favour for those who had to decide which of the competing emperors they should support in the 238 crisis.

Both emperors were elderly, notably Balbinus, who stayed in Rome – his second consulship in 213 would imply an age by 238 in the sixties – while Pupienus went out into Italy and took charge of the defence of the peninsula. Balbinus attempted to intervene in a battle between the Roman crowd and the Guard, and this would suggest he had taken some responsibility for public order in the city. So if one was on campaign, a position of danger, the other could hold the administration together in his absence, or take over if he was killed. It may be relevant to events in Rome that only Pupienus appears to have had living children, two sons and a daughter. No reference is known to the succession, but it must have been considered, if only in private or in conversation. Maybe the aim was to continue the elective practice.

The news of the imperial election was published to a crowd that, inevitably, had gathered at the capitol. It produced immediate protests on behalf of the third Gordian, a grandson of Gordian I, and the thirteen-year-old nephew of Gordian II, the son of his sister. It would appear that this protest had been arranged in advance on the assumption that the boy would not be selected, or perhaps on the assumption he would be. The reaction is an interesting demonstration of the hold the practice of heredity had on even the ordinary Roman citizens and population, not to mention the vulnerability of the Senate to popular manipulation. Evidently, there were Gordian partisans in the crowd, who had been organised in the short time since the news of the deaths in Africa had arrived. Their protest produced a riot, in the usual Roman way, and in the usual Roman way, this was quieted when the authorities gave in to the rioters' demands. The boy was accepted as the heir to the new imperial pair, as Caesar.[10] Pupienus had adult sons, so the adlection of the third Gordian would likely store up dynastic trouble for the future. The succession system was thus at least temporarily solved, though the younger Pupieni did not receive the title of Caesar.

It is unlikely that the boy's claims had been ignored by the Senate, either by the full assembly or by the Twenty, but no one wanted an adolescent as emperor in this emergency. There were too many memories of children as emperors – three in the past half-century – for Gordian III to have been elected as full emperor. The riot and the acquiescence were perhaps therefore not unexpected, and may even have been programmed in as a way of settling the issue; the Gordian partisans could hardly be dissatisfied, though they had other issues as well. The whole election process had resulted in a well-upholstered new regime, two fully experienced emperors sharing the work, and an heir who in ten years' time would be of sufficient age to take over – not to mention Pupienus' own sons. Gordian III would do so as soon as one of the emperors died, and could be guided by the survivor; such at least may well have been the theory. The whole process, however, certainly stored up trouble for the future, and if heredity was to determine who should be emperor, there would be a dispute; and the almost formal riot-and-acquiescense process was one that might be used by others.

The choice of the two men as emperors was perhaps typical of the members of the Senate, but in particular their choice of elderly men. Senators as a whole – and the word 'Senate' derived, after all, from *senex*, 'old, senior' – habitually showed excessive respect for age and experience. In 96, the plot against Domitian was intended to hoist Nerva, sixty-eight years old and ill, to the throne and he then rewarded all his aged pals with second consulships in the next year or so. And now in 238, it seemed that the same thing was happening.

The senators of the Committee of Twenty had been appointed, or elected, from the main body.[11] It had the traditional title of *vigintiviri*, the 'twenty men', but this was not in any way a body of the traditional sort – the original was a group of young men beginning their careers, and this new group was a set of experienced, sometimes elderly, senators. (In fact, one suspects that this may have been a jocular title.) They had the primary task of organising the defence of Italy against Maximinus. This election took place probably after the news came that the two Gordian emperors had died. There are contradictory notices of the purposes and powers of the Twenty in the *Historia Augusta*,[12] but it is most likely that only in the situation of no existing or acceptable emperors would such an unusual means as election by a committee be resorted to. Such a body is unprecedented in Roman constitutional history, and one book of the *Historia* is reduced to explaining that the Twenty were then each given a section of Italy to supervise, organise, or watch.[13] Apart from the inefficiency of such a method, the political situation does not require that such a strange division of responsibilities be made – though, of course, Italy was in fact already divided into that number of subsections for purposes of local government. It was, in fact, a misunderstanding of what the Twenty did, for some of its members were certainly sent off to different parts of the peninsula, but usually with a variety of tasks, above all to drum up recruits for an army.

The overall purpose was evidently to rouse Italy to its own defence, and so the main emphasis must be on the north, for it was clearly from Sirmium, by way of the passes through the Julian Alps, that danger would arrive. Further, by suggesting that twenty separate sections of the peninsula needed to be defended, the Senate would have fatally divided its military resources. On the other hand, by using a committee of the Senate to arrange the defence, the Senate as a whole had a way of involving a large number of the members of the House in opposition to Maximinus, and recruiting in the whole peninsula did the same for Italy.

The speed with which the Senate took these measures raises the suspicion that they had already been preparing for an attempt at usurping Maximinus' powers. The further suspicion thus arises that the riot in Africa had been prearranged, and that the Gordians' usurpation was part of an empire-wide plot.[14] In support of this, the participation of a man called Mauricius or Mauritius, said to be a decurion of the local government, if the events in Thysdrus is adduced.[15] However, the only other evidence that can be found is in the very speed of the Senate's initiative. And the evidence for Mauricius turns out to exist only in the *Historia Augusta* book on the Gordians, and this is not good enough for conviction. In fact, the name Mauricius appears to be one of those invented by the writer of the *Historia*, and appears to be derived essentially from the Mauri, the name of the local tribe in the Mauretanian province – that is, the author is simply saying that he was a native African, an unlikely person to be a decurion of a city of Africa Consularis.

Apart from the two men of the Twenty who became emperors, we know the names of just five other members of that committee. Two of them were sent to take command at the city of Aquileia, at the head of the Adriatic, which would be the first fortified obstacle for Maximinus and his army on the march against Rome, once he had transited the Julian Alps. Of these two, Tullius Menophilus is otherwise scarcely known, though he was a provincial governor later; it must be assumed that he had some military expertise.[16] He was probably, judging by the records of the other men in the group, of consular rank, and with governmental and military experience.

The disposition of the Twenty through Italy seems to have been decided with due regard for their earlier experience. Menophilus' colleague at Aquileia was Rutilius Pudens Crispinus, whose long career is by contrast known; he had been governor of several provinces.[17] He was by origin an *eques*, adlected by Septimius Severus, one of those many men who were chosen to fill up the depleted senatorial ranks after Septimius had executed so many; he was thus in all likelihood a Severan loyalist. He had served in several Italian posts, and had been consul in the 230s.

L. Caesonius Lucillus Macer Rufinianus was, as is typical of the Twenty, of consular rank when he was included in the committee; he had wide connections in the Greek and Roman aristocracy, notably through his wife Ovinia, and their descendants were prominent into the next century and more.[18] He had not had much of a military career; he had been curator of the Tiber Banks and *curator acquarum*, and before these offices he had been legate to the governor of Africa, then consul in the 230s. He was thus an administrator rather than a soldier, and his later career, as proconsul of Africa and *praefectus urbi*, would tend to confirm this; no doubt, he was assigned responsibilities in Rome commensurate with his experience.[19]

L. Valerius Claudius Acilius Priscilianus is recorded as a member of the Twenty in an inscription, unusually.[20] He had ascended to consul by 233 through the usual *cursus* ladder for a patrician and was curator of the Tiber Banks; he again later became *praefectus urbi* (in 255), and consul for the second time in 256. He was also a cousin of the Emperor Pupienus.

The last man we know of was M. Cn. Licinius Rufinus, who was, despite his Latin name, from Thyateira in Asia Minor. His long career was detailed in an inscription from his home town, and other details are recorded in some other inscriptions from other parts of the east where he had been employed.[21] He was mainly a lawyer, beginning as an *eques* and went through a series of secretarial and administrative posts in the imperial government; adlected to the Senate he served as praetor, and as governor of Noricum (where he may have had some military experience). He is not recorded as consul, despite the details of his career in his inscription, and it is best to assume he never reached that rank. He had been thus busy in a long series of posts for perhaps the previous thirty years, and may have been in his fifties in 238.

Clearly, with only seven of the identifiable members of the Twenty, the sample we know is only approximately representative, but it may be noted that out of the seven, two, Menophilos and Rufinus, were from the east, one (Balbinus) was from Spain, and others were from various parts of Italy – Pupienus (from

Etruria), the Roman suburbs (Licinius) – but this also had connections in other parts of the empire. Two had begun their careers as *equites*, and were adlected into the Senate by Severan emperors. At least three of the seven were double consulars, and Rufinus' long and distinguished administrative and secretarial career put him as equal to them in experience, even though there is no record of him as consul. And despite my comments as to age above, at least two of the Twenty were in their thirties (Caesonius and Valerius). If this really is a representative sample of the full Twenty, the preference clearly was for a variety of origins, experience, military, governmental, administrative, and legal; these were clearly intelligent men.

The disagreements and riots over the appointment of the new emperors brought the Praetorian Guard's attention. The Guard as a whole was distinctly unhappy about the revolution that was taking place in the city, which was continuous, without their participation. Most of the Guard in fact was not present, but was with Maximinus on the Danubian frontier, but it seems that, even so, those guardsmen who were in the city were confident enough to object to the revolution going on without them. It is conjectured that the men still in Rome were veterans who had been due to retire, and had been retained briefly as a Roman garrison for the time being; they were probably only a few hundred in number.

Two senators spoke to a crowd in the Senate House, and some off-duty guardsmen arrived to listen. The senators are identified only by their *cognomina*, Gallicanus and 'Maecenas'. Gallicanus is fairly confidently to be identified as L. Domitius Gallicanus Papinianus, who was from Carthage, which would suggest that he had identified himself as a supporter of the Gordians in part because the Gordians were active in Carthage.[22] His colleague 'Maecenas' is not easily identified, and the name is clearly wrong, but one suggestion is that he was another African, P. Messius Aequitius Maecinianus, of praetorian rank,[23] but since it was Gallicanus who was the leader in this development, his precise identification is less important.

The two senators spoke to the crowd, favouring the young Gordian, and when they spotted the guardsmen, who had moved to the entry of the Senate House, the senators drew daggers they had concealed in their clothing, and stabbed them to death. The surviving guardsmen who were present, unwounded and unarmed, escaped to their camp, pursued by the crowd that had been aroused by the senators' speeches – no doubt the Guard's discontent was public knowledge. When the crowd reached the camp, the gate had been shut; the crowd's attacks on the walls were repelled without too much difficulty. Several guardsmen had been felled by the crowd in the rush, just the thing to bring the guardsmen to a pitch of anger.[24] When the assault died away and the crowd began to leave, the guardsmen, now fully armed, came out to get their revenge.

This, as Herodian notes, was a civil war.[25] The two senators were, it seems, both from Africa, and were Gordian supporters, perhaps hoping to see Gordian III elected as emperor in place of Balbinus and Pupienus. This was the method – rousing a crowd – that had made him Caesar in the first place. Hence their antipathy towards the guardsmen, who were understood to support Maximinus. There were therefore at least three factions active in the city within a few days of the news of the deaths of the elder Gordians – the Guard and others who would be supporting Maximinus, the two new emperors who had gathered a personal guard of young men of *eques* rank,[26] and probably had a majority of supporters, and the supporters of the Gordianic succession. Balbinus attempted to broker a truce between the Guard and the crowd without much success;[27] he was acting presumably as a neutral between the Gordian party and the Guard.

The guardsmen, heavily outnumbered, were eventually driven back to their camp. This was not the only time that the city crowd succeeded in defeating the Guard, and the fighting is as much a sign of the enmity between the two as it was a dispute over the person of the emperor. The Guard was eventually forced to surrender by the interdiction of the water supply to the camp; the men came out but became entangled in the city streets and were bombarded from the buildings with 'tiles and a hail of stones and broken pots'. They retaliated by setting fire to wooden buildings. There followed much destruction and death, gleefully exploited by looters.[28]

By this time, the attention of the Romans had also shifted towards the north. Maximinus' army was fast approaching Italy. The Senate, having gone so far, now cast about for support. It was in itself unarmed, but there were two resources available, the armies in the provinces, and the population of Italy. The first were informed of events by senatorial representatives and notable *equites* – men of sufficient rank to be assured of an audience – who were dispatched to the governors of the provinces. Italy, where there were considerable numbers of trained, if retired, soldiers among the population, was the region where men were to be recruited by members of the Twenty. The precise effect of the appeal to the provinces was ambiguous and necessarily slow to emerge. Herodian claims that there was widespread support for the Senate, but as will be seen later, and as he admits, this was an exaggeration. He does note that some of the messengers were arrested, others executed, and some sent to Maximinus, in effect a sentence of death; in provinces where the revolution was welcomed, officials who remained loyal to Maximinus could themselves be executed.[29] No governor with sense would commit himself in opposition to Maximinus.

The senators issued instructions to gather a force to defend Italy.[30] This meant, since the threat came from the north-east, a levy of recruits particularly in northern Italy, and particularly in the Po Valley and Transpadana. There is one inscription naming a man placed in charge of part of this area, L.F. Annianus, who was based at Mediolanum, and organised the force in Transpadana.[31] In addition, Tullius Menophilus and Rutilius Pudens Crispinus went to Aquileia to prepare the city for a siege, collecting supplies and organising armed forces; the city was soon crowded with refugees, some of whom will have been recruited, and others used to work to strengthen the walls.[32]

Herodian's description of this has strong elements of the formulaic about it, suggesting he was personally repeating what ancient historians expected to take place in preparations for sieges. The same goes for his description of the advance of Maximinus' army. In both cases, however, there is enough hard fact elsewhere to allow a reasonably convincing description of what happened.[33]

Annianus at Mediolanum was somewhat distant from the crucial danger point at Aquileia, but an army at that city would likely give pause to any invader hoping to move south. At Ravenna was the imperial fleet, a likely source of armed men and arms so long as the sailors and marines accepted the new regime. Pupienus was sent there personally to secure the naval base and mobilise the armed forces. These included a force of German allies who had arrived to support Pupienus, of whom they had fond memories in his role as governor there. They had probably marched from Germania Superior or Raetia over the western Alps from the Rhine Army.[34] Like Annianus in Mediolanum, a force here would pose a threat to Maximinus if he got past Aquileia, or even if he formed the siege of the city. All this was done quickly, on the assumption that Maximinus would emulate Septimius and march rapidly into Italy, heading for Rome.

Maximinus' army may have been slow off the mark.[35] He and his forces were camped at Sirmium, though, since it was March, he had probably spread the units out for the winter. He is said to have started his march only four days after receiving the news from Africa. How long that news had taken to reach Sirmium is impossible to sort out; it could have travelled direct from Carthage to Aquileia or Salonae by sea, and then on by land to Sirmium – but March is not a good time for sailing in the Mediterranean, or travelling through the Dalmatian mountains. Perhaps more likely it arrived by way of Rome, where he certainly had supporters. The news reached the Egyptian Fayum between April and June,[36] but in Rome the proclamation of the replacement emperors Balbinus and Pupienus took place about 10 May.[37] That is, the news had taken at least an extra month to reach Egypt from Africa, either by sea or by way of Rome. The message of the original usurpation thus began to spread a month earlier than the elections of the new emperors of Rome, or some days more.

The journey from Rome to Sirmium would take perhaps two more weeks for a fast messenger. So Maximinus could have learnt of the threat about mid-April, though perhaps a few days later. He then marched after four days, which would suggest he started out the last week of April.

He probably did not take the threat seriously at first – after all, it came from Africa, a virtually ungarrisoned region, and the news of Capelianus' success will have travelled to him as quickly as the Gordians' usurpation, no more than a few days after it. Nevertheless, he mobilised a formidable army. The news of the African usurpation probably came to him by way of Rome, and would therefore be accompanied by news of the anti-Maximinus reaction in the city, and quite probably at any other Italian city the messenger(s) had passed through on the way to Sirmium. He did not need the news of the Gordians' deaths and the proclamation of the new emperors to get his forces moving.[38] Given that he had to assimilate the news, plan his response, decide on his destination, and muster his forces for the march, four days seems to be good going.[39] But it was necessarily done in haste, and he certainly anticipated armed opposition, including the need to besiege and assault walled cities. Therefore, his march was accompanied by a baggage train of provision wagons – food would be short at that time of year – artillery, and other war machines, which slowed up the speed of the march considerably.[40]

No doubt, he assumed that further supplies could be collected along the route. He marched with three legions, II *Parthica*, I *Adiutrix*, and II *Adiutrix*, and several units of *auxilia*, cavalry, Mauretanian troops, possibly javelin men,[41] and 'eastern' archers, possibly the Osrhoenians, though there were plenty of Syrian archers in the army.[42] The legions would amount to a minimum of 12,000 men, possibly more, and the *auxilia* would add perhaps another 2,000 – this would thus be a similar-sized force to that used by Septimius in a similar march, but in that case he did not bring a large train with him, not expecting much opposition.

But Septimius had not marched through a land where the crops were not ready. Fodder for the horses was probably available in the fields in April, but food for the soldiers had to be obtained from the inhabitants, who, at the end of winter and before the harvest, had little to spare. No doubt the troops resorted to theft and foraging, arguing that their need was the greater. This will have worked for a time, but the news of their activities soon travelled ahead of the army, and alerted future possible targets. Further, the large baggage train, wagons, artillery, and so on, moved only slowly, probably at the pace of the mules, or even oxen – the latter usually move at 3 kilometres an hour and then need several hours' rest and feeding.

The army was therefore going hungry even while marching through Pannonia, a march of 350 kilometres (in a straight line, more in fact), from Sirmium before reaching the western boundary of that province. As the prospect of requisition, theft, and ravaging spread ahead of the march, the inhabitants collected their food and valuables and moved out of the way. Herodian only notes this reaction by the population of the city of Emona, where the people evacuated the city, having burnt their belongings to defy looters, and fled out of the reach of the army, but no doubt other settlements in Pannonia had already done this before the army reached Emona.[43]

This action was not necessarily a gesture of support for the usurping emperors, but the army's march must have persuaded many who lost belongings, food, and accommodation to Maximinus' army and whose lives were disrupted by it, to turn against Maximinus, though that would not necessarily mean supporting any other emperor – nor do anything active about it.

Along the way, the emperor would have been kept informed of events in Rome, and will have learned of the deaths of the Gordians (which Herodian synchronises with the start of his march, though vaguely).[44] Such news may have led him to relax the pace of march, but the further news of the elevation of the two replacement emperors probably puzzled him. Some at least of the soldiers will have known of these two men, perhaps having served under them – Maximinus is said to have been well regarded by the German auxiliaries because of his governorship there.[45] The information of their election, which surely reached the soldiers as quickly as it did the emperor, and that they had been formally chosen by the Senate will have impressed the ordinary soldiers. They, like Maximinus, might not have had much respect for individual senators or politicians, but the collective decision of the Senate itself would certainly have impressed them.

The army came through the Julian Alps, therefore, after a march of 500 kilometres, already in rather poor shape and short of food, perhaps somewhat nonplussed at what they were supposed to be doing, and immediately faced the prospect of besieging of a major city, well fortified, garrisoned, and prepared. The march had taken long enough for the new regime in Rome to collect its soldiers and install garrisons and senatorial commanders, above all in Aquileia, but elsewhere other garrisons were known at Ravenna and Mediolanum. By now, after surviving a barbarian siege in the time of Marcus' Marcomannic Wars seventy years before, it was regarded as the bastion of Italy. This, of course, also meant that the city and the citizens were in a sense already mentally prepared for the siege; the preparation procedures were understood and the defence moved into gear without delay, impelled by the two senators sent from Rome, and the nearby presence of the new Emperor Pupienus. There were soldiers stationed in the city already, according to two inscriptions from the city,[46] and, given that it was an important site, there were stocks of supplies, food and military already held within the walls and these were supplemented from the neighbourhood.[47]

The slow and steady approach of Maximinus' army to Aquileia, which probably took at least three weeks plus the two or three weeks that elapsed between the election of the new emperors and the start of Maximinus' march from Sirmium, had allowed a considerable time for the defences of Italy to be manned. It also allowed the news of events to spread to the rest of the empire. Gordian I's letters from Carthage when he was sending Valerian to see the Senate and the death squads to pick off his enemies were probably not the only means by which the information of the usurpation was spread. After Gordian's death, the events in Rome were broadcast by the Senate.[48]

The direct evidence of the reception of the news in regions other than Africa Consularis and Italy, both of which were supporters of the Gordians and their successors (though the former was reclaimed for Maximinus by Capelianus), consists in part of scattered references in literary texts, but also, in Egypt and the east, of dated papyri, and there and elsewhere of inscriptions. These last exhibit local allegiances in two ways. Maximinus had been busy in encouraging the repair and construction of military roads, and this was as usual commemorated in inscriptions, often milestones.[49] This applies also to the emperors of 238, though they hardly had time to become widely commemorated in that way. But there was time for inscriptions naming Maximinus to be defaced, by having the emperor's name chiselled out. This, of course, only emphasises who had been commemorated, and the name can usually be easily restored, but the removal of an imperial name also means that his condemnation as a public enemy by the Senate was accepted, though the chiselling out may have taken place after the end of the civil war. Conversely, if his name was not removed this may imply either that nobody could be bothered, or he continued to be recognised as emperor in defiance of the Senate's resolutions. The practice is thus not by any means definitive in locating support for either side at the time.

With these items, it is possible to suggest, in gross terms, how each province reacted to the events in Africa and Italy. The possibilities of the issue is best illustrated by the evidence from Britannia. Gordian I had served a stint there as governor of Britannia Inferior, the northern part of the province, in about 216.[50] (He was the first known governor after the division of the island into two provinces.) His name had been noted in various ways in three inscriptions, at High Rochester on the Wall, at Ribchester, and at Chester-le-Street. The first two inscriptions show Gordian's name erased, so we may assume that orders went out from the governor who was in office in 238 – though we do not know who he was – that any record of Gordian be eliminated; that governor therefore was a partisan of Maximinus.[51] The governor in 237 was a man known only by his *cognomen* [T]uccianus, whose term of office was certainly at Maximinus' gift, and so possibly he served all through his reign.[52] He may be the man who ordered the erasure of the Gordian names, possibly in 238. If he was an obvious partisan of Maximinus, Tuccianus was no doubt replaced during 238, and so his emperor's name was erased, probably by his successor.[53]

An even more enticing possibility is that Tuccianus was retained in office by Gordian and his successors and that he had to swiftly reverse his policy, having first ordered the removal of Gordian names, he now had to order the removal of Maximinus'; we do not know the name of the new governor in 238, if there was one, but if Tuccianus had been in office throughout Maximinus' reign it would take some time for the word to arrive to replace him, and still longer for his replacement to turn up; there would certainly have been time for him to reverse his course, and so perhaps to survive, either dismissed or in another office. By the time he was replaced, the political situation had no doubt changed again.

In other words, the evidence has to be examined with care, but even so, it can be deceptive. In the African provinces we know that Africa supported the Gordians, probably all the more so after Capelianus' purges, but Numidia under Capelianus did not. There are no inscriptions providing evidence for either province. In the two Mauretanian provinces to the west there are inscriptions with Maximinus' name undamaged, but none with the Gordians' names. We are left to assume that these provinces were loyal to Maximinus, but it may be that they were simply slow to decide, or, in view of events in the African province, just cautious. The eastern province, Mauretania Caesariensis, along from Numidia, certainly commemorated the successors of Maximinus and the Gordians, on milestones at several places, but this could have happened during the reign of Gordian III after the murder of his older colleagues.[54] This province was evidently less than engaged in the contest, but, to be fair, the whole process from Gordian I's rising to the emergence of Gordian III as sole emperor lasted only six months or so; the speed of transmission of news in the Roman Empire, combined with the necessity to make decisions, means that it was quite possible for news of yet another change of emperors to arrive before any decision had been made to erase or celebrate.

So, in many cases, the evidence tends to be ambiguous and conclusions can be argued in more than one way. There is clear evidence of support for the Gordians in Britannia, as noted above, but only after an early support for Maximinus. In other regions, notably in the eastern provinces, the minting of coins can be used to support the understanding of local decisions, though since these are not dated it is always likely that the coins that were commemorating the Gordians and their successors were minted later. The apparent concrete nature of the evidence of war and usurpation is therefore much less than firm and is often ambiguous.

The details of these items of evidence have been pored over more than once, most recently by Karen Haegemans, and for want of anything more definitive – which is unlikely to be forthcoming – I will adopt her conclusions, with some reservations.[55] It is usual to work from west to east, through the several provinces. Mauretania has already been noted, and appears to have remained loyal to Maximinus, at least no doubt because of Capelianus' decisiveness in Numidia, which allowed him to march out of his province, a practice normally thoroughly discouraged by emperors.

In Spain, the governor of Tarraconensis (Hispania Citerior) was Q. Decius Valerinus, whose name has been assumed to be an adaptation for C. Messius Quintus Traianus Decius Valerianus, the future Emperor Decius. Yet the distortion is somewhat extreme, and is not easy to accept. Nevertheless, even if this was not the future emperor, he held his province in loyalty to Maximinus until well after that emperor was dead. He had only a single legion under his command, however, which was not enough to make a military mark on events elsewhere than in his province, though the other Spanish provinces, Baetica and Lusitania, had no choice but to go along with Tarraconensis.[56]

Apart from this governor, there is little to suggest any widespread Spanish support for his stand. In Gaul, one may say the same. Aquitania has produced a single inscription on the base of a statue, found at Bordeaux; it was originally apparently of Gordian I, though the statue itself has vanished;[57] Belgica has produced nothing relevant. The German provinces are equally devoid of evidence. In Narbonensis only a single inscription has Maximinus' name erased, which could have been done after his death, but nothing on the Gordians.[58] There is no evidence from Noricum and Raetia either way. This could only mean that the governors of these provinces did not feel the need to support the men from Africa and Italy, or that it did not occur to them to damage public inscriptions. It is perhaps more significant, however, that the Gallic provinces did not have garrisons of any size, and that there was an influential Gallic council which could have imposed some direction. The lack of garrisons does not apply, however, to the German lands; the military might have been expected to support Maximinus, after his successful German campaign, and his generosity to the troops, though it is possible that he had removed many of the men for his expeditions into the Danube expedition, and then, to Italy.

The fact that there are only two examples of direct action in the whole of the region, with the exception of Spain, where Maximinus' name continued to be commemorated even after he was dead, cannot be taken as an indication that those provinces were supporting one or other of the candidates. In Baetica at

Italica there has been found a bust of Balbinus – but again this means nothing, since he was from that province and perhaps from that city, and the bust may have been an element of local pride set up before he began to be emperor (he had been a double consular, after all, since 213, and had no doubt continued as patron of his home town), or one commemorating him after his death.[59] In the Mediterranean islands, Corsica, Sardinia, and Sicily, there is no evidence either way.

From the evidence, or its absence, it cannot be said that the western half of the Roman Empire was seriously involved in the crisis, at least in so far as the epigraphic evidence is concerned, and always with the exception of Britannia Inferior.

The northern frontier, beyond Raetia and as far as the Black Sea, may be taken as a special case. This was a heavily militarised region, and one where Maximinus had been busy for a couple of years; not only that, but he was stationed at Sirmium, in Pannonia, when the news of the African problem reached him. This would be a major collection of good reasons for the northern provinces, from Pannonia to Moesia, to remain loyal. In fact, they may have known little about events in the south; the assumption of their loyalty to Maximinus would deter the publicists for the revolution from attempting to contact any of the officers. At any rate, there is little to discuss on the issue in the north. (These considerations may apply also to the well-garrisoned German provinces, where Maximinus had campaigned first.)

The eastern provinces, from the Adriatic to the Syrian Desert, were much more productive of records, both inscriptions and papyri, as well as coins, at this period, but the responsibility for coining and inscriptions lay largely with the cities, so that it is difficult to assume that the epigraphic and numismatic evidence can be applied to the whole province. The regions probably received the news of events by sea, first from Africa, then from Rome, and later from Pannonia, but more slowly; it is symbolic that a statue pair depicting Balbinus and Pupienus as Jupiter reached Peiraios, but was then sunk in the harbour, to be recovered in the modern era.[60] The reign of these two emperors was so short that the market for such statues was clearly brief. Similarly, the reign of the trio of Balbinus and Pupienus with Gordian III as Caesar was also brief so that inscriptions in their name, or coins naming them, are likely to be contemporary with the joint reign of the first two or just after. There are examples from several places in the Balkans: Philippopolis in Thrace,[61] and Nicopolis in Epeiros, Korkyra, and Thessaly,[62] as well as statues from Athens.

The relevance of coining to the issue is complicated by the wide practice of forgery, not to mention the related practice of issuing coins in the emperors' names later, to commemorate them – and perhaps to suggest local support for them all along. But a further complication is that coining was in the hands of the cities, so any such coins would only give an indication of a city's allegiance, not that of a whole province.

It is equally difficult to discern the loyalties of the governors of the eastern provinces. First, only a few of them are known, and second, as with all decisions in this difficult year, events went so fast that a decision could well be overturned before it was assimilated as information of new events came in, and the further away from Africa and Rome a place was the more likely it is that confusion would exist. In Cappadocia the governor Sex. Catius Clementinus Priscillianus appears to have been appointed by Maximinus, but stayed in office under his successors, perhaps a man of deft footwork; but he was replaced by Balbinus and Pupienus (and so before August 238), which might suggest that his footwork was not in fact deft enough.[63] In Asia, Maximinus' name was excised at Pergamon, and at the city's port of Elaia.[64] This is not evidence of local decisions, only of the progress of time and the reception of news by individuals.

In Egypt, the writers of papyri faithfully used whatever emperor's name was known in their dating formulae, and this is useful in detecting the spread of news; it does not, however, mean that the governor, L. Lucretius Annianus, adhered to the Gordian cause quickly.[65] The same may be said of Syria Palestina, where one milestone in the name of Gordian II was set up, the only one in the whole empire[66] – but why not Gordian I and II, since they were joint rulers? In fact, the stone had only been prepared for carving, with the intended words marked out in red paint, so this is evidence of the interruption of the work by the arrival of further news – but also of the appeal of the Gordians and the rejection of Maximinus. In Syria Coele, the mint at Antioch produced coins in the name of Balbinus, which suggests a rapid acceptance, even possibly before Maximinus' death was known, but Balbinus was still emperor for three months after his predecessor's death;[67] the two emperors plus Gordian III are on a milestone in Arabia, which says nothing about any possible change of allegiance, only their acceptance.[68]

The more one looks at this collection of evidence, however, the less convincing most of it is. The busy period between the uprising in Africa and the death of Emperors Balbinus and Pupienus must have led to confusion as news (and rumours, and guesswork) arrived successively and probably out of sequence – and the whole affair was no more than about six months in duration. It would be natural for governors and cities' councils and army commanders alike to be cautious until something acceptable such as a valid official communication arrived, possibly with a clear and verifiable account of what was going on. The governors were all adults who could recall the several changes between 217 (the death of Caracalla) and 222 (the accession of Alexander). It is also known, for example, that some messengers arriving in provinces with the news of the Gordians' actions or deaths were imprisoned or even executed by excessively suspicious governors, and opponents of the new regime were also killed.[69] The absence of evidence in the western provinces is more convincing of caution and ambiguity, and perhaps fear, than the variety of collected items from the eastern regions; the apparent decisiveness of Decius in Tarraconensis and Lucretius Annianus in Egypt stand out as the only clear cases of any governors publicly supporting anyone in that difficult year; another thirty or so items provide no clear evidence, and it would be reasonable to suppose that they had carefully waited to see what was happening, who was involved, and who won.

While many dithered, or simply ignored the problem and got on with government, the issue was brought to a decision at Aquileia – though this was not, as it happened, a final decision.

Maximinus' army marched down from the Alpine pass towards Aquileia. An advance force had been sent on and was expected to have captured the city without difficulty before the main force arrived, but it was resisted.[70] When the whole army then arrived, it found that it had first to construct a bridge over the Sontius (Isonzo) River, a day's march from the city – for the old bridge had been destroyed by the Aquileians. The main force caught up with the advance force, and apparently only then was a bridge, floating on confiscated wine barrels, built for the army to cross. The soldiers had already discovered that the river was in spate from the snowmelt in the mountains, and extremely cold. There was no question of crossing other than dry-shod.[71]

Herodian's depiction of the subsequent siege includes all the usual items to be expected from an ancient historian living and writing at a considerable distance, in space and time, from the scene – brave defenders, inventive defensive methods, rousing speeches. This is not the say that such methods were not employed, for they were also the common currency of any people in a walled city in the ancient world, and siege methods were well known. It is, however, impossible to describe the siege by retailing individual events which took place at that particular siege, since the 'events' could well be imaginary, imported from general memory.[72]

The defence was, however, entirely successful. The attackers are said to have delayed a day because of their exhaustion[73] – Herodian is convinced that an army needed no rest – though after a long march they clearly needed time to construct their camp; one day was taken before the river crossing Herodian explicitly mentions,[74] and, having crossed, they had to organise themselves; this would have taken several days. The army was distributed around the city, probably on the north and the west sides since the Nakissa River protected it on the east and south.[75]

The army was also still – or again – short of food. It is described as deliberately destroying the olive and apple orchards around the city, uprooting vines, no doubt for their heating needs and for the cooking fires and to build huts for their shelter – it was still only spring, wet and cold.[76] Foraging by the now-besieged forces before the army arrived would have scoured the countryside already, and in the usual army way buildings as well as trees suffered destruction, leaving the army without shelter other than those huts they could construct, and late spring is wet in northern Italy. Assaults on the city walls failed, and the longer the siege went on the more the army suffered from sickness and hunger, while the besieged had shelter and sufficient food (gathered beforehand from the lands the army was now foraging over unsuccessfully).[77]

Meanwhile, the recruitment of Italians into the temporary defence forces had produced a sufficient force to be able to move forward and block the roads leading to Aquileia, so preventing the more distant foraging raids.[78] The city was, of course, a major route centre; the route the army had used was the Via Gemina, from Emona and Pannonia; leading northwards from the city was the Via Julia Augusta, a route through the Carnic Alps into Noricum; westwards was the Via Annia to Concordia, the Po Valley and Rome; south was an unnamed road to the port of Grado, which had developed to replace the river port that had originally existed in Aquileia.[79] All these routes were blocked, including that to Grado, which as a port had probably contained a considerable store of foodstuffs. Herodian notes that there were even forces along the sea coast who prevented fishing and blocked news from reaching the army and Maximinus; no doubt all this was organised by the Emperor Pupienus, who was based at Ravenna, the base of the imperial fleet, and where he was collecting a force with which he presumably intended to intervene in the siege at a critical moment.

The knowledge of being surrounded, even at a distance, together with the shortage of food, and the failures of the assaults, brought Maximinus' army to a point of very low morale. Here the knowledge that the army was fighting against the Senate, and that Maximinus had been declared a public enemy, will have added more psychological pressure on the soldiers. The *legio* II *Parthica* had its permanent base near Rome, at the Alban Mount, and there the soldiers' families were living; similarly, the Praetorian Guard had its base in the same area, and their families were also there.[80] It is not known if the guardsmen with Maximinus knew that their fellow guardsmen in Rome had been compelled to surrender, but it is highly likely that this was one item of news that was not prevented from reaching its intended recipients; indeed, it may well have been widely publicised – the Guard was not popular.

There is no record that the soldiers' families living near Rome were even threatened, either in themselves or by messages to the soldiers at Aquileia, but the threat was clearly silently present, and no doubt had its effect, particularly in the knowledge of the normal state of hostility of the Roman population towards the Guard. What other propaganda ploys were directed at Maximinus' troops are not known, but given their failure, their condition of being surrounded, the problem of their families, the shortage of food, the Senate's enmity, and their emperor's damnation, not much more was necessary. Living in a camp surrounded by a devastated landscape would by itself be a further depressing element. Rumours certainly arrived, whether originating with the enemy, originating in propaganda, or developed by the soldiers' own imaginations. One such was that more rebellions against Maximinus were developing in the Balkans and Africa; a senatorial emissary, Clodius Celsinus – full name Q. Fabius Clodius Agrippianus Celsinus[81] – had in fact been sent to the troops in Moesia Inferior to urge them to join the new regime; this would be the origin of the moves the Illyrians were making.[82] Other tales were that the population of Rome was armed, that armies were mobilising throughout Italy (all true) – and that their target was always Maximinus (this last was surely an item originating from their enemies).

The effect of this pressure on the soldiers, while slow – the siege lasted for four or five weeks – was certainly sure. The two units with families in the Roman area were the ones suffering the greatest pressure, and they turned on the emperor. A joint delegation from the legion and the Guard went to Maximinus' tent and ritually and publicly tore down the imperial portraits that they carried on their standards. Maximinus and his son, whom he had recently made Caesar, came out, apparently with the intention of negotiating, but the soldiers killed them both without delay. There was therefore no chance for loyal soldiers, of which there were plenty (the army was thus as divided as the empire as a whole) to intervene. This might have happened if they had stood for a time arguing with Maximinus. The assassins went on to kill the praetorian prefect and the murdered emperor's *consilium*, or at least those who were present and could be found.[83] It was a telling demonstration of the vulnerability of all emperors.

The instant murder was decisive. There were parts of the army that were annoyed at the actions of the Guard and the legionaries, but they could put up a new successor, and the killings meant there was no point in recriminations.[84] Grumbling, they had to accept the situation. But the civil war was still on, they were still surrounded, and now they were leaderless as well as hungry; none of them seem to have thought of finding a new emperor for themselves, and apparently no one put forward a claim. A delegation, presumably representing the whole army, but unarmed, went to the city walls, and asked to be admitted. It is clear that those in command in the city were prepared for this eventuality; they must have been well aware of the condition of the besiegers. The death of the emperor was their main aim, after all, and the obvious way of achieving this was to get the besieging army to do the job itself; it would, amongst other considerations, eliminate the possibility of a continuing vendetta. But nobody in the city was prepared to allow several thousands of recently enemy soldiers into the city, particularly when they were armed and hungry. The gates remained shut, and the army was required to swear allegiance to Balbinus, Pupienus, and Gordian, whose portraits were displayed for their edification, before being admitted. The soldiers were informed – it seems to have been news to them – that the elder Gordians were dead.[85]

Then a market was organised 'on the ramparts', where the hungry soldiers could purchase what they needed, it being made clear that the city was well supplied, and that no free handouts were available. Perhaps this reconciled those annoyed at Maximinus' death to their defeat. The city kept its guard up, even when the market was in full flow.[86]

Chapter 10

The Revolution Endangered

The Emperor Maximinus' head was cut off, put on a spear and carried to Rome, first going to Ravenna for Pupienus to have proof of his victory. (The former emperor's son's detached head accompanied his father's.)[1] Its arrival in Rome several days later stimulated a great celebration,[2] perhaps as much relief that his army was not let loose on the city as at the death of an emperor detested by the Senate – though actually he was scarcely known by anyone in Rome or in the Senate, other than his earlier sponsors.

Pupienus dismissed most of his voluntary army, and sent some of the German auxiliaries who had arrived from the German provinces back home. He retained part of the group as a guard, all volunteers,[3] clearly understanding that the Praetorian Guard in Rome was not trustworthy. The murderous *legio* II *Parthica* and the main body of the Praetorian Guard, which had been with Maximinus, and had killed him, no doubt also went to Rome, where the separate sections of the Guard were reunited; those who had been in Rome all along had had much trouble in the past six months, and those who had been on campaign were reunited now with their families, as were the men of the legion. Pupienus used the Germans as an alternative to the praetorians, not that the Guard appreciated its own sidelining.

Pupienus was also fortunate that the division of imperial responsibilities in the crisis had put him in a position where he could accept credit for the victory. Balbinus had had a much more difficult task in attempting to exert control over the Roman crowd and the rebellious guard fragment. So Pupienus, no doubt fully apprised of the situation by Balbinus, was careful to be accompanied to Rome by his own protecting force.

Apart from the problems of controlling the city of Rome and its people, and establishing some control over the Praetorian Guard, and perhaps over the legion as well (which had become as addicted to murdering emperors by now as was the Guard – it had been involved in the murder of Caracalla, rebelled against Macrinus, possibly involved in the murder of Alexander Severus, and now had killed Maximinus in addition). The two emperors had a long list of other problems to face as well. In the Senate they needed to conciliate those who had failed of election in the emergency when the news of the death of the elder Gordians had arrived; another party was composed of those who had agitated for the election of the younger Gordian, who were not satisfied that he was still only a Caesar. There was plenty in Rome for the emperors to attend to.

In the wider empire, the army was the major problem. It, or rather those elements who had fought under Maximinus, had liked him. He had been generous to the soldiery, commanded them well, and had led them to victories. Above all, perhaps, he was a soldier who had risen by his own abilities to become emperor. He had clearly despised the politicians in Rome, and no doubt, the soldiers appreciated his disdain for such men and his insistence that the rich must contribute a larger share of their wealth to the common good – by which he and the soldiers meant themselves, of course. But the army was not united. Maximinus had not managed to convince the eastern armies, so it seems, in part because the donative he had promised was given to the men guarding the German and Danubian frontiers and the eastern army had to wait, existing on promises. There was potential here for a civil war.

All this was in addition to the usual problem that emerged whenever there was disruption in the empire – invasions from outside. It is likely that Maximinus' campaigns had sufficiently pummelled the German tribes and those north of the Danube into submission, so that those areas remained relatively quiet, though the Carpi were in arms in 238, despite being the people celebrated in one of Maximinus' acclamations as *Imperator*. Others had not been affected, but they will have been apprehensive, in view of Maximinus' capability and violence, that they were likely to be on his list for punishment. The death of the military emperor and the civil war and confusion in the empire that came as a result, amounted to the usual opportunity for enemies to take advantage. There was trouble in the Black Sea area, where the Goths now emerged as Roman enemies, raiding Olbia and Tyras in 238; they were leagued with the Carpi, who had been battered by Maximinus and now presumably sought revenge;[4] and a new war was threatened in the east, where the Sassanids had moved against Singara and Nisibis and Dura Europos, an attack which apparently came late in 238 and lasted into early 239.[5] These problems on the Danube and in Syria were probably the source of the curious note in the *Historia Augusta* that the two emperors were to set off for war, Balbinus to Germany and Pupienus to the eastern frontier.[6] If the latter would almost certainly see fighting, the former would probably need only to be on his guard, for neither the Franks nor the Alamanni were making hostile moves at this time.

The new rulers had therefore taken power in a difficult political and military environment, both internally and internationally. This may be the source of the division of responsibilities which is suggested by Herodian, who, to be precise, did not really know a great deal about the court and its problems. He may have assumed that the division of responsibilities between the emperors in the crisis of 238 was intended to be permanent, but whether he was correct in such an assumption is not clear, and this may be the source of the elaboration in the *Historia Augusta*.

The return of Pupienus to Rome was certainly necessary in the summer of 238 if the two men were to work together; if they were to work in tandem, or by dividing the necessary imperial tasks, the matter had to be discussed and settled. The precedents for such a situation at the top were varied. Septimius could, just about, work with Caracalla in the former's last years, but the latter was never able to work with his brother Geta. Marcus Aurelius and Lucius Verus worked well enough with each other, but perhaps mainly because they were separated for much of their joint rule, and then Verus died soon after returning from the east. In both of these cases, also – and in the joint rule of Marcus and Commodus – one partner was the clear superior in authority, Septimius as the father, Marcus as the senior to Lucius, both in age and in date of appointment; Marcus had been responsible for hoisting Lucius to imperial authority. Similarly, Augustus had paired with Agrippa, and later with Tiberius, but he was always the superior. Going back to the Republic, the paired consuls of that period frequently disagreed with each other, but were directed to their (mainly military) tasks by the superior authority of the Senate; when the imperial regime developed, the authority of the Senate was lessened, which was the issue again in 238.

The two emperors of 238, on the other hand, had equal authority. Pupienus is usually named before Balbinus, but Balbinus was the older of the two – and the Senate respected age above other qualifications. It had apparently been Pupienus who had proposed the dual-emperors policy to the Senate. The decision to divide the imperial responsibilities in the crisis of the succession to the Gordians was pragmatic, as well as avoiding a probably bitter dispute in the Senate by a neat compromise.[7] Pupienus, it appears, had the more, or at least some, military experience, according to his career; Balbinus may have seemed, as the senior consular (cos II 213, whereas Pupienus had been 'cos II' only in 234) to have had a better, or at least longer, purely political experience. Balbinus was unfit and old, whereas Pupienus had shown a good deal of vigour.[8]

In addition, since Maximinus had ignored his role of supervising the Senate's usual occupations of passing legislation and considering judicial decisions, no doubt problems in these areas had accumulated and were requiring resolution. There was, in other words, plenty of work for the emperors in Rome, as well as the international problems, and establishing their authority over the army; division of the work made sense. Much of this is speculation since the sources for their joint reign are typically inadequate – Herodian is elaborate, rhetorical, wordy, and inaccurate as usual, and the over-imaginative *Historia Augusta* relies largely on Herodian; there are fragments of other historians, usually out of context and composed much later.

It is clear that the two men soon developed a mutual antagonism. Perhaps in the minds of some of the senators there was the notion that the Senate might re-adopt the authority of the Republican Senate and direct the emperors to their separate tasks, but such a reversion to the by then distant past is unlikely to have worked; this notion might be behind the proposal that they should go to command on separate frontiers, presumably leaving the Senate in charge of the imperial government in Rome, though another part of the putative plan was for Gordian III to stay in Rome; he might be considered to be exercising imperial authority, though he would clearly need a regent – and this would be yet another problem.

The problem was that there had been two and a half centuries and more of imperial authority since the Senate had had such power, and the government system had adapted to the condition of obedience to an emperor. The empire was no longer an entity capable of being directed by a group of several hundred senators – this had been a major factor in the failure of the Republic. The basis of imperial authority had become located in the army ever since Augustus' victory in the civil war that ended the Republic and these two emperors had a very precarious hold on the army, if at all. The field army had been Maximinus', and his death had been the result of a plot by a small group of soldiers who were normally stationed in and near Rome. It would take a deal of effort by the two to establish their own unchallenged authority over the soldiers. (This is perhaps another source for the suggestion that they should go off to different frontiers.) It would take, however, in the short term, money; in the long term, it would take much more than simply money.

In fact, Pupienus had made a start on exerting their authority over the army before returning to Rome. He had travelled from Ravenna to Aquileia to celebrate the victory.[9] The army of Maximinus there had, of course, already accepted its defeat by submitting to the two members of the Twenty in the city, though there is plenty of evidence that many of the soldiers were disquieted at the murder of Maximinus.[10] Pupienus spent two days sacrificing to celebrate the victory and no doubt being briefed on the condition of the forces he faced. He made a speech to the former enemy forces which is suggested by Herodian to have included a rhetorical flourish about the army being the servant of the Roman people and the Senate, such as might be expected of a senator, but which also included, more convincingly for the soldiers, the promise of a rich donative and an amnesty for their 'rebellion'.[11] The several units that were present were then, over the next days, returned to their stations on the frontier.[12]

Pupienus waited at Aquileia to ensure that matters on the frontier were calm – 'everything safe and undisturbed up to the Alps', as the *Historia* put it[13] – and possibly to receive reports on the submission of the governors of the other provinces, and by the armies which had not been involved in events so far. The cities of Italy had heard the news as quickly as Pupienus, and had sent delegates to join the celebrations.[14] News of the result of the fighting at Aquileia had also been sent out by the Senate, by messengers wearing laurel wreaths as a mark of Roman victory.[15] Aquileia, of course, was a very convenient place, geographically, for watching events in the northern provinces and the frontier, and was one of several northern Italian and Pannonian cities to be used for this purpose in the next century and more – Maximinus' headquarters at Sirmium was another similarly well-placed city, used by Marcus in the past.

This will have taken some time, perhaps two or three weeks, and then the emperor travelled back to Rome. Meanwhile, Balbinus had been carrying through his own celebration, including a large sacrifice (described as a hecatomb).[16] Another celebration occurred when Pupienus approached the city and was greeted by Balbinus and a celebrating crowd that had come out from the city.[17] Submissions, no doubt accompanied by congratulations, came in from most of the provinces, though two held out – Numidia and Hispania Tarraconennsis, Capelianus and Decius.

From Aquileia, Pupienus sent one of the victorious generals of Aquileia, Rutilius Pudens Crispinus, to take over Tarraconnensis.[18] It seems that this was accomplished peacefully, though possibly only after extensive negotiations, for Decius was not punished, other, perhaps, than not receiving any imperial tasks for some time; Crispinus appears to have remained in Tarraconensis until 241, the normal term of three years. In Africa, on the other hand, Capelianus, who had been responsible for the deaths of two now-revered emperors, resisted, and was supported by his legion, III *Augusta*.[19]

In the dearth of other information it must be assumed that the other provinces remained quiet, the governors perhaps stunned by the news from Aquileia. There was no doubt a major replacement of governors, to ensure future loyalty. Tullius Menophilus, for example, took over the governorship of Moesia Inferior, where he also remained for the next three years, and where he had to bear the brunt of the attacks of the Goths during his governorship, the first of a series lasting for a generation.[20] Any governor who had been appointed by Maximinus, unless he had come out very early in support of the Gordians, was liable to supersession by a replacement. Tuccianus in Britannia Inferior, who was actually attested only in 237, would no doubt be as good a case for replacement.

Tullius Menophilus had been sent to Moesia Inferior, probably because of his reputation for generalship acquired in the siege of Aquileia, and as a reward. The province had two legions, IX *Claudia* and I *Italica*, plus the usual complement of auxiliary regiments, but whether this was sufficient to stem the attacks by the Goths is not clear; they certainly reached as far as Marcianopolis, well within Moesia Inferior, in 241 (and so possibly after Menophilus' replacement). The attack by the Sassanid king, Ardashir I, into Syria in 238–239 captured some places in the Adiabene province, notably Nisibis and Singara, so much so that it can be claimed that the whole province was taken. He then turned to attack the independent city-state of Hatra, but by then the term of the two emperors had run out.[21]

The plan for the emperors to separate and each take control of a sector of the frontier was never implemented, if it ever existed. (It left out the most active part of the frontier, along the Danube, which would be a very good reason for presuming that the very idea was an invention of the author of the *Historia*.) Instead, both emperors stayed in Rome, and their personal relations steadily deteriorated.

The details of the personal animosity that developed between the emperors appear to have been a mixture of political strife, personal ambition, fear, and jealousy, a toxic mixture, but not perhaps unexpected. It is portrayed in the *Historia Augusta* with some imagination, but much less so than by Herodian.[22] In this case, we must take the *Historia* seriously, since rather more than what Herodian suggests clearly lay behind the ultimate disaster, and the *Historia*'s remarks are reasonably convincing.

There was professional jealousy revealed when Pupienus accused his partner of lazing away his time in Rome while Pupienus himself was actively working in Ravenna; to which Balbinus replied that Pupienus had in fact done nothing while at Ravenna except sit and watch the siege of Aquileia from a safe distance. As usual with accusations made in the heat of an argument, there was some truth on both sides, but also much exaggeration and a too-personal denigration. In neither case is it in fact reasonable to suggest that either of the emperors sat back and let the other do the work; both had been busy attending to this particular set of problems. The generous promotion of Menophilus and Crispinus after the siege was over, presumably arranged by Pupienus while in Aquileia, is a clear sign that he fully appreciated their successes. In a sense, Balbinus was correct in decrying Pupienus' victory as one he had not gained, but that was the Roman system under the empire, in which all victories were gained in the name of the emperor – that by Capelianius in Africa counted as one of Maximinus' *Imperator* acclamations despite its military insignificance.

Even more personal and very typical of Roman social attitudes is their quarrel over social place. They contrasted in their origins. Balbinus claimed precedence because of his aristocratic ancestry, and denigrated Pupienus as of inferior social position because he was the son of an *eques* (though Balbinus was the type of man who had reached no higher than the praetorship.) Balbinus' prior second consulship was also cited to prove his superiority. Balbinus had inherited his status as a patrician; Pupienus had been adlected relatively recently. Pupienus laid stress on his term of office as *praefectus urbi* and his experience as a successful administrator, as if having reached the consulship a second time in a lifetime and adlection as a patrician was not distinction enough; interestingly enough, neither made any reference to a contrast in military experience, which might suggest its total absence, or its insignificance, in both their lives. To an outsider, however, the distinctions they emphasised were really of limited importance; they were arguing these minor differences in their social status in the thin layer of nobility, senators and *equites*, which covered the vast majority of the Roman population. Balbinus' superior nobility by birth was balanced by Pupienus' greater experience of government; they should have, with good will, been able to work together on these terms, and the suggestion of dividing responsibilities for imperial affairs might imply that such was intended.

Both men undoubtedly harboured ambitions to be sole emperor, an ambition not at all surprising given the strength of ambition in the Roman nobility and the normal imperial system. This is not suggested for Balbinus, but his noble birth probably did not prevent him from being jealous at Pupienus' administrative achievements, and to a degree perhaps he harboured feelings of inadequacy. Pupienus, on the other hand, though this is not actually suggested as a source of the quarrel, had adult sons, probably two of them, both of whom had already been consuls. Heredity, as Balbinus certainly is said to have claimed, was vital to Roman aristocrats, and enhancement of social position was one of the aims of any noble Roman family. Balbinus, as far as we know, had no offspring, and appears to have been the elder of the two men. Pupienus may thus have been able to contemplate continuing as sole emperor when Balbinus, older, fatter, and probably in less robust health, pegged out. Getting rid of Gordian III would not be difficult. Pupienus' eldest son would then be the next emperor. Of this (unstated) ambition we can be sure Balbinus was as conscious as was Pupienus, with the added fear in Balbinus that Pupienus might well anticipate matters with a quiet murder, something Balbinus is said to have actively feared.[23]

The fear they jointly apprehended was the threat from the army. There were three units of the army of which to be wary. First was the Praetorian Guard, its sections probably now reunited in the camp outside Rome. It was collectively angered at having been forced, on the one hand, to have been defeated in battle with the Roman populace and, on the other, to have stood by while the legionaries killed an emperor. They knew they were supposed to protect the emperor, but had found that it was that emperor – Balbinus – who had directed the attack on their camp, while that part of the Guard with Maximinus took part in that emperor's murder. The guardmens' feelings must have been mixed in this tumultuous year because of the events in which the Guard had been involved.

Second, there was the legion, II *Parthica*, some of whose members had also participated in the murder of Maximinus. It is doubtful if anyone felt it was a trustworthy unit after this (and the other imperial murders it had taken part in). It was perhaps less confused than others at its own behaviour than the Guard was, but the legion was not camped at the Alban Mount in order to protect the imperial ruler; instead it had been placed there by Septimius as a way of reducing the influence of the Guard and its murderous potentialities, and as a threat to the Senate. This, of course, did not work, for the Guard and the legion found that they had plenty in common. (Did it never occur to any emperor or praetorian prefect that the best way of ensuring that the Guard and the legion stayed out of politics, and neutralised each other, would be to limit their appointments near Rome to a brief stay, and to rotate units regularly?)

The recent events at Aquileia and Ravenna had resulted in yet another attempt to neutralise the Guard and the legion, by multiplying the separate forces in Rome. This was Pupienus' recruitment of a volunteer group of German soldiers as his personal guard. How large a group this was is not known, but probably not more than a few hundred men at most. Their presence in Rome set up several areas of tension. The first was between this new guard and the Romans, who would not be too keen on the presence of a considerable group of armed men in the city, men who had no loyalty to the city; second, there was the old Praetorian Guard, who were not at all pleased at being displaced as the Guard of the emperors in favour of a bunch of foreigners. That it was the Guard's own fault – its murderousness – which had compelled Pupienus to resort to this expedient, probably passed the Guard completely by; third, was the fact that these men had been recruited by Pupienus, and that they appeared to have looked to him for their orders and functions. Balbinus was apparently being bypassed.

What actually triggered the final crisis is not clear, but it was probably the result of a group of disaffected members of the Guard working themselves into an angry mood. They approached the palace, where both emperors were in residence, but apparently could not find either of them at first. The attendants at the doors fled when the guardsmen arrived, and possibly one or more warned Balbinus. He had at least some of the German guard close by, but it appears that Pupienus had not, and sent a message to Balbinus asking for them, but Balbinus would not let them go, fearing that it was a ploy by Pupienus to leave him exposed and so acquire sole rule; or the Germans were separated from both emperors.[24]

This raises the possibility that the whole scene was plotted by one or the other of the emperors to do exactly that – either by Balbinus, who kept the German guard with him because he knew this would leave Pupienus defenceless, or by Pupienus, who wanted the German guard to leave Balbinus vulnerable – all depending on which account is believed. If so, neither plot – not too convincing, in fact – was trumped by the guardsmen, who attacked both emperors, when they had met and were arguing over the issue. Since both emperors died, and it is unlikely that any of the Guard provided an account of events, or explain their reasons, confusion is not surprising, and motives can scarcely be distinguished.

It seems that when the attackers finally located the emperors, they were together, disputing about command of the German guard, which was not there.[25] The two 'old men', as Herodian describes them, were then beaten and stripped and tortured, and either killed there and then and their bodies dragged out to be displayed, or they were dragged out of the palace still alive and were murdered in the open.[26] (There were two versions of these events, and there are clear parallels with the Guard's attack on Nerva, though the target there was to kill the chamberlain and the former praetorian prefect, who had been involved in the death of Domitian, and were being sheltered in the palace by the emperor.)

The boy Caesar, Gordian III, was apparently either present or easily locatable while all this was going on – or the plot was to kill the two 'old men' so as to put Gordian forward as the sole emperor. It seems unlikely that he would be able to organise this himself, but there were undoubtedly people around him who were not unhappy that this should happen – the group in the Senate referred to as the party of Gordian would be the prime suspects in this. The German guard had come out to rescue the victims, but were too late.[27] The murderers seized Gordian, hoisted him up, and proclaimed him emperor, then carried him off to their camp. They did this because 'there was no one else' they could find worth proclaiming. The wording, in both Herodian and the *Historia*, is very similar, and suggests, therefore, that the murders were spontaneous, without any sort of plan made in advance. It was not a coup aimed at seizing control of the government of the state. Gordian may have been the only possibility the men could imagine for promotion, or could locate, but they certainly knew of his status as Caesar, and so he would be the prime possible candidate.[28]

It is much more likely that the soldiers proclaimed Gordian as a pre-emptive move, to prevent the Senate from carrying out another imperial election, which from their point of view had turned out so badly. They are said to have jeered at the Senate (and people) while transporting their new emperor to their camp. The whole situation is best accounted for as a delayed guard reaction to the original crisis of the African rebellion and the death of Maximinus, with the Senate as one of the soldiers' targets.

There was a clear potential for a new episode of civil war in the city following the killings. If such a conflict broke out it is probable that it would spread to involve the provincial armies. Some of them we know had been opposed to two emperors all along, though they had not been involved in the Italian fighting – *legio* III *Augusta* in Africa, and *legio* VII *Gemina* in Tarraconensis in Spain were the obvious members, but there are indications of similar feelings in Britannia under Tuccianus (if he was still in office), and in Cappadocia, where the two emperors replaced the governor with their own nominee, a *novus homo*.[29] The obvious recourse would be for an army, say in Syria, or in Britannia, or on the northern frontier, to set up its own emperor-pretender. The result would be a rerun of the conflict following the murders of Nero and Galba in 68–69. The fact that no provincial army made any such move must be down to the speedy resolution of the issue in Aquileia and then at Rome.

It is necessary to resort to this sort of conjecture because the sources available up to 238, Herodian and the *Historia Augusta*, fail at the accession of Gordian. Herodian's account ceases abruptly, the *Historia* has a section on Gordian III, and then there is a gap for the next decade. Yet the aftermath of the murders is clearly an important moment, of which something must be made, and conjecture, based on what had happened before and what can be seen of later events, is a reasonable expedient. Most accounts simply slide over the events after the murders, with brief accounts of the period and a general moan about the lack of source material, and about the way the empire was in such trouble, but more can be made of the situation rather than mere despair.[30]

Neither the Senate nor the Guard made any further moves in the immediate aftermath of the killings. The Guard had the person of Gordian in its camp, and treated him as the emperor. His promotion from Caesar to Augustus could be regarded as legal, because he was clearly intended for that move in succession to the dead men, and because the army had then chosen him – he was thus the choice of the populace and the army, and this decision was accepted by the Senate. On the other hand, he was only thirteen years of age, far too young to be entrusted with any obvious responsibility. After Commodus, Elagabalus, and Alexander Severus, yet another child emperor would be yet another problem. But it was not a problem the Guard was equipped to solve. The decision was evidently made in the Senate to accept the situation, and so, as the *Historia* remarks, peace was agreed.[31] It was the Senate's role now to set up a government.

The murders had been, as the killers had indicated, directed at the Senate and at the new imperial system it had set up, by elevating Balbinus and Pupienus. Once the shock of the murders wore off, the newly invigorated Senate could set to work to make the best of the new situation. The youth of the new emperor did enable the Senate to exert itself and maintain its leading position, as with the two dead emperors. It already contained a group who could act as intermediaries between the Senate and the Guard – the party of Gordian, the men who had agitated for his promotion in the first place. The Senate had as much, or more, *esprit de corps* as the Guard, and in an emergency such as that following the imperial murders it was capable of collective action (as it had shown on the news of Gordian I and II's usurpation), as much perhaps from an instinct for self-preservation by the individuals as of such a spirit, and for the 'good of the *res publica*'. The negotiations will have been delicate, since it was a senator who had set off the civil conflict by murdering a couple of guardsmen; no doubt, he – Gallicanus – was carefully excluded from the talks, but he seems to have been included in the governing group.

There is little evidence for the Senate's actions after the grisly murders of the two emperors, men who had been their senatorial colleagues for many years until a few months before, but some such negotiations would seem to be both likely and necessary, if only to extract Guardian III from the Guard's camp, but also for the Senate to formally accept the new emperor. In past crises of the same sort, in 193 and in 96, this had been the process. In 96, to be sure, the consul in office had successfully gathered a selected number of his colleagues to install the new emperor, Nerva, in place of the dead Domitian, and in 193, the proclaimed Pertinax had been careful to seek the Senate's approval. Even peaceful accessions had been followed, or perhaps confirmed, by decisions in the Senate. In the first crisis of 238, earlier in the year, the Senate had met and had made a series of collective decisions: to condemn their imperial enemy, set up an election for a replacement, organise the defence, and so on. In the second crisis of 238 they were surely capable of the same sort of collective action.

But the situation in 238 was quite unprecedented. All earlier coups that involved the killing of an emperor had subsequently produced an adult as the replacement emperor – Nero, Septimius, the two dead emperors. But now there was no apparent successor available. Therefore, the Senate had the opportunity to seize governmental power for itself. The accession of a child had moved the Senate into taking the power that it had in effect been losing ever since Commodus' reign.

The *Historia Augusta* author has bundled the three Gordians together, avoiding any real discussion of the process of transition, remarking only that he was 'hurried to the Senate, then the assembly', which according to Herodian is completely false, since he was taken to the Guard's camp instead.[32] But the fact of his youth is the necessary clue to what certainly had to happen. The Senate could have rejected him as emperor and then gone through another process of election, which would have taken time, produced a clash with the Guard, and perhaps the *legio* II *Parthica* as well, and roused opposition. It had already agreed that he should be Caesar, and that senatorial decision was not overturned.

The Guard, representative of the army as a whole and so also of the Roman people, had proclaimed him emperor, a legally acceptable process ever since the murder of Caligula and the promotion of Claudius. Therefore, there was an emperor in office, who could be recognised in the usual way by his investiture by the Senate with the usual institutional powers – *tribunicium potestas, pontifex maximus*, and so on. This would confirm him as emperor, and give him the legal powers and the command of the legions. Because of his youth, he could scarcely exercise these powers, so he then had to be provided with a *consilium*, a group of advisers. This was the task that the Senate now had to undertake, and since it was the Senate that was making such decisions and selecting those advisers, they would inevitably be a set of senators.

It is worth pointing out that the process was clearly accepted by all those parties – the Guard, the legion, the provincial governors – who might have had the power to challenge it. Admittedly, the sources are silent, but some sort of an echo of any discussion or dissension would surely have survived; it was exactly the thing to provoke the production of source material. We may therefore make the assumption that the process was accepted and formally gone through. The reason is probably that the lesson of the previous six months had affected everyone's attitude. The slaughter of so many emperors in only a few months was shocking enough, but it was accompanied by the defeat of a powerful professional army by groups of citizens, first in Rome and then in Aquileia. The contempt of the soldiers for the Senate was hardly new, but could easily have developed into outright hostility if the senators had not been extra careful. The provincial authorities, armies and governors, were far from the action, and after the previous events they probably waited on the next instalment – with the result, in fact, that the situation in Rome was solved quickly enough to prevent any movements elsewhere.

This result was clearly a decision by the Senate with the agreement, explicit or simply by silent acceptance, by the Roman populace and by the troops in their nearby camps. A quick and possibly unanimous Senate decision could have been authoritative and therefore accepted. The Roman crowd had their preferred candidate accepted, the army had the very person in their control, and the Senate had re-established, once again, its overall authority over both and over the government system. And the Senate had demonstrated, for the second time in a year, how decisive it could be in a crisis.

Furthermore, there was a relatively recent set of precedents for this solution of a supervisory *consilium* for the child emperor until he became adult. Marcus provided the group of senators, guardians, for Commodus; the two Severan boy emperors had been provided with advisers, though that had been an unsuccessful practice, with men not selected by the Senate, and in the case of Ulpian, advising Alexander Severus, a dull lawyer. In addition, the latter two of these had been hampered by the presence of their mothers, and in Elagabalus' case by his religious eccentricity and egocentricity; Alexander, however, had served as emperor for thirteen years, almost as long as Septimius. Before that, there was the case of Commodus, a dangerous example for senators to invoke, of course, but his father had been the revered Marcus Aurelius, and it had been his solution to the problem of his son's youth and inexperience that had led him to surround him with a group of his own former advisers when he died. It had not worked very well, to be sure, but anything that limited Commodus' personal options was likely to have failed.

This, therefore, despite the problems, which could have been foreseen after previous experiences, was the model to follow. And this time the Senate was in command of the process. The emperor's mother was on hand and present, which might have caused problems (she was the daughter of an emperor, Gordian I, after all) but she seems to have been less assertive than the earlier ladies. There is no list of the members of the *consilium*, but one can be at least partly reconstructed.[33] The most obvious member is the man who eventually emerged from the pack as a sort of executive regent, C. Furius Sabinus Aquila Timesitheus. He was a former *eques* with a notably high-flying career. He had served every emperor since Septimius in a series of posts, often of a fiscal nature, and in a long series of provinces from Belgica and Spain to Syria and Arabia. In the process, he had been acting governor of several provinces and in command of the forces there. He had been fast-tracked from his first post, which was as prefect of *cohors* I *Gallica* in Tarraconensis.[34] He skipped the next steps, which would normally be two more posts of a military nature, and was quickly moved into the high peaks of the imperial administration, occupying a series of procuratorial posts. He showed a skill in serving in each administration, and in sliding comfortably into a high position in its successor – from a post under Alexander Severus to one under Maximinus, for example, where he was the procurator of Lugdunensis and Aquitania, a high post that might be regarded as a demotion from his previous post in Asia, but was a better fate than many of his gubernatorial colleagues, who were often executed. He would appear to have made himself indispensable. The revolution of 238 scarcely impeded his career, which was now centred on Rome and the imperial court.

He clearly had a high reputation, and having been demoted somewhat by Maximinus he would likely be in favour with his successor. It is perhaps unlikely that he was the first choice of the senators for a position on the new *consilium*. His ability and wide knowledge of the empire and its system may well have made him indispensable soon enough, however. He was made praetorian prefect in 240, though by whose nomination is not known. He was not above manipulating the social system, though, and his appointment as prefect came at the same time as his daughter was married to the young emperor. The daughter, Furia Sabinia Tranquillina, seems to have been as easy to manipulate as Gordian himself.

Other possible members in the emperor's early *consilium* in the reign of Gordian III were a careful mixture of men of various political persuasions. Not surprisingly, the senator who had roused the Roman crowd to shout for the promotion of Gordian III, L. Domitius Gallicanus Papinianus, was one of them.[35] He was probably thoroughly unpopular with the Guard, two of whose men he had stabbed when he was haranguing the crowd outside the Senate, but he had been the most prominent supporter of Gordian since the first two of the family had been murdered. He had a lengthy, if very typical, senatorial career from tribune of the plebs and prefect of the Saturnian treasury through praetor (fast-tracked again, notably omitting any military posts and skipping the quaestorship) up to consul, with governorships of Dalmatia, Hispania Citerior (i.e. Tarraconnensis) and Germania Inferior; add the fact that he was from Africa and he was clearly familiar with the western half of the empire, it is no wonder he was able to speak with authority in the Senate, and was listened to.

Any man who was consul in 239–241 can plausibly be counted as an adviser. The years are those for which the new regime would have chosen the consuls, those of 238 having been Maximinus' nominees. It is however worth including the two known consuls of 238, who were in office amid the crisis. One of these *consules ordinarii* of 238 was Pontius Proculus Pontianus. Maximinus no doubt assumed that he was a supporter, to have awarded him such an honour. If so, he rapidly switched sides, and served as governor of Germania Superior after Maximinus' death, as inscriptions in the province indicate.[36] The dating is vague, but he was certainly in office in 241, and could well have been posted to Germany after his consulship, and also in late 238 or 239 – by which time the new regime was seen to be fairly settled.

His colleague for 238 was Fulvius Pius, probably descended from the family of Septimius' mother. He appears to have played no part in affairs in 238, which might mean he simply acquiesced in what was happening, though such a supine attitude is unlikely in a man who had become ordinary consul. He had been consul first in 233, which might suggest a mixed loyalty, to Alexander Severus in 233, and to his murderer in 238. Both of these *consules ordinarii* were sons of senators from the provinces, Pontius from Macedonia, Fulvius from Africa.[37]

Gordian III took one ordinary consulship of 239 for himself, and his colleague was M'. Acilius Aviola, a man of the highest distinction in the Senate, by descent if not by achievements (no office held by him is known). He was descended from the long line of Acilius senators going back as far as the middle Republic, one or more senators in every generation. His instant participation in the new regime is significant, however, perhaps in part because an Acilius had been regarded as *capax imperii* back in 193. He cast a glow of antique distinction over the new regime.[38]

For 240, the *ordinarii* were C. Octavius Appius Suetius Sabinus and L. Ragonius Venustus.[39] The former was a veteran of the reign of Septimius (and had held offices under Caracalla, who was a friend. He had a long series of relatively minor administrative offices. He was praetor in 206, commanded *legio* XXII *Primigenia* in 211–212 and was part of an expeditionary force into free Germany the next year, along with governing Raetia. He was made consul in 214 having already governed Raetia. He then governed a Pannonian province during Caracalla's last year; he had been continuously employed from his praetorship until his time in Pannonia. After that, he had only the governorship of Africa. This was a notable career, which came to an abrupt end with the death of Caracalla.[40] Having begun his career in 193, he must have been one of the oldest men in this *consilium*. One might guess he was persuaded by the offer of a second consulship. The contrast with his colleague L. Ragonius Venustus is extreme, for Ragonius was descended from two generations of senators, but no office he had held is known.[41] Both of these men were, however, Italian born.

Gordian took his second consulship in 241, with as his colleague Clodius Pompeianus. This was, like the association with Acilius and perhaps Octavius, a connection back to the past. Pompeianus, having changed his name from the aristocratic Claudius to the more plebeian Clodius, was a descendant of the Claudius family, which came into prominence in Marcus' reign. His great-grandfather had married Marcus' daughter, so Clodius was a descendant of that emperor, another who might be thought *capax imperii*; his cousins (still using the Claudius version of the name) had been consuls in Alexander Severus' reign, and his father and uncle under Septimius. There is no indication of any offices held by this later consul, but with that ancestry he probably did not need to take any; the family came, of course, from Syria, specifically Antioch.[42]

It may be assumed that these men were a fair selection, perhaps rather more distinguished than the average, of those who surrounded the young emperor, who by all accounts was fairly pliable. (Only the ordinary consuls are known by name, none of the suffects of these years can be dated and identified.) So far as can be seen, age was one of the criteria applied, which would tend to confirm that the Senate was in charge of the choice. There were two high aristocrats, Acilius and Claudius Pompeianus; there were representatives from a variety of imperial provinces – Italy, Syria, Africa, Macedonia – and men who had served every emperor since Septimius, including both Macrinus and Maximinus, the two emperors who were least popular with the Senate. As a list, it had all the characteristics of a politicians' selection, designed to appeal to, or perhaps conciliate, all types of opinion.

A *consilium* for an emperor would be considerably larger than these four men, and one would expect at least another half-dozen to be included, though attendance at meetings would always fluctuate. In their imperial experience, however, this group may be properly representative, including, as it did, men who had pursued imperial administrative careers, and those who were no more than senators by descent. These men had, collectively, experience in many parts of the empire, not simply in their native provinces, but in other provinces that they had governed, though one supposes that the record there is less than complete. There was even a touch of the military about some of them. Octavius, for example, had been part of a German expeditionary force under Caracalla – though that was thirty years before.

There are six more men who have been suggested to have been part of the *consilium*, though there are also conditions that militate against their inclusion. L. Caesonius Lucilius Macer Rufinianus was another man whose career began in Septimius' reign; he was quaestor in about 212, and reached consul in 222. The administrative posts he had held were mainly in Italy, though he had been legate to an African proconsul. He recorded his membership of the Twenty on his *cursus* inscription, and later served as governor of Africa. He appears to have originated in Campania, and in the early 250s, he was *praefectus urbi*. His period of service was exclusively under the Severan emperors, not, of course, under Maximinus. This may thus be the basis of his attitude in 238, and it may be said that he maintained that loyalty after 238.[43]

Tullius Menophilus had been one of the successful commanders at Aquileia, and went from there to be governor of the crucial frontier province of Moesia Inferior. The other elements of his career are unknown, though it is probable that he had been consul before 238, and his name suggests an origin in the eastern part of the empire. Seven inscriptions in the Moesias bear his name and commemorate Gordian III, but Menophilus' name was chiselled out, so he clearly fell foul of the government about 241.[44]

His colleague at Aquileia, Rutilius Pudens Crispinus, was rather more well known, with a detailed lengthy cursus, from his post as prefect of cohors I *Lusitania equitata* in Egypt to a post supervising the census in Lugdunensis in the 240s. He was quaestor in 213, his fifth post, so he had begun his career, like so many others in this group, as an *eques*, under Septimius. He was fully occupied under every subsequent emperor, including Maximinus, until he chose the Senate's side in the crisis of 238. He served in Egypt, Italy, Thrace, Syria,

Gaul, and Lusitania in this long career, and went on to take over in Tarraconensis from Decius. His last post was in 244.[45]

C. Flavius Iulius Latronianus' career is unclear, but from inscriptions, we may note that he was related to the Pollienus family from Etruria, and probably had a career linking him to various parts of the empire, including Narbonensis. He became praetorian prefect under Gordian III, which presumably means he had plenty of experience and was an early supporter.[46]

L. Flavius Honoratus Lucilianus is recorded in some inscriptions in Moesia and Dacia, on all of which Maximinus' name has been deleted. In these provinces, Lucilianus appears to have been governor, but no more can be said.[47]

M. Aedinius Iulianus had a career of an odd shape. He was *praefectus Aegypti* (a post for an *eques*, after a long and successful career) in the first years of Alexander Severus' reign, and before that, he had been governor of Lugdunensis, a senatorial post. After that, there is no record until his name appears on the great inscription from Normandy, the 'Marbre de Torigny', as chairman of the Tres Galliae council. It rather looks as though, like Timesitheus, he was demoted by Maximinus, but was still kept in employment, presumably for his efficiency.[48]

Consideration of these further possible members of Gordian's *consilium* does not really alter conclusions reached from the careers of the four consuls in office between 239 and 241, except that they were distinctly less highborn than such men as Acilius. Their origins were largely in Italy so far as can be seen, and their work took them all over the empire. To have left detailed lists of their careers means they were largely typical of other senators; some of their careers seem rather unusual, but no more so than can be explained by a simple reference to the political upheavals of the previous thirty years. The possible members of the *consilium*, in other words, conform well to the pattern of senatorial careers. There seems nothing in all the detail to separate this group of ten men from the rest of the Senate, with the exception that they were active in supporting Gordian III – but then so was the Senate as a whole, at least in the end. One must presume that they were therefore well regarded, or notably compliant, or perhaps representatives of parties in the Senate. The chosen group was thus typical of what one might expect from the Senate, generally old, but also well experienced in the ways of both the Senate and the empire. They would be generally knowledgeable about provincial conditions, a group who collectively could advise on many problems or regions in the empire and its frontiers.

There was perhaps one omission. There is no indication that the army had any input into the choice, except the two former *equites* who appear to have been included, and these, though each holding the post of praetorian prefect for a time, had less to do with military affairs and more with administration and law. One of these, of course, was Timesitheus, whose *cognomen* rather suggests Greek ancestry, though from which part of the Greek Roman Empire is unknown. The other was M. Aedinius Iulianus, who had been *praefectus Aegypti* in the first year of Alexander Severus' reign. He had not served in that office under Maximinus, both of whose prefects had died during the crisis, one killed at the orders of the elder Gordian, the other murdered by his own troops at Aquileia. Aedinius had perhaps served elsewhere under Maximinus, but was regarded with respect by senators, partly for his culture, as was Timesitheus. The participation of these two widened the social basis of the reigning *consilium*, and they provided at least a tenuous link with the army.

It was also necessary to include a man, or men, who had been loyal to Maximinus. L. Flavius Honoratus Lucilianus had been governor of Moesia Inferior under that emperor, and had possibly held that post throughout the civil war. He was replaced during 238 at latest by Tullius Menophilus, but evidently he was not regarded as beyond the Pale by Gordian's regents. Menophilus would have perhaps been seen as a useful member of the Gordian *consilium*, if he had not been dispatched by Pupienus as Lucilianus' replacement in Moesia; similarly Crispinus, who was sent to take over Tarraconensis from Decius. Neither man in their relatively distant posts can be taken to be members of the Gordian *consilium*; in both cases they appear to have served a full three-year term as governor (unless Menophilus was dismissed, or dead, in 241), and it seems likely that both provinces required the full attention of a governor.

There are a considerable number of other men who might be included in this catalogue of Gordian's early supporters, but it would take us further and further away from any convincing inclusiveness.[49] It must be admitted that the half-dozen listed above are no more than suggestions, though they look pretty convincing in their experiences, ages, and senatorial positions to be a group selected by the Senate for the purpose; the consuls in particular would be in a good position to influence the government.

If they were part of this supporting group, or the *consilium*, they were the men who had to cope with the early problems of Gordian's reign. These were a varied set. The deposition of Q. Decius Valerinus from his position as governor in Tarraconensis was one of them. He had been busy during his governorship, judging by the frequent appearance of his name (along with Maximinus') on milestones all over the province.[50] To say that he only had command of a single legion, and so to imply his essential powerlessness, is to be intentionally misleading. There was no equal force anywhere near Tarraconensis, and many of the people in the army might have been very reluctant to tackle him, out of posthumous loyalty to Maximinus, a loyalty which Decius displayed by continuing to commemorate the former emperor after his death.

That issue, however, seems to have been settled quietly, and presumably, Spain was not further disturbed; Decius emerged as emperor ten years later, though his career between 238 and 249 is not known, although he was active in the Senate.[51] Africa, however, was a different matter. It was there that Gordian's relatives had been murdered, and where Capelianus had let loose the III *Augusta* legion on the province to loot and destroy. It was claimed that a large part of the aristocratic inhabitants had been killed in this reign of terror.[52] Revenge was therefore sought. The first method was to disband the legion, and to decree it into *damnatio memoriae*. What became of the dismissed soldiers is unclear, but many must have been natives of the province with their homes in the region – the legion had been present at various bases and forts in Africa for two and a half centuries.[53]

This availability of trained men, in fact, may have been an element in the attempt by a man called Sabinianus in 240 to have himself proclaimed emperor.[54] He cannot be further identified, but it is suggested that he was the new governor of Africa: but half a dozen men with that *cognomen* can be traced at this period.[55] He may have had support from some of the dismissed men, and from many of those in the province whom they had oppressed; he was as it happens suppressed as quickly as the Gordians had been, this time by a force fighting for Gordian III. The attempt indicated a distinctly unhappy province, not surprisingly; it had been badly damaged, a factor recorded with some exaggeration by bishop Cyprian.[56]

The immediate problems associated with internal imperial affairs were thus surmounted within a couple of years. But the essential point is that the revolution which began with the murder of a procurator in an obscure African city had survived the early difficulties. The purpose of the revolution that had begun with the action at Thysdrus had been provoked by the perceived excessive taxation that had been imposed by the military emperor Maximinus. The reaction in Africa had been drastic under Capelianus' unpleasant vengefulness, and the province suffered grievously as a result. Whereas in the half-century or so before 238 Africa had been a place where prosperity had grown steadily, though, as is the way with such things, the larger benefit went to a fairly small group, some benefits did trickle down to other parts of the population. The province continued to supply food to Rome, but prosperity appears to have been reduced somewhat by the time of the trouble at Thysdrus.

The subsequent reaction to these events in Africa took matters in an unexpected and different direction. In Rome, the Senate took the opportunity to seize control of affairs out of the hands of an emperor whose sole purpose seems to have been warfare, at the expense of the wealthy – that is, the senatorial class. This may have been the result of an existing plot by a group of senators, who seized the moment of the usurpation of the Gordians to implement their plot. The result was a reversion to what was believed to have been senatorial authority as exercised in the past. Six months later, after the deaths of six emperors, the Senate contemplated the task of having to cope, again, with a boy ruler. The murder of Maximinus by the Guard and the legionaries of II *Parthica* (curiously similar to the murders of the two Gordians by III *Augusta*'s legionaries and auxiliaries), was followed by the killing of the two old emperors chosen by the Senate in an extremely distasteful way, by men of the Praetorian Guard. Once more, a murder had been committed by the Guard, and perhaps with some participation by legionaries of II *Parthica* – again.

This should have disturbed the new regime of the Senate, but its control of the government continued. In no case could it be said that the murders of all six of these emperors were aimed by the army, or its commanders, at seizing power from the Senate. The killing of the two Gordians had largely been a part of a personal vendetta by Capelianus, who covered this by claiming to be acting on behalf of Maximinus, and by instituting the sack of the province; the killings of Maximinus and Pupienus and Balbinus had by contrast been an act of anger and vengeance, partly revenge for the death of Maximinus, with no obvious political content at all. Certainly the deaths of Pupienus and Balbinus were not followed up by the Guard by hoisting their own new emperor; they simply proclaimed Gordian III, who was already Caesar.

Despite all the violence directed at the several emperors and pretenders, the result of the affairs of 238 – of the revolution – was that power swung out of the hands of the emperor and into the hands of the Senate. The revolution had found its own meandering way to success, as revolutions do, but without having had any particular destination in mind for most participants. The result was an increase in senatorial influence and power, for the first time since the reign of Marcus Aurelius, or even since the Julio-Claudians. And yet it was found that the office of emperor remained a necessary one. The real test of the permanence of the new regime would come in the next generation, when even more emperors would die by violence.

Chapter 11

The Senate Empowered

The interpretation of the relations of emperor and Senate in the third century tends to concentrate on the vicissitudes of the emperors. After Marcus Aurelius, for a century and more, only one emperor, Septimius Severus, died a 'natural' death. The rest died violently, by assassination or in battle.

This version of events tends to eclipse the Senate's condition, which problem (in historiography) is made more difficult by the absence of reliable sources, after Dio Cassius and Herodian. Not only is there little information about the attitude of the Senate as a whole, even the names of many of the consuls and other magistrates are absent. Inevitably, therefore, the persons and work of emperors becomes the main historical subject. Yet despite the lack of sources and information, the Senate recovered and continued to operate with confidence. The Senate, due to the effects of the revolution of 238, was a revived power in the empire from 238. This was also because several of the subsequent emperors understood that their own power and authority depended in part on their good relations with the Senate – the lesson of Septimius and Maximinus appeared to have been learnt.

This condition operated for about a generation after 238, but with the disasters of 260 it became clear that only the power and authority of untrammeled emperors commanding the army and able to conscript the necessary resources were adequate to the task of holding the empire together, so long as the army could be controlled. It was the potential collapse of the empire into fragments that doomed the Senate into futility, for in that period of war and crisis, the Senate was unable to affect matters.

To see how this worked out it is necessary to begin with 238 and its aftermath, where it can be seen that the Senate's authority had been greatly enhanced by the result of the preceding crisis. And yet the Senate's authority was never secure, and it had to struggle against some brutal emperors; so this chapter looks at the Senate's period of some success, and the next chapter looks at how it all resulted.

The result of the crisis caused by the Guard's killing of the two emperors Balbinus and Pupienus was, paradoxically, a confirmation of the authority of the Senate. The guardsmen who murdered them were only a small minority of the whole force – just as it was only a small minority who had turned on and killed Maximinus and his son and their praetorian prefect at Aquileia. It may well be that the rest of the Guard was therefore as a result satisfied with their action, either that, or disgusted by it. The fact is that the Guard as a whole then did nothing, effectively abdicating any pretence at the exercise of power. This suggests that the officers asserted their control, especially since the new emperor was now present in their camp. If they, as Herodian commented, could think of no one else to promote as emperor[1] they had to accept the one candidate on offer, Gordian III, who was a senatorial candidate, even if pushed forward by the Roman crowd. Then the army had to leave it to the Senate, a group of experienced administrators, to solve the problem of how to run the new government of the empire. It was probably realised that the army was out of its depth in such a situation, but that the Senate had the knowledge and expertise required.

To do this the Senate first accepted the promotion of Gordian III as Augustus, thereby neutralising the Guard, but at the same time, since he was too young to rule himself, the senators seized control. It was, in a sense, a senatorial *coup d'état*, in place of a military version. By surrounding the new emperor with a group of senators as his *consilium*, adopting an old expedient that had been used several times, when the succession had passed to a child, in the past half-century, the senators asserted control. And the Guard did nothing to oppose them, nor did any other military unit.

Therefore, the Senate was in control, but this might only last so long as the emperor was too young to rule alone. By exercising control for several years, however, the Senate was able to establish itself as a power centre once more. It was the Senate that appointed new governors in lieu of those who had to be replaced, the Senate which sent commanders to suppress provincial opponents, such as Sabinianus and Capelianus in Africa and Decius in Tarraconensis. No doubt, it was the Senate that imported Aedinius and Timesitheus as skilled administrators and financial experts, of the social rank below senators, into the government, if not directly into the new emperor's *consilium*, and acquiesced when the latter achieved a dominating influence over the new emperor. The fact that Timesitheus was not a senator, and had remained an *eques*, perhaps reconciled them to the situation, since it implied that he was in some way reconciled to a certain inferiority.

The major external problem facing the new regime after the ructions of 238 was the war which had begun in the east in that year (or perhaps a year or two earlier) against the Sassanid Empire. But until the issue of the government of the empire was settled, this war in the east had to wait. It would make no sense to take the field army to fight in Syria with dissidents operating in the west, or when the army was liable to suddenly turn on its imperial commander in the midst of a campaign.

At the same time, there was some trouble on the Rhine frontier and on the lower Danube. What happened in Germany is not clear, though at least one frontier fort suffered destruction (Kunzing in Noricum) and others were damaged, probably after 241.[2] There is no sign that the frontier was seriously penetrated, but some damage inside the empire did occur. The lack of wider reactions along the German frontier suggests that Maximinus' work in that area had been lasting.

The more serious immediate problem was a full-blown invasion across the Danube by the Goths, a tribal federation only recently instituted, and presided over by a most capable king, Kniva; they were allied with the Carpi. The raiders penetrated as far as Marcianopolis in Moesia Inferior.[3] This was the province to which Tullius Menophilus had been sent in 238 by the Emperor Pupienus. He drove out the raiders and then made a peace treaty with them – the Goths gained rather better terms than the Carpi, their partners, possibly a ploy to set them against each other.[4]

So Spain and Africa were dealt with first, in 239 and 240, and elsewhere any obnoxious governors were replaced, and existing governors' loyalties were tested. On the Rhine frontier, presumably, the governors succeeded in restoring the line; but the Gothic invasion loomed larger. Meanwhile in the east, the Sasanid invasion was making progress in Syria. The Mesopotamian province was conquered and the border retreated to the Euphrates; the independent city-state of Hatra, which had defied Roman emperors, was taken in 240. The eastern legions were clearly inadequate to the task of a proper defence.[5]

Internally, there was a crisis in 241. In May, the young emperor married the daughter of Timesitheus, who in turn was now appointed praetorian prefect, traditionally an *eques* post.[6] It was a post that was in the gift of the emperor, but the social inferiority still operated, so senatorial agreement was no doubt fairly easily forthcoming. In the same year, and perhaps in reaction to these events, Tullius Menophilus was removed from his post as governor in Moesia and was at least disgraced (his name was chiselled out from inscriptions, implying *damnatio memoriae*) and probably he was executed.[7] Menophilus' loyalty had surely been presumed after his successes at the fighting at Aquileia and in Moesia against the Goths, but he was clearly provoked to do whatever he did which the Senate decided was hostile to it. It may be that he presumed too much in making a treaty with the Goths, which was the responsibility of the emperor and the Senate as a whole. It may also be that he objected to the promotion of Timesitheus as praetorian prefect.

This was perhaps ominous for the government's stability and for the frontier in Moesia as well. There had therefore been three incidents of internal and armed refusal to accept the Senate's authority; there had been invasions in Germany, in the Balkans, and in the eastern provinces. This is hardly surprising, given the unusually complicated, disturbing, and crucial events of the year 238; it was not unexpected once the internal situation in the empire became unsettled. That is to say, the revolution had produced the usual active hostility from its hitherto quiet enemies, seeking to take advantage of the confusion. It was the situation of 68–69 and 117–118 and 193 over again.

The dismissal or destruction of Menophilus may have provoked a new Gothic invasion, though the matter is not clear. If so, the provocation was probably the cancellation of the treaty, or the failure to deliver the agreed subsidy. The Roman field army that was gathered to deal with the eastern war had to fight in the Balkans on the way there. Timesitheus was a competent commander, and a good organiser of supplies, and so on, as one would expect from a man who had been doing such tasks for the past thirty years. He succeeded in restoring matters on the Danube,[8] but this caused yet another delay in dealing with the issue in the east. It was not until late in 242, therefore, that the army began its march to recover lost lands in the east, three years and more since the Sasanid invasion began.

The formal appointment of a new praetorian prefect was technically in the hands of the emperor, but Gordian was still no more than sixteen years of age, and the *consilium* (if that group which was put in position around Commodus is anything to go by) was likely to be in authority for at least two or three more years yet. Possibly the appointment of Timesitheus as prefect was Gordian's declaration of majority, as well as marriage, though Timesitheus' position as prefect and father-in-law remained controlling. Certainly one result was that the two of them (along with the new wife) went off to the east. Gordian was in nominal, and Timesitheus in actual, military command. Such a situation (Timesitheus was still an *eques*) is likely to have seemed unnatural and wrong to some senators – and Tullius Menophilus may be an example of one who was exceptionally vociferous in the matter, to his cost. Menophilus' execution (if that was his fate) was technically ordered by the emperor, but Timesitheus was the executive. It was perhaps a warning to other senators not to interfere too obviously.

Yet the Senate was not reduced to the impotence to which it had sunk under Maximinus. Timesitheus' co-option into the *consilium* had been a decision of the Senate, and it is probable that his post as praetorian prefect was actually made in agreement with the Senate's *consilium* group. Tullius Menophilus, far off in Moesia Inferior, close to the Black Sea, would be unable to influence matters in Rome, and a *fait accompli* may have simply enraged him, especially given his no doubt inflated ego after victories at Aquileia and in Moesia.

It is difficult to decide exactly how influential the *consilium* of senators was in the years when Gordian and Timesitheus were away from Rome in 241–243 campaigning in the Balkans and the east. But in the previous few years, since the events of 238, the appointment of new governors and administrators had continued, and with the deaths of the two emperors the choice of their replacement clearly fell to the Senate, prompted by the army. At Aquileia, Emperor Pupienus had sent off Rutilius and Menophilus to replace existing, but delinquent, governors in two of the provinces, but after the two emperors died, there was no one with such authority left. The Senate therefore was the obvious group with the authority to act, though probably there was a fairly small group, not perhaps precisely the same as the men surrounding the young emperor, or of the original Twenty who made such appointments. In fact, some of the Twenty were, like Crispinus and Menophilus, too far away from the city to influence its decisions. Gallianus was certainly involved, though Caesoninus went as governor to Africa to clean up after Sabinianus. Others, no doubt, were also sent abroad.

The measures taken in the aftermath of the revolution can be ascribed to the Senate, and members of the Twenty were prominent in them. The rebel in Africa, Sabinianus, who seems to have been the governor, had been appointed by someone, probably the two emperors, to replace Capelianus in Numidia. His rebellion is unexplained, but he was opposed by the governor of Mauretania Caesariensis, Fultonius Restitutianus, an *eques*.[9] He used his own auxiliary forces from eastern Mauretania, since by that time, *legio* III *Augusta* had been disbanded, and he must have been given special permission to invade the neighbouring province by the Senate. He was in fact acting in the absence of the appointed governor – or 'in place of the governor'. Again, senatorial instructions were clearly required.

The prominence of *equites* in the new regime was not particularly new. The Mauretanian procurator was a temporary replacement for a governor who had either been removed or not yet replaced by the Senate – so not a precedent. Timesitheus' career had included two periods when he was the temporary governor in Arabia. In other areas of the administration, at a level lower than procurator, it may be assumed that affairs continued in the usual humdrum bureaucratic mode. Men were recruited, dismissed, replaced, and moved in the normal way. It was, after all, a bureaucratic state and such postings and positioning did not usually require approval from the chiefs of the state, any more than low-level civil servants in modern western states do. The heads of the bureaucracy would be vetted, or chosen, by the men in command of the government, on the recommendation of others, with the emperor normally involved. In the early years of Gordian III, this would be done by the Senate, or by a committee thereof. This would be the source of the inclusion of Timesitheus, an *eques*, in the government circle. He remained at that social rank, even as the father-in-law of the emperor, though he would in earlier days have been adlected to senatorial rank years before; Aedinius was another *eques* who, like Timesitheus, had chaired the Tres Galliae council for a time.

The emergence to independent political power and authority of these *equites* had been a gradual process, of course, going on for several decades, and their own *cursus* had developed, with the posts of *praefectus Aegypti*, praetorian prefect, and prefect of the *vigiles* in Rome as the summits, together perhaps with the *praefectus annonae*. (It appears, for example, that Timesitheus had aimed for the post of praetorian prefect for a long time, hence his deliberate retention of *eques* status.) But now the *equites* were colonising more of the highest positions, without being adlected to the Senate, or wishing for that promotion. Commodus had perhaps been the major influence in this direction, with his enhancement of the powers of the praetorian prefect and his appointment to that post not only of *equites*, but also even of freedmen. This had as a result shifted the role of the praetorian prefect from the command of the Guard to a much more central administrative and legal role in affairs, a process that had gone on for some decades before Commodus, of course.

These *equites* were much better trained in administration than any senator was. They were, in effect, the heads of a professional civil service in contrast to the generally amateur status of senators. They were also less limited in numbers than members of the Senate. Timesitheus held a long series of procuratorships, being constantly employed for thirty years; his younger contemporary, C. Attius Alcimus Felicianus, had risen to a fairly high post under Elagabalus, then held a series of procuratorships, and from 233 was in charge of the Roman mint, from which position he was moved to take control of the collection of the inheritance tax in 235.[10] Maximinus, as he did with Timesitheus, demoted him to procurator in charge of the city amphitheatre, as a (minor) punishment for their service under Alexander Severus, but, significantly, did not remove him entirely, presumably, as an *eques* himself, valuing his and his colleagues' abilities.

Those men therefore re-emerged from 238, and Felicianus had charge of two of the great offices of state, the grain supply (*annonae*) and the city watch, the *vigiles*, perhaps as a precaution when the emperor went off to war after the trouble in Africa, which was a major source of food for the city. In 242, the *vigiles* went to another *eques*, Valerius Valens, who was promoted from the command of the fleet at Misenum.[11] Later the post went to Fultonius Restitutianus, the victorious governor of Mauretania. At the same time, these Roman posts were being described as 'in place of the praetorian prefects', that is, they were now part of an administrative structure headed by the praetorian prefects, and separated from the senatorial regime – though one would suppose that in the uncertain time following 238, the Senate kept a close eye on the loyalty of the *equites* in these posts. But note the wide range of offices now being held by *equites* – the praetorians, the *annonae*, the fleet, the amphitheatre, deputy governors, tax collecting, the mint, and they had early experience of commanding auxiliary regiments – and there were still other offices held by them. It is clear that despite the Senate's superiority in social and political affairs, it was the *equites* who were running the empire's administrative system; the senators, however, still commanded the legions and governed most of the provinces.

It is commonplace to remark, as above, that the areas of expertise in the administration that were taken by the *equites* had been gradually expanding in the half-century since Marcus Aurelius' death, though in fact it was for far longer than that. The succession of imperial crises enhanced the speed of the process. The crucial event, after the push given by Commodus, was perhaps the seizure of power by the *eques* Macrinus in 217. He was accepted as emperor by the Senate, if reluctantly and with grumbling, no doubt because he was involved in war in the east at the time, and he was well known to the senators for his work in Rome. But in the circumstances of 217, the Senate had no choice in the matter. Macrinus was in command of the main field army of the empire.

Timesitheus was thus following, more successfully, where Macrinus was the (failed) pioneer. From Macrinus' time on, such men as Felicianus and Timesitheus rose through the *eques* ranks with speed, filled different posts as required, and the area of their authority gradually expanded – into commanding in war, for example. They had the advantage over the senators, whose range of posts was restricted, and their terms of office short, with a year or two 'off' between posts. Such interruptions did not affect an *equites'* career. (Macrinus was the pioneer in an *eques* rising to emperor; the next man to do this was Maximinus, yet he evidently demoted the senior men he found in office – possibly this was intended as a conciliatory gesture towards the Senate, but if so, it evidently failed in effect, and those demotees were appointed to high offices by the Senate after Maximinus was gone.)

This Sasanid Empire had its own succession crisis. In 240, King Ardashir yielded the command of the army to his son and joint-king Shapur. The Roman advance in the subsequent years recovered the Mesopotamian province and Timesitheus gained a victory at Resaina on the Euphrates. Osrhoene was recovered, and the king of the region, Abgar X, was returned to his position.[12] The Sasanid forces appear to have withdrawn from the conquered cities of Singara and Nisibis, thus evacuating their earlier conquests in the Mesopotamian province. The war, however, was not yet over. Ardashir died in 242. Then, in the year of his victory (243), Timesitheus also died.[13]

He had taken, or had been given, a colleague as a second praetorian prefect the year before, C. Julius Priscus, who now became the senior man, and promoted his more capable brother, Marcus Julius Verus Philippus, to the post he himself had recently filled.[14] These men came from the village of Shahba in the province of Arabia, and were citizens of *eques* rank. Priscus' career is partly known. He had held a series of procuratorships, like Timesitheus and Felicianus and other *equites* already mentioned,[15] and it is likely that his brother had had the same sort of career – though it is equally possible that he had had a military career.

When Timesitheus died, therefore, Priscus inherited the military command as the sole praetorian prefect, though by this time Gordian was old enough to take part in the fighting. The death of the victorious commander may have disheartened the troops, so the emperor stepped forward to lead, even if Priscus assumed the actual command. On the Sasanid side, the new king perhaps did the same for his troops. Priscus' brother Philip was promoted, just as Shapur had been promoted by Ardashir. The war went on, with the Roman invasion of the Sasanid territory following, unusually, the route of the Euphrates River. This was a difficult route, for the river flows through a desert; the alternative and more popular route, along the Tigris, had its own difficulties, besides being much longer, though it had better supplies of food and of fodder for the animals. The Romans were aiming to take the Sasanid government centre at Ctesiphon, on the east bank of the Tigris opposite Seleukeia-on-the-Tigris, and had, by marching along the Euphrates route, made their aim clear. The Sasanids were able to muster a new army and meet the invaders at Meshike, the present al-Anbar, a forward defence post for the cities. The Romans were defeated there.[16]

The major casualties of the defeat were, first, a considerable proportion of the Roman army, though there were soldiers enough surviving to prevent a swift Sasanid recovery, and there seems to have been no interference with the Roman retreat. The second victim was the Emperor Gordian. His fate is the subject of at least four contradictory explanations in Roman sources, but the most convincing is that he was wounded in the battle and died of his wound (said to be a broken thigh).[17] The news of the defeat was apparently suppressed (it is not related in any Roman source), and the several explanations of the emperor's death certainly rouse suspicions that the truth was being evaded. The Sasanid source for the event is similarly unclear and ambiguous; neither government was apparently interested in relating the truth.

So the Roman army had lost both its actual and its nominal commanders within a year. After the defeat in the battle of Meshike, the two brothers, Priscus and Philip, quite correctly, assumed a joint command and brought the army back along the Euphrates as far as Circesion. Close to that city, in a region called

Zaitha, a monument to the dead emperor was built, possibly because that was where he actually finally died.[18]

The senior officers of the army now had to decide what to do. The precedents were numerous from the last generation. Septimius, Caracalla, Macrinus, and Alexander Severus, were all killed or died while well distant from Rome, and in command of a major army, and only Septimius had nominated heirs who assumed the rule at once. The others, in the emergency – it was always an emergency when an emperor died – were succeeded by men chosen by the army. This had even happened when the emperors were killed in Rome itself. This was clearly a legitimate means of accession, but also required validation by the Senate. Augustus had made it clear that the imperial power rested on his command of the army, and emperors were often chosen by elements of that army, and by the third century the process was clearly understood and certain.

The relations between the two brothers are unknown. Though Priscus' career had clearly been in advance of his brother's, it was Philip who emerged as the commander of the army. Possibly the defeat had been in part Priscus' fault, possibly Philip was the more popular of the two, but he was at once faced with a major difficulty; the army was stuck in enemy territory, defeated, and was retreating; it and urgently needed a recognised commander. Any man who emerged from this group as the new emperor would inevitably be blamed for Gordian's death, simply because he would be believed to have profited by it. The leading group of officers, therefore, headed by Priscus, held back from claiming the imperial office, though no doubt some of them hoped to be persuaded. Priscus, it appears, no doubt because he was the senior man present, suggested Philip, and he emerged from the group as the new emperor.

Philip had certain advantages. He was relatively young (Priscus was the elder brother). He was married and had a son, so there was the prospect of a dynasty being founded. He was the son-in-law of a Roman senator, and it may also be that he was in favour of close cooperation with the Senate; this would make him an adherent of the revolution of 238, which would short-circuit all sorts of problems. Many of the officers (and men) had no doubt been involved in the fighting in that year when Maximinus failed, and would not wish to repeat that experience. They also knew – who in the empire did not? – that a swift replacement for the deceased emperor was the best way to prevent any new frontier invasions.[19]

This is a crucial moment, of course, in the history of the revolution. The Senate had no role in these events, though some senators had surely imagined the possibility of the emperor's death in battle, or by disease in the infectious east (several emperors had died in the region), and it is likely that the name of the man whom the army proclaimed as Gordian's successor was not unknown to the Senate. His brother had clearly been prominent as an administrator before being promoted, and Philip was certainly known at Rome, even if he was regarded as an Arab and had been born on the eastern edge of the empire. In fact, to refer to him as an Arab may well be accurate in racial terms, but he and his brother were Roman citizens and the sons of a citizen. He had the social rank of *eques*, so, like his father and his brother, he was tolerably wealthy. He had, like his brother, ascended through a career of more than twenty years, occupying a series of *eques* offices. We do not know the offices he held, though to have risen as he did requires that he was an able administrator and had good Roman connections. He was married to Marcia Otacilia Severa, said to be the daughter of a provincial governor (and so the daughter of a senator).[20] He was therefore a member of the elite of the empire, clearly, and was no doubt almost as well known to the senators as his brother and Timesitheus.[21]

So far, the conduct of the army and its leaders in the face of the deaths of its main men was perfectly normal. The emergence of Philip as the new emperor was exactly the sort of answer to the crisis that had been concocted as far back as the death of Trajan, or even Claudius, and had been repeated in Syria at the deaths of Caracalla and Macrinus. So an Emperor Philip was only a surprise in that neither his more prominent and senior brother, nor any of his other fellow commanders, had taken up the post. He conducted affairs in a sensible, even respectful way, erecting the monument to Gordian near Circesion,[22] then by opening negotiations with Shapur.

Evidently, both rulers were in a condition that moved them to make peace. Both armies had achieved victories and suffered defeats, and both chose to emphasise their victories and ignore their defeats. The Roman forces had retreated from their attempted conquest, as had the Sasanids. Neither wished for a longer, more intensive war, which had been originated by their imperial predecessors, in part because both emperors were recently emplaced and needed to attend to internal affairs. So they made peace on the basis of the restoration of the former boundaries.

Shapur, a new king, had to attend to dissidents, Parthian partisans, in various parts of his empire; Philip had to get to Rome and establish his position as emperor and arrange relations with the Senate. So the Persians gave up the Mesopotamian province, which they had already lost, and the Romans pulled out of Babylonia, which they had already left. To sweeten the deal, Philip agreed to pay a subsidy, a lump sum, and possibly a continuing annual payment to Shapur.[23] It was certainly a cheaper alternative to fighting, and once peace was signed, both rulers were assured of its continuation while both of them lived. Payment of an annual 'tribute' might deter Shapur from resuming the war, since such payments would automatically cease in that case.

Philip, if it was he who conducted the negotiations, was acting in a properly statesmanlike way. He was now free to pull the field army out of Syria and return to Rome. He did so with a stately progress, taking the body of his young predecessor with him for burial at Rome, and halting to erect a monument at Circesion, on the border of the Roman state – a clear statement of intent. He reached Rome in July 244. He established a cordial relationship with the Senate, which must mean he deferred to the assembly and left it to conduct its share of affairs without his interference, while he continued with the traditional tasks of an emperor, which were essentially foreign affairs and war. He promoted road repairs, he used sailors and marines from the Ravenna fleet to suppress bandits. In Syria, he promoted new games celebrating the victory at Actium in 31 BC, and the local deity Dusares at Bostra, the capital of Arabia province, in which province he had been born;[24] and he built up his home village of Shahba into a new city, Philippopolis.[25]

He fought a campaign in the Balkans against invaders from the north. These were the Carpi, who had not gained what they expected from Tullius Menophilus' peace treaty, together with the Quadi, their neighbours, old Roman enemies. With neither of these peoples had Philip agreed a treaty, and any treaties already agreed with earlier emperors had ended with their deaths. Philip only claimed victories over the Germans and the Carpi, but the Goths were annoyed enough to go to war in 248 when Philip ceased paying the subsidy agreed by Timesitheus and Gordian III. The Senate was not involved, but when he returned he was given – perhaps he took – the complimentary titles *Germanicus maximus* and *Carpicus maximus*, and his ten-year-old son was promoted from *princeps iuventutis* to Augustus – and he was therefore proclaimed as his heir – and his wife became Augusta.[26]

We may therefore say that the relations between emperor and Senate that had been established after the murders of 238 had been restored under Gordian and had simply continued under Philip. Philip is classed as one of the 'soldier emperors', but he was nothing of the sort in fact. His pre-imperial career, so far as we understand it, was similar to that of his brother, and to that of Timesitheus, largely administrative, but probably with a military beginning and possibly with episodes of command – not necessarily in warfare. He was clearly capable of conducting military operations, and succeeded in driving out the Carpi and the Quadi when they invaded, but the Roman army was largely an automatic organisation, and had long experience of various sorts of combat. An emperor did not need long experience of warfare or military expertise to conduct the war, though he did need competent sub-commanders at the legionary level, and these were generally senators, since legions were actually under command by men of praetorian rank – these also would rely on the forces they commanded operating without detailed supervision. The only emperor actually trained to war, or perhaps one should say, experienced in warfare, in the previous century had been Maximinus; no other emperor since Hadrian had been a warrior, though some had thought they were, and many had conducted military operations. Maximinus had been a conqueror, but he had also been a disaster in internal affairs. An emperor needed expertise in domestic matters – that is, Roman politics – perhaps more than in foreign affairs and in war he could operate as a commander successfully so long as he could rely on competent officers.

That is, the revival of the authority of the Senate which had taken place in 238 continued to operate through the reigns of both Gordian III and Philip. It began to look as though the period of 238 onwards represented the success of the revolution that had taken place in that year.

Philip, at some point in his rule, made some interesting appointments, which were both replications of past versions, but also anticipated later experiments. Probably before leaving the Syrian region he appointed his brother Priscus as overall governor of the eastern provinces, first apparently as prefect of Mesopotamia (he was *eques*, therefore could not, in theory, be a governor), and later with some such title as *rector Orientis*, or possibly *corrector Orientis*.[27] Priscus' authority covered Syria, Palestine, Osrhoene and Mesopotamia, at least. Later, Philip's brother-in-law, Servianus (presumably Otacilius Servianus), was appointed to a similar position in the Balkans, overseeing the two Moesian provinces and Macedonia.[28] (Macedonia was a separate province, of course, but it is odd to find it linked with the Moesias in this way; Thrace would have been geographically and strategically much more fitting.) Priscus and Servianis were no doubt intended to be essentially frontier guards, facing the most active Roman enemies. Philip himself had direct rule over Italy and the west, including the German frontier, probably from Pannonia west to Britannia. From the complaints made about him, Priscus evidently had taxation powers – he was accused of being unpleasantly rigorous, but then so was Philip; the imperial government was always short of money and so concerned with taxation.[29]

There were precedents for this sort of delegation of geographical responsibility. The Roman Empire was an awkward shape from a government's point of view, and large areas were not Latin- or Greek-speaking. Even by the first century AD, there was a tendency to appoint natives of Greek provinces as governors in the eastern regions. Perhaps the most important precedent was the large responsibility given to Avidius Cassius by Marcus Aurelius in Syria and the east generally; this was in fact a continuation of the command of the Emperor Lucius Verus, but was particularly noted because Cassius was a commoner. And, of course, later in the third century AD, large sections of the empire broke away for a time, and another delegated scheme was developed by Diocletian, which lasted for two or three decades until Constantine demolished it. Philip's scheme had both precedents and a future.

How well this scheme worked is unclear. On the one hand, Priscus' guardianship of the east caused problems internally, largely concerned with taxation, and there was trouble also along the frontier, especially in Armenia. This last may have been a result of the problems faced by Shapur in extending his full authority throughout his own territories. Parthian partisans were active east of the Tigris. If Priscus had to fight to hold the frontier, that would be one good reason he would have felt compelled to tax his region heavily. His rule provoked opposition, and Marcus Iotapianus went so far as to claim the throne, without success, quickly suppressed no doubt by Priscus.

Iotapian's *cognomen* connected him with a series of queens and princesses called Iotape who had ruled in various parts of the Eastern Roman Empire since Hellenistic times; he also claimed descent from Alexander. There was already, of course, a certain tradition of attempted usurpation in Syria – Elagabalus would be the prime example, but not the only one. The sources for this usurpation are however late and vague, as for much of this period, but it appears that the usurper was eventually killed by his own soldiers. Oddly, he does not get a mention in the *Historia Augusta*.[30]

Philip, or perhaps originally Severianus, faced the same problem in the Balkans. The invasions by the Carpi and Quadi are supposed to have left the soldiers of the region dissatisfied, though it was probably a feeling stirred up by an ambitious governor. After Philip had dealt with the situation, which involved subsidising the invaders after their defeat, as before, the soldiers complained. (The situation when Maximinus complained about Alexander Severus' similar tactics was being replicated.) The instigator was Ti. Claudius Pacatianus, who may have been a governor of a Danube frontier province; he survived only long enough for C. Messius Decius Valerianus to complain in the Senate about him, and for Philip to send Decius himself the deal with the problem. This he did, but Decius was then proclaimed emperor by the same troops who had supported Pacatian, and who had surrendered to him; these recruits evidently were cleared of punishment and then resorted to repeating the offence.[31]

This has all the hallmarks of a plot, with Pacatian as the sacrificial goat, and Decius, an old Maximinus supporter when governor of Tarraconensis, as the chief plotter. He was a senator, evidently the beneficiary of a pardon, and had been *praefectus urbi* at Rome for a time, where he had no doubt gathered political support. Philip, faced by invasions and revolts, may have offered to resign, but this was not an acceptable solution, and does seem highly unlikely. In his new command, Decius had control of a sizeable army, one rather more potent than that in Spain he had commanded when the Senate sent Crispinus against him, and he enlarged it by recruiting Pacatian's army, which clearly had the same Maximinan sentiment as Decius himself. He was now aiming to succeed where Maximinus failed.

He invaded Italy, was met by Philip at the head of an army recruited in Italy and so much less competent than Decius' own, hardened as it was by frontier fighting. (The Italian levy may have been energised by memories of the fighting at Aquileia.) Decius may have suggested negotiations, but this could only have been to demand that Philip stand down, after which Philip's life would have been worth nothing. The two armies fought in open battle at Verona. Philip was beaten, and then was hunted down and killed. In Rome, his son was killed by soldiers. Neither Severianus, who had in fact probably vanished earlier, nor Priscus, survived.[32] This was a counter-revolution, an attempt to reverse the verdict of the revolution of 238, and to return to the practices of Maximinus, high taxation, frontier warfare, and the suppression of the Senate.

Chapter 12

The Senate's Authority Maintained

Decius, as his past suggests, must be assigned to the anti-senatorial, Severan-Maximinan persuasion. He had continued to 'support' Maximinus in Spain after the emperor's death, and he stood in the Senate and attacked Philip, thereby making good use of the increased freedom and authority of the Senate. He was also an imperial eccentric. He believed he was a great soldier, and took the additional *cognomen* 'Trajan'. He was the first emperor, indeed probably the first senator, to emerge from Pannonia.[1] He looked back into the Roman past for inspiration, which was all very well, but he also instituted measures intended to revive the 'good old days'; it was said that he attempted to reintroduce the office of censor, though that had been exercised by the emperors themselves for two centuries. He insisted that all Roman citizens must sacrifice to the 'ancestral gods', a phrase which had the probably unintended consequence of singling out Christians for punishment, since they refused to acknowledge any god but their own.[2]

He was also the first usurper to seize the throne since Maximinus, and eventually the first emperor to die in battle (but not the last). He issued a set of coins celebrating selected emperors of the past, which may be counted as a manifesto of his own original policies. In the list he included several of those who had seized the throne by violence or by usurpation – Augustus, Vespasian, Nerva, Trajan, Hadrian, Septimius, Alexander Severus – together with a leavening of less enterprising men – Pius, Marcus, Commodus – a most curious grouping, though the last three are presumably included for nostalgic reasons.[3] It all suggested that his own usurpation was justifiable and was in the grand Roman tradition; the inclusion of Pius, Marcus, and Commodus might indicate something of his aims, though, like his religious decree, it was notably vague, and could be interpreted several ways, which was perhaps the intention.

Given all this, it is not surprising that Decius' reign was a comprehensive disaster. With an army at his back he was inevitably accepted as emperor by the Senate, which was clearly under threat. But then, so far as can be seen, he ignored the Senate, quite in the Severus-Maximinus mode – and this despite his active senatorial career before his elevation. But his reign involved two intractable problems. There was what the Christians happily called a 'persecution', though it was essentially an attempt to make them obey Decius' misjudged sacrifice decree; and probably not a deliberate persecution of Christianity, the Christians welcomed the attention. He appears to have been a stubborn type, and when things went wrong, with Christian objections to his religious policy, instead of adjusting the decree to bring them into conformity, such as classifying the Christian God as an 'ancestral' one, he resorted to compulsion. Christians, after all, had a habit of drinking and eating at their sacrifice, just as other faiths did. Christians embraced this discrimination, since it brought welcome publicity and some public sympathy, as well as a roster of dead Christians who were supposed to have ascended to heaven forthwith as martyrs. If Decius became anti-Christian, he was provoked into it by Christian defiance, searching for 'martyrs'.

The second consuming difficulty of his reign was Balkan warfare. He was already familiar with the Danubian frontier region. He had been born in a village near Sirmium in Pannonia, a city which was emerging as a major strategic base of the Roman forces defending the nearby part of the frontier – Marcus had used it as such, as had Maximinus, who was camped there when summoned to Italy to counteract the senatorial usurpers. Decius had, after his consulship in 233,[4] served a term as the governor of Moesia Inferior,[5] the eastern part of the Danubian frontier, and by this time the most sensitive part of it. Philip's campaign against the Carpi and Quadi had been interrupted by the rebellion of Pacatian and Decius, and Decius in power had in turn at once to continue Philip's work. Decius despised Philip, but he had to deal with the same problem in the same way – so much for his researching of the deep past.

At first, he was successful. The Quadi are not mentioned, but the Carpi were still occupying part of Dacia, which their own lands adjoined. Decius took his army north and drove out those Carpi who were still in occupation.[6] Probably this was only a matter of following them as they withdrew, but he was able to proclaim on his coinage that 'Dacia is recovered'.[7] He could thus count two victories: that against Philip's Italian scratch force at Verona, and that against a minimal Carpi force in Dacia. It seemed that the Trajan name had been properly earned.

Not so, as was demonstrated when King Kniva led a new invasion across the Danube in 250. The invaders are called Skythai by the historian Dexippos, another who looked into the past for inspiration, only to fox modern historians who are trying to identify the actual invaders. Exactly who the invaders were is thus unclear, but they ultimately developed into one of the elements of the new tribal confederation that became the Goths, though it may be premature to use that term in the 250s.[8] Decius spent the next year (250) and half of 251 fighting this force, and losing. He was defeated in battle at Beroea (Augusta Traiana), in southern Moesia Superior, on the border with Thrace. The invaders captured just one city, Philippopolis in Thrace, and then withdrew northwards, apparently in a leisurely way, carrying their booty. Decius decided to prevent them getting home, and caught up with them at Abritus, some way short of the Danube. There the Roman army, through Decius' own military incompetence, suffered a heavy defeat. Both Decius and his son Herrenius Etruscus were killed.[9]

During this campaign, the prospects of an emperor failing in the face of barbarian invaders had been becoming steadily more likely. This provided the opportunity for opposition to him to emerge, helped by Decius' almost constant absence from Rome. During the campaigning, the governor of Thrace, T. Julius Priscus, was captured by the invaders when the city of Philippopolis fell to them: Kniva, no doubt gleefully, supported Priscus' self-proclamation as emperor. Priscus died soon after, hardly surprisingly.[10] But at much the same time in Rome, the Roman crowd (the same group that had forced the Senate to accept Gordian III) demonstrated its displeasure by proclaiming its own candidate, a senator called D. Julius Valens Licinianus.[11]

This rather suggests that there was a division of opinion among the senators. When Valens was proclaimed in the city, there were Hostilianus, Decius' second son (the first, Herrenius Etruscus, was with the emperor in the fighting and was killed with him) and P. Licinius Valerianus, who was left there, in charge of law and order by Decius, that is as *praefectus urbi*; he would have had command of the *vigiles*. If Valens was really a senator, as it appears, he probably had more support than just the Roman crowd, even though that itself was a powerful political force at times.

Decius, after all, had systematically ignored the Senate. He appears to have been in the city only in the first months of his reign, after which he was in the Balkans, inefficiently fighting the empire's enemies, and, of course, emulating his adopted patron, Maximinus, but without the military skill. This lack of success could hardly be concealed or ignored. Priscus in Philippopolis in his own lunge for the empire thought he had better support among the invaders – and certainly Kniva successfully outfoxed his Roman enemies at every turn. In Syria, a man called Mariades, a prominent Antiochene, had also raised a local rebellion and had then fled to Sasanid territory.[12] Presumably, all these usurpers expected support to be forthcoming from somewhere. Valens, for example, in Rome, might look to Hostilianus and Valerianus, and then to other members of the Senate. It had worked before.

The final blow to Decius and his reign came, not just in his defeat and death at Abritus in June 251, but, as before, from the failure of the governor of Moesia Inferior to act decisively in his support. This was C. Vibius Trebonianus Gallus, who was alleged to have deliberately withheld his support in the battle. (The ancient sources, usually pagan in religious sympathies, are pro-Decius, and therefore look for a scapegoat for his death, and since Gallus appeared to benefit, he was fingered.) Since Decius was leading his army into a swamp, a trap all too obviously laid by Kniva, it is more probable that Gallus simply had more sense than to follow his emperor and so compound one disaster with a second. Decius and his eldest son Herennius Etruscus' deaths were thus hardly unexpected, and Trebonianus must not have been surprised when both were killed in the battle.

Decius' army – the same military community that had in the past supported Pacatianus and then Decius in their usurpations – now turned to Trebonianus and proclaimed him the new emperor. This was evidently quite acceptable to him, an attitude that will have reinforced the rumours that he had conspired against Decius – and with the invaders – in the battle. The latter were easily persuaded to accept a new peace treaty, including a Roman subsidy payment, on top of the booty they were carrying away.

Then Trebonianus rapidly headed for Rome to ensure his acceptance by the Senate, and to establish his hold on the city after Valens' attempted coup. Perhaps to counter the hostile rumours he adopted Decius' younger son Hostilianus into his family, and made both him and his own son Volusianus his co-emperors. That, and his acceptance by Decius' army, strongly suggests he had nothing to do with Decius' death.

On the other hand, his actions after the army's proclamation of him as emperor resulted in the abandonment of many of Decius' policies. His first action was to seek the Senate's approval – after buying peace, also not a policy approved by Decius, or Maximinus – while his adoption of Hostilianus would seem to be a deliberate attempt to heal the political divisions, as did his promotion of Decius' defenders. Decius' name was cut out from a number of inscriptions, and Trebonianus proceeded to cancel some privileges Decius had awarded to various cities. The persecution of Christians also ceased, which probably means his general religious policy of promoting the 'ancestral gods' was also abandoned.[13]

All this probably did not heal all the rifts in Roman political society, nor in the Senate, but it did show willing. The new emperor faced greater difficulties even than Decius did, though the Goths at least were now quiet. In the east, however, the atrocities of Mariades had roused Shapur of the Sasanids, whose peace treaty with Philip had expired with the latter's death. He invaded Syria, defeated a Roman army, which suffered very high casualties, and then set about plundering the province, including probably the city of Antioch.[14]

The failure of the Roman defence in Syria evoked a rise of local resistance, emanating particularly from the city of Emesa, which had been the Syrian base of the Severan dynasty. The leader was L. Julius Aurelius Sulpicius Uranius Severus Antoninus, whose success in repelling the Sasanids, probably when they were retiring with their booty – they had apparently reached only as far south as the town of Arethusa, some distance north of Emesa – persuaded him to be proclaimed emperor. The collection of names he sported – surely, a concoction for the occasion – implies a claim to the empire by way of the Severan dynasty. He appears to have been a priest, presumably, like Elagabalus, of the Emesan sun god El.[15] There was clearly by this time a powerful local feeling in Syria, probably inspired by the local origin of the Severan family, but also by the recent imperial career of Philip, whose home was not far distant from Emesa, and the revolts of Iotapianus and now Uranius Antoninus.

Trebonianus Gallus was thus even more thoroughly beset than his predecessors were. It was surely ominous that anyone, anywhere, who could claim a local grievance (like Iotapianus) or a minor victory (like Uranius Antoninus) or could kill an emperor, could then lay a claim to the empire itself. Not even a large armed force in support was needed, just a few soldiers – another lesson of the events of 238. It was the beginning of the break-up of the empire, which became manifest by 260.

To the Senate in Rome the situation verged on the farcical, but it was also clearly heading for tragedy and imperial disaster. Since the revolution of 238, which had so boosted the Senate's authority, there had been two emperors, Gordian III and Philip, who had paid due attention to the assembly. Philip's killer, Decius, though paradoxically a distinguished senator, had reverted to the Maximinan attitude of ignoring it, perhaps to avoid criticism, such as he himself had voiced against Philip in the Senate, perhaps because he was busy losing the war in the Balkans. Yet he had been a disaster as emperor, more likely because he had been a Maximinan all along.

He had faithfully replicated Maximinus in his contempt for the Senate, though not in his military abilities. If in Rome he had pursued a sensible policy, or had succeeded in his wars, he might have both lasted longer and possibly been able to cooperate with the Senate. But he had been a comprehensive failure. From the Senate's point of view, the usefulness of an emperor began and ended with his command of the army, and with all that implied. If he failed, any emperor was instantly vulnerable to being removed. And his success would be measured in part by his cooperation with the Senate.

Now Decius' replacement, a senatorial emperor on the pattern of the successors of the Revolution of 238, was falling into as deep trouble as Decius, which was dangerous since it would suggest that the Senate's recovery of authority was a danger to the empire as a whole. The city and the empire was being ravaged by a new outbreak of plague – Hostilianus Caesar probably died of it soon after his adoption.[16] The wealthiest province of the empire, Syria, was suffering destruction by a Persian invasion, the worst since the end of the Republic. Usurpers emerged all too easily and often, and the methods of usurpation were now so well understood that it had become easy. The Senate could see the answer: an emperor supported not just by the army but also by the city and by the Senate. The cooperation was necessary for victory, since this was not just a matter of defeating invaders, but of controlling the internal regions of the empire; victory, once again, would quickly quash further disturbing attempted usurpations. An emperor should be a mature and experienced man – that is, a man who had had experience of the Senate and of government in the empire – with an adult son to succeed him; this had been one of the favourable qualities of Philip, and now of Trebonianus; military skill would obviously help.

Trebonianus Gallus might have been the man required. His measures were conciliatory, including his adoption of Hostilianus. He had gone to Rome as soon as he was free of the Gothic war, in order to be accepted by the Senate, thus, unlike all the other emperors at the time, displaying a due regard for that body. He organised the burial of the plague victims, no doubt for good sanitary and medical reasons, but he was given credit for helping the poor in this.[17] He began to prepare an expedition against Shapur, to be commanded by his son Volusianus. He appointed Valerian, who had supported every emperor since Gordian I and II, and probably Maximinus and Severus Alexander before them, to the Rhine frontier, probably with orders to assemble an army to join in the eastern expedition. He ordered the mint to begin production of coins to finance an expedition to the east.

The crucial province of Moesia Inferior, whence had come more than one recent usurper, including Trebonianus himself, though he was only marginally a usurper, was now guarded by M. Aemilius Aemilianus, who appears to have taken, or been assigned, authority over Pannonia as well – though possibly only Pannonia Inferior. Thus, Trebonianus was in the process of copying Philip's construction of larger military commands based on linking neighbouring military provinces under one man, so overriding the old rule forbidding governors to operate outside their assigned provinces, except by special permission – which Aemilian probably had. Valerian in Germany appears in Trebonianus' final crisis to have had a wide command along the German frontier, from which he was to collect his contribution to the Persian expedition. Aemilianus must have felt he was in tune with the emperor when he proposed himself as commander-in-chief along the Danube. He also suggested that the Senate should be left to conduct the ordinary imperial administration, which would include the appointment of provincial governors, presumably.[18] It was another stage in the political disintegration of the empire, but it was also a reaffirmation of the Senate's authority.

Perhaps Aemilianus' mistake was in proposing that a formal agreement to this effect was required. This was hardly something an emperor could agree to since it would look very much as though too much independence of action was being permitted to his subordinate. (Maybe Avidius Cassius was remembered.) It did not help Aemilianus' argument that a band of 'Skythai' raiders from the north had bypassed Moesia and got into Asia Minor, where they raided and burnt the great temple of Artemis at Ephesos, among other places.[19] Clearly, it was much more urgent in Moesia Inferior to develop a defensive fleet on the Danube and the Black Sea than to discuss dividing up the empire among governors. It may also be that Aemilianus was blamed for the raid, while Trebonianus himself had been in command in the area until very recently. The absence of a fleet on the river, and possibly in the Black Sea, was plainly the fault of earlier administrations, but someone had to be blamed and the man in office was the patsy. Nevertheless, it is evident that Aurelian cleaved to the Senate's policy rather than to that of Maximinus. His quarrel with Trebonianus was the result of his province being invaded.

That was in 252, and Aemilianus fought and won his battle in Moesia Inferior early in the next year. As a result, his army, as after every other recent bout of violence in the region, proclaimed him emperor, and so compelled him to make an attempt to overthrow Trebonianus.[20] It was this same army that had rebelled with Pacatian, had raised Decius and then Trebonianus himself to the throne, and no doubt everyone in Rome had become distinctly weary of its behaviour. Aemilianus immediately marched on Rome, perhaps unexpectedly. Trebonianus, though he had been collecting forces for the Persian expedition, seems to have still had to rely mainly on the amateur soldiers of Italy. These had perhaps not yet been adequately trained, so that, even though his forces outnumbered those of Aemilianus, so giving him a misplaced sense of confidence, he was defeated. The Rhine forces under Valerian had been summoned to assist and were on their way to support him, but had too far to march. Trebonianus and his son were both eventually killed, possibly in the process of retreating north to link up with Valerian's forces.[21]

Aemilianus would seem by his record to have been an imaginative governor and a competent soldier, but his victories, like those of Decius, were against relatively minor forces, professional army against amateurs. There are several versions of Trebonianus' death, including one where his own troops, after an initial defeat at Interamna on the via Flaminia in the Apennines, killed him and went over to the enemy. Trebonianus and Volusianus had survived their original defeat, and moved north, presumably hoping to link up with Valerian's army, but their troops prevented the junction. By killing them, the army therefore opted for, and joined, Aemilianus.[22] Their defeat meant that Aemilianus now collected both armies. He was then attacked by Valerian's army.

Valerian had been proclaimed emperor at some point in his army's march from Germany to support Trebonianus. The dating is not clear, nor is the sequence of events in Germany and Italy, and communications between them, but the proclamation took place in Raetia,[23] north of the Alps, which implies that Valerian had already covered two thirds of the way to Italy. It thus seems likely that it was the news of Trebonianus' defeat and death (which took place in August 253) that preceded and provoked his elevation. This was a different army than the persistently usurping Balkan army, one that had been gathered from the soldiers of the Rhine garrisons. Perhaps it was jealous of the Balkan force's exploits, perhaps it was as weary of the constant changes as everyone else was.

Aemilian began his move back north from Rome, but was intercepted at Spoletium by a dissident group in his own army, which killed him. Valerian therefore did not need to fight for the throne, for Aemilian's own army (which included that of Trebonianus and those of earlier emperors, joined him. Valerian's reign is usually dated from September 253.

It is significant that, despite Valerian's looming approach, Aemilianus at once had gone to Rome to gain the Senate's approval and support.[24] Trebonianus had done the same, and had remained in the city, leaving the fighting in Moesia to Aemilianus. In the short time that Aemilianus spent in the city before he had to march out to defend his stolen position, he must have understood that the Senate's approval of him was less than enthusiastic – they had originally declared him a public enemy at Trebonianus' behest.[25] Their lack of approval was probably transmitted to the soldiers, either directly or by rumour, and they then killed him. He had left a lieutenant in Rome, a man called Salbannianus, who may have tried to make himself emperor, but failed.

Now Valerian was welcomed by the Senate as the next emperor – the fourth in the year – even before he reached Rome, and his son Gallienus was made Caesar, to be promoted to Augustus by his father not long after he had reached the city. Both the soldiers and the Senate were weary of the chaos, no doubt.

Valerian had had a substantial senatorial career already, back to the reign of Alexander Severus and before, unlike his two predecessors. Many of the details of the offices he held are not known, but he was of consular rank by 238, and so he was born about 190, growing to adulthood under the first two Severan emperors. His son Gallienus was born about 218, so Valerian had been married earlier than usual for a Roman of high rank; his ancestry, however, is not known, though the Licinius *nomen* was a distinguished one. To have been of consular rank by 238, he was clearly a patrician. He married Egnatia Mariniana, daughter of Egnatius Victor, a member of another notable family of senators during the past century, and he was linked by that marriage with the Triarii (as in the crisis of 193), the Erucii (ditto), to Iunii Rufini and the Pomponii.

He was thus unusual amongst the sequence of emperors in his wide range of aristocratic contacts and relatives.[26] As a result he not only had an adult son when he became emperor – Gallienus was thirty-five in 253 – and had other children as well, but he was fully enmeshed in the senatorial aristocracy.

He had been active in supporting the first Gordians, and had been sent to Rome by the elder Gordian as his envoy, a journey that may well have saved his life considering what then happened in Africa, and his message was crucial in stimulating senatorial support and action. He had also accepted office under Decius, which extended into Trebonianus' reign, and he was actively supporting Trebonianus when the emperor was defeated and killed. This was a man who was politically in favour of the revolution of 238 from the start, but who was also politically adept enough to survive under Decius, who was of the Maximinan persuasion. (He had also accepted office from Maximinus.)

The *Historia Augusta* claims that Decius attempted to revive the office of censor, one of his backward-looking schemes and notions, but Valerian is said to have refused the post when the Senate offered it to him;[27] the whole story is probably fictitious, but the author hits exactly the right note for Decius (his antiquarianism) and for Valerian (his senatorial popularity and his modesty). He was evidently trusted by both parties, just as, probably, Trebonianus had been, and Decius had left him in command in Rome when he went off to the wars in the Balkans. Trebonianus had also apparently trusted him to collect an army and bring it to him without using it to make himself another usurping emperor. His record puts him in the middle-of-the-road, with contacts on both sides of the political argument in the Senate-emperor dispute, and perhaps surprisingly, trusted by both. His accepting of the emperorship would seem to be the result of a general accession of common sense after the farce of the previous years – and in the knowledge of the damage that had been caused to the empire in their wake.

The upheavals in the empire from Decius to Valerian were, inevitably, attracting foreign invaders. The Sasanid Persians in Syria were probably the most formidable; they might have been defeated in part here and there by local militias such as that of Emesa, but they did not give up their war; in the Balkans, various groups had invaded from the north; and the formidable tribal confederacies in Germany and the Ukraine – Franks, Alamanni, Goths – which had developed, all at more or less the same time, could put much larger invading forces into the field than their individual member tribes. This latter development was the barbarian equivalent of the professionalisation of the Roman army. This Roman change had been happening, rather more slowly, from Septimius onwards, and was to receive a significant boost from the measures taken by Valerian and Gallienus to combat these powerful enemies.

But reforms of an empire take time to be implemented, and more time to be accepted and to take effect, and can only be done piecemeal. Valerian, an elderly man of over sixty when he became emperor, could scarcely spend much time on such matters, since, on the one hand, he was conservative in his politics and disliked change, and on the other, he had to fight wars almost continuously during his reign. He was not, so far as can be understood, any more a soldier than any other tradition-minded senator; he had been born about 190, before Septimius seized the throne, and had presumably gone through the traditional senatorial *cursus*, possibly serving as a military tribune in his late teens, and going on to become consul in the 220s – as a patrician he could have been consul by that time. There is no indication that he ever commanded a legion, or governed a province, elements in a career which, given his later prominence, might have been recorded somewhere even when the contemporary records are so abysmal. (The so-called biography in *Historia Augusta* – 'the two Valerians' – is largely a work of fiction.) There are no inscriptions recording his presence in any province.

The known items of his life before his elevation to emperor are therefore the occasional notices in the written sources which add up to a political life as a senator in Rome, except that he was in Africa when Gordian I usurped the throne (as was the Gordians' message to the Senate), and he was then in Rome when the Senate moved against Maximinus.[28] (This pair of coincidences might seem to have put him at the centre of a wider conspiracy, even one of its originators.) He was employed by both Decius and Trebonianus Gallus for delicate tasks in Rome and Germany. But, apart from the gathering of an army from the German garrisons in 253 to fight the Persians in Syria, he does not seem to have had any military experience of any sort before then. Yet when he became emperor, he became the commander-in-chief of an army of perhaps 500,000 men, legions, *auxilia*, *numeri*, fleets of warships, all commanded by men of greater military experience than him, and probably of greater physical vigour, whom he was expected to command in battle. In many ways Valerian was a prime example of the faults of the amateur Roman command system as it had developed. His own son could perhaps discern these faults more clearly than he could.

This new emperor's reign was thus dominated by war, for which he was badly prepared, though he could command, so long as the traditional legion-and-*auxilia* army was functioning. But the new warfare demanded much more adaptability by both soldiers and commanders. A barbarian invasion was not really a deliberate and carefully ordered campaign, but often was a scattering of plundering bands who only came together as an army when necessary, as when serious opposition appeared. They formed into a campaigning army only when a major enemy force approached or when they were withdrawing, burdened by loot – as in Decius' final disaster, whose principal cause, apart from Decius' incompetence, was the existence of an intelligent commander, Kniva, on the barbarian side. To counter this sort of warfare smaller Roman fighting units than the legion were needed, to be commanded by men of lower rank but fully professional, including new and better cavalry units as well. Senators who were parachuted in for a brief period of command were no longer sufficient. Yet at the same time, a Persian war was a much more organised and systematic affair, and would certainly require to be countered by a mass Roman army, legions and all, unless, as with Uranius Antoninus' encounter with the Persian force at Arethusa, the enemy had also scattered to collect plunder, like the Balkan barbarians, after defeating the main Roman forces.

The demands of warfare from 249 onwards, therefore, required the use of smaller units, capable of mobility and adaptability. Emperor Valerian, by his whole life and upbringing, was out of touch with this requirement. He could command, from a rear position, a major army, since the older army functioned largely automatically once it was given a task; for other warfare, he required inventive subordinates who could act on their own initiative.[29]

Valerian took a western army, gathered in Germany and the Balkans – which had been planned by Trebonianus – to Syria, arriving in 254. He supervised the reoccupation of that part of Syria which the Persians had conquered, but which they had now, or earlier, relinquished.[30] Whether Valerian had to fight at this time is not known, but if so it was probably only to dislodge a few tardy Persian detachments. In 256, the town of Dura Europus, beside the Euphrates, south of Circesium, was being repaired by the prefect of Osrhoene,[31] implying that there was no immediate Persian threat or presence in that area. Valerian may have campaigned into Cappadocia in 256, when it was raided by 'Skythai', but they were fast moving, and seaborne, so it is unlikely he had much success. He is recorded in the west, at Cologne, Sirmium, and Rome during 255–257, clearly moving about, probably dealing with minor local problems, and being seen to be doing so.

He had spent only a brief time in Rome in 253, at first to accept the Senate's acclamation as emperor, and to make the usual arrangements necessary for the start of a new reign, and then again in 257. Then there was the need for him to go to the east again. The Persians, in what seems to have been an isolated action, captured Dura-Europos in 256–257,[32] and this might have been seen as the precursor to a new, much larger, attack on the Roman provinces. It did not come, then, possibly because Valerian turned up once more at Antioch with more forces. But it was evident that the Persians did not believe that their war had finished; the main attack came two years later, in 259, in massive force, systematically conquering.

In the west, the presence of Gallienus, Valerian's co-Augustus, and Valerian's second son Valerian II, now Caesar, made it clear that there was now a new imperial dynasty, for adult imperial sons was one of the preferred conditions for supporting a new emperor. Valerian's authority was mirrored by Gallienus', who was of an age (in his late thirties) and capable enough to be left to govern by himself in the western half of the empire, and basing himself at Rome, and so in touch with the Senate while, like his father, travelling to local trouble spots. This was by now the sort of action to be expected of new emperors. The Senate, with friendly 'senatorial' emperors in charge, was no doubt content. The Senate probably saw more of Gallienus than of Valerian in the 250s; Gallienus, however, does not appear to have shared his father's political opinions, and he developed his own ideas during that time, but he was obedient to his father. He was as likely to be at Milan or Cologne as at Rome, and the young Valerian II was stationed, with an experienced commander at his side, in Pannonia, probably normally at Sirmium. All this imperial movement was understandable, but it did separate the Senate from its emperors.

Gallienus in Italy saw to the development of a much larger cavalry force than was usual with the old Roman army, using his general Aureolus as trainer and commander.[33] This force was, of course, more mobile and faster moving than the infantry legions, and more adapted to the pursuit of scattered barbarian invading forces. (The Sasanid army also had a major cavalry contingent, as the Parthians also had.) Gallienus had to fight fairly regularly along the Rhine frontier during the 250s, including combating a large raid by Franks, which reached as far as Spain. It was on this occasion that Valerian arrived in the west and stayed for a time at Cologne.[34] It was perhaps not coincidental that while he was preoccupied in Asia Minor and the west, the Sasanid assault on Dura Europos took place.

Valerian was a firm believer in the authority of the Senate and of senators. Gallienus was not, so it appears. The latter's work on the army in the west built on the gradual shift away from employing senators as legionary commanders and as provincial governors, a development which had been in process by this time for fifty years – the rise of the *equites*, personified by Timesitheus and his contemporaries, was the most visible element. Yet the new development was not a shift in the traditional direction, in which *equites* rose to supplement and replace senators in both roles. Instead, in the military the new process was to promote from within and below, and to put the command of the smaller mobile sectional forces, smaller and swifter than the legions, under the command of non-*equites*, non-senatorial, commanders, men who had been promoted from the ranks. The origins of the smaller military forces were in fact the old auxiliary regiments, infantry and cavalry, and the new units were generally commanded by sons of senators or *equites*. This new system became interpreted by the historians writing in the next century as Gallienus issuing a decree forbidding senators from taking up the command of military forces.[35] There is no actual evidence that he did so, but the effect of his military reforms was to institute such a practice in the army. Senators continued to be employed as provincial governors until the end of the third century, and probably longer, but were no longer to be preferred for command of military units, and fewer of them were employed.

Gallienus was therefore deliberately developing a new kind of Roman army, specifically designed to deal with barbarian raids. His father, more tradition minded, was commanding a traditional Roman legionary army, especially in the east. Gallienus is credited with the regulation that senators should no longer command armies, which, though apparently a myth, was a condition that later prevailed. That is, the decisive shift from Senate to emperor in power and authority began with Gallienus, and was not halted thereafter.

Chapter 13

The Reversal

The culmination of the disputes, usurpations, civil wars, and invasions of the empire since Commodus' reign finally came in 259–260. In 258, as Valerian was returning to the east after helping out in Gaul in the face of the invasion of the Franks, a usurpation took place in Illyria. The usurper was Ingenuus, who may have been Valerian II's mentor, and who was hoisted to emperor by his soldiers in the face of a threatened invasion by the Marcomanni.[1] This did not prevent an invasion by the Iuthungi, which reached far into Italy, where they were stopped by one of those *ad hoc* Italian armies, and later destroyed by Gallienus.[2] Ingenuus' usurpation had brought Gallienus from the Rhine to suppress the usurper. In the process, Valerian II died; the cause of his death is not specified and is not said to have been part of the revolt, but the coincidence is very suggestive. Gallienus had left his son Saloninus at Cologne, more as a symbol of his authority than in command (he was still only a boy); he was soon killed in another usurpation.[3]

The concentration of Valerian, Gallienus, and Valerian II during the period from 254 on the condition of the frontiers is a clear indication that there was an obvious problem all along the line. As a result of the frontier problem, none of the three emperors spent much time in Rome; Gallienus was more frequently in Milan and on the Rhine; Valerian II was more or less permanently in Pannonia, possibly at Sirmium; Valerius himself spent much of his reign in Antioch; they all moved about in their regions. It is clear that invasions were expected at any time or place; but it seems just as obvious that no clear military solution was available, other than attempts to interrupt the raids. Theoretically, it should have been possible for a Roman army to make a pre-emptive strike to disrupt any perceived preparations. The organisation of the new tribal confederations beyond the northern frontier was an obvious threat, for they could hardly have been developed for any other reason than to invade the empire, and their size and human resources enabled them to field larger armies, while not abandoning their homelands. In the east, the new Sasanid dynasty was keen to prove its strength by attacking the old enemy, which had repeatedly battered its Parthian predecessor. But the Roman army could not cope with the universal pressures, and since Maximinus it does not seem to have had the strength for pre-emptive strikes.

What is more, it seems obvious that the various parts of the frontier – Syria, the lower Danube, Pannonia, the upper and lower Rhine – were all sensitive to events along the whole line. So there was an increasing likelihood that simultaneous attacks would take place. These were not necessarily deliberately co-ordinated, but the four main Roman enemies, Persia, the Goths, the Alamanni and the Franks, were now geared up to war on a near-permanent basis. In this they were possibly belated copies of the Roman professional army, and this opportunism was an extension of established procedure of attacking the empire in moments of crisis, particularly at the death of an emperor.

The Romans' enemies were thus able to take speedy advantage of the movements of the Roman army, or of an emperor, from one base to another. As Gallienus moved from Cologne to deal with the Iuthungi and with Ingenuus in Italy and Illyricum, this will have alerted the Franks and the Alamanni to the opportunities available; the news of a new Persian war beginning in 259, which will have reverberated along the empire's frontier, would alert other Roman enemies to the possibilities.

The storm broke in 259–260. In the east, the new Persian invasion was aimed at the Mesopotamian province and Oshroene, with Karrhai and Edessa as the immediate targets.[4] At much the same time there was another seaborne expedition from the north against the Black Sea coasts of Asia Minor and the Balkans.[5] Valerian was in Antioch. He moved his army forward to counter the Persian advance and put himself into Edessa as his headquarters. This was a trap, as it happened. The city was besieged and either captured or betrayed. Valerian attempted to organise a breakout of his soldiers, but was himself captured, allegedly by a trick of Shapur, which Valerian fell for; a whole collection of senior officials were also seized, effectively decapitating the eastern army.

It was probably news of this momentous event – the capture of an emperor had never happened before – which set off the trouble that followed in the west. Gallienus, after the suppression of Ingenuus in Illyricum, had the responsibility for defending an extremely long frontier, from the North Sea to Pannonia and perhaps to the Black Sea. He placed his headquarters at Milan, but the invasions happened more or less simultaneously across the Rhine and across the Danube. Dacia was attacked by its neighbours, Vandals and Iazyges attacked the Pannonian line, Alamanni broke through into Raetia and the Agri Decumates and then into Gaul; some of these territories were never recovered by the empire.

The reaction in the empire to these several attacks was to look to local commanders, and to resort to self-help, something that had become increasingly common in the last half-century. A rash of proclamations of usurping emperors spread from Pannonia to Syria. Gallienus attended with difficulty to the Alamanni, who penetrated the frontier fortifications and spread throughout

Gaul and into Italy. At Carnuntum the defending soldiers elevated Regalianus to emperor and fought to defend the local area; Pannonia was already partly defended by the Marcomanni, with whom Gallienus had made an agreement, but others could get through and Pannonia was badly damaged by a systematic campaign of looting and destruction by a combination of Sarmatians, Quadi, and Roxolani. Gallienus met and defeated the Alamanni when they reached Italy, but by then the Gallic provinces had, like Pannonia, chosen their own defender, M. Cassius Latinius Postumus, the imperial governor of Germania Superior, who seized power at Cologne, and in the process killed Gallienus' son Saloninus. He succeeded in establishing a regime, which at one time included Britannia and Hispania as well as the Gallic and German provinces, and lasted more than a dozen years.[6] It was not, however innovative in any way; the emperors had only a short stretch of frontier to defend, and considerable resources in their part of the Roman Empire with which to do so. Postumus set up a regime with the traditional Roman institutions, which included frequent *coups d'état* and imperial assassinations.

In the east, the disappearance of the emperor into captivity, and the defeat of his army, forced the emergence of more than one local defence force. One force was commanded by Marcianus, who promoted his two sons to Augusti, while another commander, Callistus, merely took command of part of the eastern army. In the desert city of Palmyra, Odenathus, who had acquired a certain status as a Roman official, did the same, but with greater cunning, since he claimed to act as a Roman commander and got Gallienus to agree to this.[7] These local forces in Syria were similar to the reaction of Uranius Antoninus several years before, and of Ingenuus and Regalianus in Pannonia in the west in 258–260, so that they were reacting to the invasion of their own regions and fighting back with whatever forces they could collect. They were also successful, and Odenathus in particular was able, by his command of the cross-desert routes, to attack the Sasanid economic centre in Babylonia, and so compel the Persian forces to withdraw from Syria.[8]

The empire, however, was so rigid in its inability to adapt to new conditions that only by claiming to be emperors could most of the usurpers command the loyalty of the troops they collected. Thus there was, on the one hand, a devolution of authority by the emperors to family members, and on the other, the more spontaneous elevation of local commanders to command local forces. These were essentially similar reactions to the crisis, but they were also perceived as antagonistic; Odenathus was thus the only one whose enterprise became accepted – and this was presumably because he was seen as the most easily suppressible, his political base being only a single small city in the desert. Once these usurpers had a certain recognition as emperors they had no choice but to operate as if they were the rulers of the whole empire, and their destruction became the main task of the 'legitimate' emperors, at the expense of the defence of the empire as a whole. So Ingenuus had to be crushed by Gallienus, and the Marciani had to expand their territory, aiming to overthrow the 'legitimate' emperors, until defeated. One of them, Quietus, who was holed up in Emesa and was essentially inoffensive, was murdered at Gallienus' order. Just two of these local enterprises, Postumus in Gaul and Odenathus in the east, made any real progress towards the firm establishment of their own regimes.

These two breakaway regimes actually fairly swiftly failed, destroyed by the Emperor Aurelian within a couple of years once the other major crises in the empire were surmounted. Neither was actually any more viable as a long-lasting state than the old pre-260 empire had become. Postumus set up an imitation of the old empire, consuls, Senate, and all; Odenathus' regime was too narrowly based on a single desert city to last, and once he was dead his widow Zenobia and her infant son could not possibly continue for very long. Neither regime showed any indication that they had any real political imagination. The expanded and reformed Roman army instituted by Gallienus was too good for both of them, as was the military autocracy that Aurelian represented.

These local ventures were, of course, only informal versions of the divisions and devolutions of imperial authority which had been attempted by Philip and by Valerian, and were to be more firmly founded by Diocletian, but even then only for a single generation. For half a century after the crisis of 260 the empire was in effect divided between many emperors, either 'legitimate' or 'usurpers' – it is often difficult to decide between them. Constantine reunited the several parts, but in the end, this was only temporary – his sons divided the empire again. The end result was the definitive break-up of the empire between successful usurpers, delegated junior members of the ruling family, and barbarian invaders; civil warfare, invasions, and usurpations continued relentlessly.

The Senate had virtually no role in all this. All the power in the military emergency was concentrated in the army commanders, emperors or usurpers. This was the end, and the failure, of the Revolution of 238; and in effect, the end of the Roman Empire, for what followed, when the chaos died away, was hardly recognisable as Roman. This second revolution had attempted to reverse the decision of the 193 revolution, which reduced the Senate to impotence; in 238 this was an attempt to rebalance the Senate-emperor relationship, returning to something resembling what was thought to have been the situation in the first and second centuries AD, which was seen as a time of partnership between the two institutions.

· The balance of power between emperor and Senate had oscillated since the death of Marcus – indeed, it could be said to have done so since Augustus.

But Commodus had deposed the Senate from any real involvement in affairs, governing through his selected choices of men as praetorian prefects, and he had cut a swathe through the members of the Senate by executions so that the survivors were cowed into submission; then Septimius did the same. A revival of the Senate with his death came when Pertinax briefly held the imperial authority, but neither Julianus nor Septimius were interested in anything but their own power. In effect, they confirmed and continued Commodus''system', and the Senate succumbed again, continuing in that mode until the killing of Elagabalus. The reign of Alexander Severus pretended to restore the Senate's position, but he was despised because he depended so obviously on his mother, and he was involved in warfare for most of his reign as an adult, which kept him out of Rome for much of the time. Even that feeble attempt at restoring the balance essentially failed, to be emphasised brutally in Maximinus' clear soldierly disdain for the Senate. His reign was a revival of the system of Commodus and Septimius, even more disdainfully of the Senate, and it was a clear sign that ruling the empire as a military autocracy was perfectly possible.

The revolution of 238 was thus, like so many other revolutions, an attempt to return to a condition recalled from the past, and of course, it did not work in the long run. The system put in place by Augustus was, in the very long term, quite unviable. It depended too much on restraint by both parts of the regime, but the empire was too large and complicated for either of them to manage, so that the bureaucracy emerged to rule, and to provide the emperors with an alternative to the Senate. The Senate-emperor duopoly became rigid and unadaptable. That it lasted for two centuries (plus the revival between 238 and 260) was a testimony to the self-interest of all involved, emperors and aristocracy – and perhaps the continuing fear of a return to the civil warfare out of which Augustus had emerged as autocrat, as Vespasian and Domitian did after the civil war of 69. Its continuation was also due to the lack of a serious external challenge. But it did not take much effort to overthrow it, as was almost done more than once between Augustus and Septimius. But Septimius, following on from Commodus, upset the system so badly that it was becoming unrecognisable, and then returning to what had been the old situation proved to be too difficult. This was especially so when the pressure was on to survive by warfare, with the development of much more capable and determined enemies. And so the balance decisively tilted towards the army commanders, which was, as Augustus had shown, the emperor's role.

One must admire the way the Senate, knocked down repeatedly – by Commodus, by Septimius, by Elagabalus, by Maximinus – always got up and resumed the contest, even recovering after the Decius disaster – as a former active senator his betrayal and then failure might have been encouraging. The emperors who followed him – Trebonianus, Aemilianus, Valerian – once more attempted to make the duopoly work through the 250s, but the disasters of 259–260 administered the final knockout, a verdict accepted by Gallienus and his successors, who once more ignored the Senate in their constant travelling and fighting. The Senate-emperor duopoly ended decisively when the senatorial emperors of the 250s all failed, and the capture of the Emperor Valerian – perhaps the quintessential senatorial emperor, old, distinguished, tradition-minded – brought an empire-wide collapse. Pure military autocracy followed, symbolised by the myth that Gallienus, a purely military emperor, is supposed to have excluded senators from military commands – by imperial edict. The irony is, of course, that while Valerian was acting as a normal, traditional Roman emperor, his son was devising the military and eventually the political system that would replace it.

The two Roman revolutions considered here, therefore, in one sense saw the final realisation of the implications of Augustus' system, which put the emperor above the Senate and in command of the army. The Augustan system was based on the army, but also on the emperor's ability to control membership of the Senate – Augustus, of course, repeatedly purged the Senate. This was distorted by Commodus and his successors by reducing the Senate to an unconsidered role in the imperial system, a situation confirmed by the victory of Septimius in the civil war that followed the revolution of 193. The revolution of 238 was an attempt to reverse that, and to restore the role of the Senate, but only to its relationship to the emperor as understood from the period before Commodus, not to any true independence. As soon as a military emergency of empire-wide proportions arrived, as it did in 260, the Senate was again sidelined, this time without hope of recovery. The Augustan system had therefore worked itself out to its inevitable destination, the military autocracy that ruled the empire for the century after Diocletian, and, of course, failed in its turn, oversaw the final disintegration of the empire.

Notes

Chapter 1

1. Dio Cassius 71.33.4–34; *HA, Marcus,* 27.11–12, 28; Herodian 1.3–4; Antony R. Birley, *Marcus Aurelius* (London, 1966), 287–288.
2. John D. Grainger, *Nerva and the Roman Succession Crisis of 96–99* (London, 2000), 23–25.
3. Herodian 1.51.8.
4. Dio Cassius 72.8.1–2; the general who was killed is not named; there is some difficulty in naming the governor, but Ulpius Marcellus is certainly named as 'returning' to the province to deal with the problem; John S. McHugh, *The Emperor Commodus, God and Gladiator* (Barnsley, 2015), 58; for the governor, Antony Birley, *The Fasti of Roman Britain* (Oxford, 1981), 135–142.
5. Herodian 1.6.1–6; Dio Cassius 72.1–2.
6. Dio Cassius 72.3.1–3.
7. Dio Cassius 71.16.2; the governor who arranged this, Q. Antistius Adventus, was present at the *consilium* in 180.
8. Dio Cassius 72.2.1–4.
9. David S. Potter, *The Roman Empire at Bay* (London, 2004), 86.
10. It is not clear where Marcus was when he died; Vindobona (in Aurelius Victor, *de Caesaribus,* and the *Epitome,* 16.14) or Sirmium (in Tertullian, *Apology,* 25). The former is preferable for geographical and textual reasons; Birley, *Marcus Aurelius,* 268.
11. Dio Cassius 72.1.2.
12. Dio Cassius 72.2.3–4.
13. Herodian 1.6–8.
14. Herodian 1.7.1.
15. *Ibid.*
16. Herodian 1.7.5, describes his appearance, though not at first hand; but there seems little doubt of his essential accuracy, since his sculptured likeness and coins imply the same.
17. Herodian 1.7.2–4.
18. *HA, Commodus* 2.3–4; and *Marcus* 22.12.
19. *HA, Commodus* 3.6; not a reliable source; neither Dio Cassius nor Herodian mention this.
20. *PIR* C 1024; Rupke, 1236.
21. *PIR* C 973; Rupke, 619.
22. Dio Cassius 72.4.5.
23. *PIR* P 474; Rupke, 2725.
24. *PIR* P 311; Rupke, 833.
25. *PIR* A 792; Rupke, 639.
26. *PIR* B 163; Rupke, 959.

Chapter 2

1. On all aspects of the emperor's work, see Fergus Millar, *The Emperor in the Roman World* (London, 1977), especially chapters 3, 5 and 8.

2. Cassius Dio 59.6.3.
3. Plutarch, *Life of Demetrios* 42.7; Serenus, quoted by Stobaeus, *Flor.*, 3.13.48 (about Antipater).
4. So it is assumed; but it may be that the resentment was based on the fact that such men stood between the senator and the emperor.
5. Tacitus, *Annals* 1.9–15; Cassius Dio, 56.
6. Grainger, *Nerva and the Roman Succession Crisis of 96–99* (London, 2000), 22–23.
7. Suetonius, *Titus* 11.
8. John D. Grainger, *The Roman Imperial Succession*, Barnsley 2020, ch. 6.
9. So suggests McHugh, *Commodus*, 70.
10. She is named in an inscription of 191: *CIL* 8.2366.
11. Josephus *AJ* 19.105–113; Cassius Dio 59.29.7.
12. Suetonius, *Domitian* 15.
13. *HA, Marcus* 20.
14. *PIR* C 973.
15. A. Aymard, 'La conjuration de Lucilla', *REA* 57, 1955.
16. *HA, Commodus* 1.4.1; Cassius Dio 78.4.4–5; Herodian 1.8.4–5.
17. Herodian 1.8.5–6; *HA, Commodus* 4.1–2; Cassius Dio 78.4.4.
18. Herodian 1.6.4–7.
19. Herodian 1.7.1–2.
20. *HA, Avidius Cassius* 8.6, and *HA, Marcus* 25; the *Historia* is probably fairly reliable still at this point.
21. Herodian 1.8.8; *HA, Commodus* 4.1–2.
22. *HA, Commodus* 4.1.
23. This had been one of the arguments of Marcus in refusing a wider punishment for supporters of Avidius Cassius: *HA, Avidius Cassius* 8–9.
24. *HA, Commodus* 4.4; Herodian 4.5–7; Cassius Dio 78.12.2.
25. *HA, Commodus* 4.5; Cassius Dio 78.5.1.
26. *PIR* S 135.
27. *PIR* Q 22 and 4.
28. Cassius Dio 73.6 .1–6; the hunt resulted in many false identifications; these were killed, and their heads sent to Rome, but by the time they arrived they were unidentifiable. It is clear, however, that the fugitive had plenty of help.
29. *PIR* V 349.
30. *PIR* E 17.
31. *PIR* A 1309 (Atilius).
32. *HA, Commodus* 5.1; Cassius Dio 73.4.1, claims that 'Commodus killed a great many people', but this is not specific to the plot.

Chapter 3

1. Susan Bingham, *The Praetorian Guard: A History of Rome's Special Forces* (London, 2019).
2. Britain: Dio Cassius 73.8.1–6; Anthony R. Birley, *The Fasti of Roman Britain*, 140–142, 'Ulpius Marcellus'; Balkans: J. Fitz, 'The Military History of Pannonia from the Marcomannic Wars to the Death of Alexander Severus (180–235)', *Acta Antiqua Academiae Scientiarum Hungaricae* 14 (1962), 25–112; North Africa: *HA, Commodus* 13.8.
3. *HA, Commodus* 5.7; Dio Cassius 73.9–10; Herodian 1.93–96; P.A. Brunt, 'The Fall of Perennis', *Classical Quarterly* 23 (1973), Birley, *Fasti*, 142.
4. Dio Cassius 73.9.1.

5. *HA, Commodus* 6.
6. Dio Cassius 73.12.3; *HA, Commodus* 6.
7. *PIR* A 757.
8. *HA, Commodus* 11–12; *Pertinax* 9.2.
9. So notes John S. McHugh, *The Emperor Commodus* (Barnsley, 2015).
10. Anthony Birley, *The African Emperor, Septimius Severus*, 2nd ed. (London, 1988), makes Severus responsible for Sabina's later marriage (and that of her sister, Cornificia); others assign the responsibility to Commodus; both husbands were *equites*, which supposedly put them safely out of reach of the throne.
11. Herodian 1.10.1–3.
12. Herodian 1.10.4–7.
13. *PIR* A 69.
14. These results were calculated from the consular list in Wikipedia 'List of Roman consuls', and *PIR*.
15. L. Ragonius. Quintianus, *PIR* R 17; Triarius Maternus Lascivius, *PIR* T 341; cf Settipani 369 and 401 for their descendants.
16. Dio Cassius 73.12.4; *HA, Commodus* 6, *Severus* 4.4; neither historian attempts an explanation, other than Cleander's selling of offices.
17. Reminiscent of the use made of a similarly beautiful woman by the Athenian tyrant Peisistratos to bedazzle the citizens into believing his ambitions were approved by the gods; in this connection note Papirius' Greek surname.
18. Dio Cassius 73.13.1–6; Herodian 1.13.8; *HA, Commodus* 16.8–9.
19. McHugh, *Commodus*, 152–153.
20. Dio Cassius 73.14.3; Herodian 1.14.6; *HA, Commodus* 17.1–2.

Chapter 4

1. *ILS* 1327; *HA Commodus* 10.3; Dio Cassius 73.14.1.
2. *HA Commodus* 7.5; all accusations of poisoning in the ancient world must be regarded as guesswork.
3. *HA Commodus* 7.5 and 9.2.
4. Anthony R. Birley, 'The *coup d'état* of the year 193', *Bonner Jahrbucher* 169 (1969), 24–38.
5. Birley, *Fasti* 142–146; *AE* (1963), 52 for his early career; *HA, Pertinax* seems fairly accurate.
6. Dio Cassius 73.3.1; *HA, Pertinax* 1.6.
7. *HA, Pertinax* 2.10–11.
8. *HA, Pertinax* 4.2–3.
9. Dio Cassius 73.19.4.
10. Confiscated on the execution of the owners in 182; cf G.W. Adams, *The Emperor Commodus, Gladiator, Hercules, or a Tyrant?* (Boca Raton, FL, 2013), 193–195.
11. Plague: Dio Cassius 73.1 4.3–4; fire: Herodian 1.1 4.2–6.
12. Dio Cassius 73.15.1–20.3 for his extravagances.
13. *HA, Commodus* 7.2–3.
14. *HA, Commodus* 7.2.
15. Ronald Syme, 'The Biographer Marius Maximus', in *Ammianus and the Historia Augusta* (Oxford, 1968), 89–93; and 'More About Marius Maximus', in *Emperors and Biography: Studies in the Historia Augusta* (Oxford, 1971), 113–134, and 'Marius Maximus Once Again', in *Historia Augusta Papers* (Oxford, 1983), 20–45.
16. *HA, Commodus* 14.8–9; Herodian 1.1 7.1–6.
17. *PIR* E 96 and P 655; Settipani, 320.

18. Details in Birley, '*Coup d'état*'.
19. *HA, Pertinax* 4.3.
20. Dio Cassius 73.21.1–2.
21. Dio Cassius 73.15.2–16.1; Herodian 1.16.9; *HA, Commodus* 11.1 and 15.1.
22. *HA, Commodus* 11.3 and 7.5; Dio Cassius 73.14.1.
23. Herodian 2.1.5.
24. Dio Cassius 74.3.1–3.
25. Herodian 2.1.5, says they were 'a few men who were in the plot', and that they were 'soldiers'. It could be that there were two separate groups with Laetus; as praetorian prefect he was obviously entitled to an armed escort.
26. Dio Cassius 74.2.3.
27. Dio Cassius 74.1.2.
28. Herodian 1.17.7–11; *HA, Commodus* 16.7 (very brief); Dio Cassius 73.22.4–5.
29. Dio Cassius 79.16.5.
30. Dio Cassius 74.1.2–3; *HA Pertinax* 4.4; Herodian 2.2.1–10.
31. Grainger, *Nerva*, ch. 2.

Chapter 5
1. Dio Cassius 74.1.4.
2. Herodian 2.3.3–4.
3. *HA, Pertinax, passim.*
4. *HA, Pertinax* 5.1.
5. *HA, Pertinax* 5.3.
6. *HA, Pertinax* 8.1–8.
7. *HA, Pertinax* 7.1.
8. Dio Cassius 74.6.3–5.
9. *HA, Pertinax* 6.1.
10. *HA, Pertinax* 6.7.
11. Augustus ruled from 30 BC to AD 14 (forty-four years), and died at the age of seventy-seven; Tiberius ruled AD 14 to 37 (twenty-three years) and reached the age of seventy-six; together they ruled the empire for sixty-seven years. It was this long, long period of careful rule by two capable men that was one major reason for the empire's own longevity.
12. Grainger, *Nerva*, ch. 8.
13. *HA, Pertinax* 10.1.
14. Dio Cassius 74.3.3.
15. Dio Cassius 74.7.1–3; Herodian 2.6.8.
16. Dio Cassius 74.8.2 ('at the coast').
17. Dio Cassius 74.12.2.
18. *HA, Pertinax* 6.7.
19. The date of the refusal of the title of Caesar for his son is not obvious from Dio's account, but he included it along with Sulpicianus' appointment as *praefectus urbi*, a post it was clearly necessary to fill once Pertinax had become emperor, and so it was probably within a few days of his accession.
20. *PIR* T 34; Settipani 399–404, makes several attempts to find his ancestry; E. Champlin, 'Notes on the Heirs of Commodus', *American Journal of Philology* 100 (1979), 288–306; both of these have references to other discussions.
21. *PIR* F 373 and 190; H. Halfmann, *Die Senatoren aus dem östlichen Teil des Imperoum Romanum bis zum Ende des 2 Jh. n. Chr.* (Gottingen, 1979), 183.

22. *PIR* C 973.
23. *PIR* A 69.
24. Champlin, 'Notes'.
25. *PIR* E 97.
26. *PIR* S 1016; Halfmann, 'Senatoren', 212; their son was sufficiently well integrated into Roman society to become an Arval Brother.
27. Dio Cassius 74.6.8.
28. Dio Cassius 74.8.1–2.
29. Dio Cassius 74.7.1.
30. Herodian 2.5.1.
31. *HA, Pertinax* 11.1.
32. Dio Cassius 74.7.3–4.
33. Herodian 2.5.3–8; Dio Cassius 44.9 .4–10.1.
34. *HA, Pertinax* 11.4–5.
35. *HA, Pertinax* 11.5.
36. Herodian 2.5.3.
37. *HA, Julianus* 2.4.6, naming the tribunes.
38. Dio Cassius 74.11.2–4; the only source implying an auction and describing events as such.
39. Herodian 2.6.10.
40. *HA, Julianus* 2.6–7.
41. This is not a particularly large sum for a donative; Marcus had paid 20,000, and Pertinax claimed to have promised the same.
42. *HA, Julianus* 27; Dio Cassius 74.11.5–6.
43. Dio Cassius 74.12.1–3.
44. Dio Cassius 74.12.4–5.
45. *HA, Julianus* 1.2.
46. *PIR* D 77; *ILS* 412; *HA Julianus* 1.1–2.5 is wrong in several details.
47. Herodian 2.6.6; Dio Cassius 74.11.2.
48. *HA, Julianus* 2.5.
49. Herodian 2.6.13: *HA, Julianus* 4.1–2; Dio Cassius 74.13.3–4.

Chapter 6
 1. Dio Cassius 73.2.5–6.
 2. *HA, Severus* 5.8; *Niger* 2.4.
 3. Dio Cassius 74.11.5; Herodian 7.6.6; *HA, Julianus* 9.1–2.
 4. The date comes from a military papyrus from Dura Europos in Syria, which listed such things as imperial birthdays: *Feriale Duronum*.
 5. A.R. Birley, *Septimius Severus, the African Emperor* (London, 1988), 97.
 6. Birley, *Fasti*, 155–157.
 7. Birley, *Septimius Severus* 97.
 8. *HA, Commodus* 16.2; *Niger* 3.3–5.
 9. *HA, Severus* 2.4; Birley, *Septimius Severus* 49–50.
10. Barbara Levick, *Julia Domna* (Oxford, 2007).
11. I have discussed Syrian participation in the empire in *Syrian Influence in the Roman Empire* (London, 2018).
12. *HA, Pertinax* 15.5; *Severus* 7.9.
13. For the propaganda processes in this crisis see Z. Rubin, *Civil War Propaganda and Historiography*, Collection Latomus 173 (Brussels, 1980).

14. Dio Cassius 76.15.2.
15. This is the force suggested by Michael Sage, *Septimius Severus and the Roman Army* (Barnsley, 2020), 47.
16. Herodian 3.2.4.
17. Dio Cassius 73.13.2–5.
18. This support emerges from the later campaign; the governor of Asia, Asellius Aemilianus' children were rounded up at the same time as Niger's.
19. *HA, Severus* 5.5; Herodian 2.10.1.
20. *HA, Severus* 6.9–10 names an envoy, Heraclitus, sent by Severus to secure Albinus' support; cf also *HA, Niger* 4.7 and *Albinus* 3.6.
21. Dio Cassius 74.16.1–4; Herodian 2.11.8–9; Sage, *Septimius Severus* 47–48.
22. Calculations by Whittaker in the Loeb Herodian vol. 1, at 214, note 1.
23. *HA, Julianus* 8.4.
24. *HA, Julianus* 5.8.
25. *HA, Julianus* 5.6–7; Dio Cassius 74.17.1.
26. *HA, Julianus* 6.3.
27. Dio Cassius 74.17.1.
28. *HA, Julianus* 6.2; Dio Cassius 74.16.5.
29. *HA, Julianus* 8.5.
30. Dio Cassius 74.17.3.
31. Dio Cassius 74.1 7.1–3.
32. *HA, Julianus* 8.7; Dio Cassius 74.17.4.
33. *HA, Julianus* 8.8; *HA Severus* 5.9.
34. *HA, Severus* 6.1–2.
35. *HA, Severus* 6.2; Herodian 3.2.3; *HA, Niger* 5.2.
36. Herodian 2.13.1–11; briefly in Dio Cassius 74.1.1–2 and *HA Severus* 6.11.
37. Herodian 2.13.3; Eric Birley, 'Septimius Severus and the Roman Army', *Epigraphische Studien* 8 (1969), 63–82.
38. Dio Cassius 75.1.3–5; *HA, Severus* 7.1 says he was armed; Herodian 2.14.1–2; cf Millar, *Cassius Dio*, 139 for Dio's account, and some suggestions on its flattering nature.
39. Dio Cassius 75.4.1–5.5; *HA, Severus* 7.1; not in Herodian.
40. *HA, Severus* 7.5; Herodian 2.14.3–4.
41. Dio Cassius 75.2.1–2.
42. *HA, Severus* 7.6.
43. Dio Cassius 75.2.6.
44. As Herodian pointed out, 2.14.1.
45. *HA, Albinus* 6.8.
46. Dio Cassius 75.6.3; *HA, Severus* 8.12–13; Herodian 3.1.5–2.1.
47. *HA, Severus* 8.7.
48. *PIR* A 988; *HA, Severus* 5.8.
49. Summarised in Birley, *Septimius Severus*, 106–107.
50. Herodian 2.14.6–7; Dio Cassius 75.2.4–5; E. Birley, 'Septimius Severus and the Roman Army', 67–68.
51. *HA, Severus* 8.6–7.
52 *HA, Severus* 8.6.
53. *HA, Severus* 8.9.
54. Herodian 2.14.6.
55. Herodian 3.2.10; Dio Cassius 75.6.4–6; *HA, Severus* 9.1–3 (inadequate); Birley, *Septimius Severus* 109–110; Sage, *Septimius Severus and the Roman Army* 55–57.

56. Birley, *Septimius Severus*, 110.
57. Dio Cassius 75.6.3; *HA, Severus* 9.2.
58. Herodian 3.3.6.
59. Herodian 3.3.3–5; Birley, *Septimius Severus* 112.
60. Herodian 3.4.1–5; Dio Cassius 76.7.1–8; Z. Rubin, *Civil War Propaganda and Historiography*, Collection Latomus, Brussels 1980, 66–68.
61. Dio Cassius 75.8.4; Herodian 3.6.9.
62. Dio Cassius 76.1.1–3.
63. Dio Cassius 76.2.3; Stephen Ross, *Roman Edessa* (London, 2001), 49–54; Sage, *Septimius Severus and the Roman Army* 63–66.
64. Birley, *Septimius Severus* 117.
65. Dio Cassius 75.10.1–14.6.
66. *HA, Severus* 10.6; H. Halfmann, *Itinera principa, Geschichte und Typologie des Kaeiserreizen in Römische Reich* (Stuttgart, 1986), 220.
67. Dio Cassius 76.4.6–7; Birley, *Septimius Severus* 120.
68. Herodian 3.5.1–4; *HA Albinus* 7.2–8.3.
69. Dio Cassius 75.4.1.
70. *PIR* C 1186.
71. *ILS* 1140.
72. Herodian 3.8.6.
73. *HA, Severus* 12.5–6; Glen Bowersock, *Roman Arabia* (Cambridge, MA, 1983), points out that the legion had been awarded the title *Severiana* already, and had been consistently loyal to Severus.
74. *PIR* F 554; Birley, *Septimius Severus* 221.
75. Herodian 3.6.10; *ILS* 1368.
76. Dio Cassius 75.6.2.
77. *AE* 1957, 122, recording Trier's gratitude.
78. Described with varying accuracy and at varying length by Dio Cassius 75.6.1–8, Herodian 3.7.2–6; *HA, Severus* 11.2; modern accounts include Birley, *Septimius Severus* 125, and Sage, *Septimius Severus and the Roman Army*, 73.
79. Herodian 3.7.3–4, and Whittaker's note on this passage in the Loeb edition.

Chapter 7

1. Herodian 3.8.3.
2. Dio Cassius 76.7.1–8.3; Herodian 3.8.6–7; *HA Severus* 13.1–2.
3. Dio Cassius 76.8.1–4 gives the numbers; a series of names is given in *HA Severus* 13, but only one (Novius Rufus, the governor of Tarraconensis) seems accurate; the rest were either invented or garbled. There is no reason to doubt the numbers – at least as a minimum – only the accuracy of the names; cf G. Alfoldy, 'Eine Proscriptionsliste in der Historia Augusta', *Historia-Augusta-Colloquium 1968–1969* (Bonn, 1970), 1–12.
4. Herodian 3.8.7.
5. Summary in Birley, *Septimius Severus*, 125–126.
6. Birley, *September Severus*, 128; D.R. Walker, *The Metrology of the Roman Silver Coinage, III, from Pertinax to Uranius Antoninus*, BAR S40 (Oxford, 1978), 59–61, 129–132.
7. As in 197; Herodian 3.8.9.
8. R. Develin, 'The Army Pay-rises under Severus and Caracalla, and the Question of the *Annona Militaris*', *Latomu*s 30 1(971), 687–695.
9. G.R. Watson, *The Roman Soldier* (London, 1968), 102–108.

10. Birley, *Septimius Severus*, 128.
11. *HA, Severus* 12; this is notably vague as to details, but is probably a reasonable summary of what happened.
12. *HA, Severus* 12.
13. *Ibid.*
14. *HA, Severus* 14.3; it had been run by private individuals until then.
15. Dio Cassius 77.15.2.
16. Dio Cassius 78.2.1–5.5; Herodian 4.3.1–6.5; *HA, Caracalla* 3.1–4.10.
17. Dio Cassius 78.5.1–6.4; Herodian 4.1 3.3–7.
18. Dio Cassius 78.9.1–3 and 11.5–6.
19. Dio Cassius 78.11.5–12.2.
20. Dio Cassius 78.13.1–2.
21. Dio Cassius 78.31 (garbled); Herodian 5.3.9; *HA, Heliogabalus* 2.1.
22. Dio Cassius 78.4.4–5.3; Herodian 4.12.2–13.2.
23. Dio Cassius 78.37.3–4.
24. Elagabalus attracts salacious biographers; for two better than usual studies see George C. Brauer Jr, *The Decadent Emperors, Power and Dynasty in Third Century Rome* (New York, 1995) (originally, and better, entitled *The Young Emperors*), and Martijn Icks, *The Crimes of Elagabalus: The Life and Legacy of Rome's Decadent Boy Emperor* (London, 2011) (with an extensive biography), though this is less a life than the 'legacy'. In truth, his life was so short and the sources for it so bad, there is really little worth saying, except astonishment that he became emperor at all.
25. Noted in Potter, *Roman Empire at Bay*, 152–153.
26. *HA, Elagabalus* 11.1.
27. Potter, *Roman Empire at Bay*, 152–154.
28. *HA, Elagabalus* 16.1-2.
29. See the suggested restoration of the temple as reproduced in Icks, *Crimes*, plates 11 and 12.
30. Brauer, *Decadent Emperors*, ch. 15.
31. Dio Cassius 80.9.4.
32. *HA, Elagabalus* 10.3; Herodian 5.7.4; Dio Cassius 80.17.2.
33. Herodian 5.7.5.
34. Dio Cassius 80.16.6 and 21.2; Herodian 5.7.6.
35. Herodian 5.8.8; Dio Cassius 80.20.1–21.3.
36. The date is uncertain; Ronald Syme, 'The Reign of Severus Alexander', in *Emperors and Biography, Studies in the Historia Augusta* (Oxford, 1971), 147.
37. Dio Cassius 80.2.2–3.
38. Syme, 'Reign of Alexander', 184–185.
39. Dio Cassius 80.2.2.
40. Syme, 'Reign of Alexander'.
41. Ronald Syme, 'The Careers of Maximus and Dio', *Emperors and Biography*, 142–145, and 'Reign of Alexande", 158–159.
42. Herodian 6.4.1.
43. Herodian 6.4.2.
44. Herodian 6.6.5–6.
45. J.F. Drinkwater, *Roman Gaul* (London, 1983), 88 and 214–215, and M. Todd, *The Northern Barbarians* (London, 1975), 32.
46. Whittaker in the Loeb Herodian, vol II, 125, note 3.

47. Halfmann, *Itinera principum* 232.
48. Herodian 6.8.1–9.8.

Chapter 8

1. The most useful modern account, restricting myself to works in English, is Karen Haegemans, *Imperial Authority and Dissent, the Roman Empire in AD 235–238*, Studia Hellenistica 47 (Leuven, 2010), which has an enormous bibliography, and her 'Representation and Perception of Imperial Power in AD 238, the Numismatic Evidence', in L. de Blois (ed.), *Representation and Perception of Roman Imperial Power* (Amsterdam, 2003). The biography *Maximinus Thrax*, by Paul N. Pearson (Barnsley, 2016), relies too much on the *Historia Augusta*, but is useful. Brauer, *The Decadent Emperors*, has a ten-page chapter on the emperor, unfortunately entitled 'The Peasant and the Aristocrats', 192–202. Ronald Syme discusses the source material particularly in 'The Emperor Maximinus', in *Emperors and Biography*, 179–193, and is perhaps the most useful of the short discussions. Prescott W. Townsend, 'The Revolution of AD 238, the Leaders and their Aims', *Yale Classical Studies*, 14 (1955), 49–105, is perhaps the earliest good examination of the issue. For a careful prosopographical approach there is Karlheinz Dietz, *Senatus contra principem: Untersuchungen zur senatorischen Opposition gegen Kaiser Maximinus Thrax*, Vestigia 29, (Munchen, 1980).
2. It may be noted that, apart from a visit in 233, Alexander Severus had paid little attention to the Senate between 231 and 235 – thus the Senate was already feeling ignored and neglected for several years before Maximinus' coup.
3. Herodian 6.8.9–10.
4. Herodian 6.8.2.
5. Herodian 6.8.8.
6. Haegemans, *Imperial Authority*, 41–42 and chapter 4.
7. Herodian 7.3.5–6.
8. Herodian 7.3.1–4.
9. Potter, *Roman Empire* 169.
10. Syme, 'Emperor Maximinus'.
11. Herodian 6.8.1–2, 7.8.4.
12. Herodian 7.1.4 and 9.
13. Herodian 7.2.2–9; *HA, Maximinus* 12.1; *CIL* VI.2001; A. Bellezza, *Massimino di Trace* (Geneva, 1964).
14. For example Pearson, *Maximinus*, ch. 7; note the elaborate map p. 106, which is entirely fiction.
15. Herodian 7.2.8.
16. P. Southern, *The Roman Empire from Severus to Constantine* (London, 2001), 275–276, and note 39.
17. Herodian 7.2.1–9.
18. Pearson, *Maximinus*, 96–97.
19. Whitaker, in the Loeb edition of Herodian, 168, note 1.
20. Herodian 7.4.2–3; Whittaker, in the Loeb Herodian, vol. II, 177–178 notes; Haegemans, *Imperial Authority*, 131–140; Frank Kolb, 'Der Aufstand der Provinz Africa Proconsularis im Jahr 238 n. Chr.', *Historia* 26 (1977), 440–477.
21. Herodian 7.4.5–6.
22. Herodian 7.5.3.
23. A.R. Birley, 'The Origin of Gordian I', in M.G. Jarrett and B. Dobson (eds), *Britain and Rome: Essays to Eric Birley* (Kendal, 1966), 56–60; J.H. Oliver, 'The Ancestry of Gordian

I', *American Journal of Philology* 89 (1968), 345–347; K.D. Grasby, 'The Age, Ancestry, and Career of Gordian I', *Classical Quarterly* 25 (1975), 123–130; Settipani, 135–139.

24. Birley, *Fasti* 181–186.

25. Syme, in *Emperors and Biography*, 167.

26. Herodian 7.5.2.

27. Herodian 7.5.5–7.

28. Zosimus 1.14.1; some doubts have been expressed over the precise identity of this 'Valerianus'; such is the effect of these inaccurate sources.

29. T.D. Barnes, 'Philostratos and Gordian', *Latomus* 27 (1968), 581–597; V. Nutton, 'Herodes and Gordian', *Latomus* 29 (1970), 719–728. Philostratos in fact claims that Gordian was a descendant of the Athenian millionaire and consul *c*.143, Herodes Atticus; this has proved difficult to substantiate, involving the supposed marriage of Herodes' daughter, which is unrecorded. The *HA, The Three Gordians*, also claims he was descended from the Gracchi and Trajan, which is nonsense.

30. Herodian 7.6.1–3.

31. A selection of the chronological discussions includes C.E. van Sickle, 'A Hypothetical Chronology of the year of the Gordians', *Classical Philology* 22 (1927), 416–417; Prescott W. Townsend, 'The Chronology of the year AD 238', *Yale Classical Studies* 1 (1928), 231–238; C.E. van Sickle, 'Some further Observations on the Chronology of the Year 238 AD, *Classical Philology* 24 (1925), 285–289; P.W. Townsend, 'A Yale Papyrus and a Reconsideration of the Chronology of the Year 238 AD', *American Journal of Philology* 51 (1930), 62–68; Giovanni Vitucci, 'Sulla cronologia degli Avvenimenti del 238 d.C.', *Rivista di Filologia* 32, (1954), 372–382; R.A.G. Carson, 'The Coinage and Chronology of AD 238', in H. Ingholt (ed.) *Centennial Publication of the American Numismatic Society* (New York, 1958), 181–199; J.R. Rea, 'O. Leid. 144 and the Chronology of AD 238', *ZPE* 9 (1971), 1–19; Michael Peachin, 'Once More AD 238', *Athenaeum* 67 (1989), 594–604; Haegermans, *Imperial Authority*, appendix 1, 257–258; Dietz, *Senatus contra pricipem*, 345–347 (a summary account). Those listed in this note also contain discussions of this issue, which is clearly unresolved.

32. Whittaker, in Loeb Herodian, vol. II, 214, note 1.

33. Herodian 7.9.2.

34. Twenty days in the *Chronographer of 354*, twenty-two days in Zosimus 12.17; it could be some days longer, depending on the assumed date of his accession, either at Thysdrus, opposition to the enrobement at Carthage, or his recognition by the Senate; this can leave several weeks unaccounted for; both of these sources are much later than the events, are no more than guesses, and do not name their own sources.

35. Herodian 7.9.7.

36. *Ibid.*

37. Herodian 9.10.11.

38. Herodian 7.6.4; *AE* (1957), 278, and Whittaker's note in Loeb Herodian, vol. II, 195.

39. Herodian 7.6.9.

40. *Ibid.*

41. Herodian 7.7.1–3.

42. Herodian 7.7.4.

43. *Ibid.*

Chapter 9

1. Birley, *Fasti*, 168–172 and 181–186.

2. Herodian 7.10.3.

3. *PIR* C 126; Barbieri 49; Rupke 1003.
4. *PIR* C 1179; Barbieri 99; Rupke 1266.
5. *HA, Maximus and Balbinus.*
6. *HA, Maximus and Balbinus* claims he ruled seven provinces, but none of this can be accepted, and no province is specified.
7. There are summaries of the careers in the Whittaker, Loeb Herodian, vol. II, 269 note; for Balbinus see also Mahia Gramatopol, 'Decimus Caelius Balbinis (cos P.P.), *Latomus* 25 (1966), 824–830.
8. Wikipedia, 'Balbinus'; Settiapani 224.
9. Settipani, 120.
10. Herodian 7.10.5–9.
11. Herodian 7.10.3.
12. *HA, Maximinus* 32.3; *Gordians* 10.1–2.
13. *HA, Gordians* 10.2.
14. Townsend, 'The Revolution of AD 238', works hard to expand events from Africa outwards.
15. *HA, Gordians* 7.4; Syme, 'The Usurpation of Silvanus', *Emperors and Biography*, 54, used the form Mauricius (Mauritius in *Gordians*), and classes the name with a large selection of clearly invented men and women's names.
16. Herodian 8.2.5, with Whittaker's note; *AE* (1962), 265; Settipani 346–351; Dietz, *Senatus contra principem*, 233–245 (no. 81).
17. Herodian 8.2.5, with Whittaker's note; Rupke 2943; *PIR* R 257; CIL 6.41229 = *AE* 1929, 158 and 1995, 124; Haegemans, *Imperial Authority*, 168; Dietz, *Senatus contra principem*, 210–226 (no. 75).
18. *PIR* C 209; *CIL* 14.3402 = *ILS* 1826; Rupke 1031; Dietz, *Senatus contra principem*, 108–109 (no. 17).
19. Haegemans, *Imperial Authority*, 162–169.
20. *ILS* 8974: *AE* 1903, 337; Haegemans, *Imperial Authority*, 169; Dietz, *Senatus contra principem*, 245–246 (no. 82).
21. *PIR* L 236; *SEG* 47, 1656; Rupke 2253; F. Millar, 'The Greek East and Roman Law: the Career of M. Cn. Licinius Rufinus', *JRS* 89, 1999, 90–108; Haegemans, *Imperial Authority*, 169–170; not in Dietz, *Senatus contra principem*.
22. *PIR* D 148; *IL Africa* 322; Aurelius Victor, *Caesaribus*, calls him Domitius, which makes the identification clear; Dietz, *Senatus contra principem*, 140–143 (no. 32).
23. Haegemans does not venture an identification, but Whittaker, in Loeb Herodian 235, note 2, made the suggestion for Messius; Dietz, *Senatus contra principem*, 185–187 (no. 53), not identifying him with Messius.
24. Herodian 7.11.2–6.
25. Herodian 7.11.6.
26. Herodian 7.10.7; this might be particularly annoying to the Guard traditional function was to protect the emperors.
27. Herodian 7.12.2–3.
28. Herodian 7.12.4–7.
29. Herodian 7.7.4–6.
30. Herodian 7.12.1.
31. *CIL* 12.6763; Haegermans, *Imperial Authority*; Dietz, *Senatus contra Principem*, 47–54 (no. 4).
32. Herodian 8.2.3–6.
33. Herodian 7.8.9–11; 12.6; 8.1.1–5.

34. Herodian 8.6.3.
35. Haegemans, *Imperial Authority*, 197, criticises Maximinus for delays, unjustifiably.
36. *P.Oxy.* 43.3107, two documents, of 7 April and 13 June.
37. *CIL* 6.816.
38. He may have sent instructions to Capelianus, but the latter had certainly moved against the Gordians before any imperial message could reach him.
39. He made a speech on the third day, and next day issued directions for the march (Herodian 7.8.3 and 9); Haegemans, *Imperial Authority*, 197, says he was 'not in a hurry'.
40. Herodian 7.8.10.
41. Assumed to be so perhaps because Caracalla learnt the skill from them; but javelins were hardly a desert warrior's weapon; later he calls them archers.
42. See the lists in G.L. Cheesman, *The Auxilia of the Roman Army*, Oxford 1914.
43. Herodian 8.1.4.
44. Herodian 8.1.1.
45. Herodian 8.6.6.
46. *AE* (1934), 230 (by the Prefect of *Cohors* I *Ulpia Galatorum*); *CIL* 5.889.
47. Herodian 8.2.4–7.
48. Herodian 7.7.5.
49. There is evidence of road repairs in the Aquileia region during Maximinus' reign, and the city had commended him as *restitutor et conditor* (*CIL* 5.7489); Haegemans, *Imperial Authority*, 202–203; Whittaker, Herodian, vol. II, 264 note. None of this can be translated as local support for the emperor; he may be commemorated on the milestones, but he probably knew nothing about the actual work.
50. Birley, *Fasti*, 181–186; he would have been governor for several years; the next man known is dated to 219.
51. *RIB* 1279 and 590; the Chester-le-Street inscription (*RIB* 1049) shows a less definitive erasure.
52. Birley, *Fasti*, 196–197; Dietz, *Senatus contra principem*, 232–233 (no. 80).
53. *RIB* 1553, from Carrawburgh, also on the Wall.
54. Haegemans, *Imperial Authority*, 259, with references.
55. *Ibid.*, appendix 2, 259–276.
56. *Ibid.*, 261–263; Dietz, *Senatus contra principem*, 190 (no. 54, on Messius).
57. *CIL* 13.592
58. *CIL* 17.155.
59. Haegemans, *Imperial Authority*, 262–263; the identification is not universally accepted.
60. A. von Schlieffen, 'Eine romische kaiserstatue in Piraus Museum', in *JOAI* 29 (1935), 97–108; C.C. Vermeule, *Roman Imperial Art in Greece and Asia Minor* (Cambridge, MA, 1968), 310–314.
61. *IGBulg* 3.1.1510 = *AE* 1900, 23.
62. *BMC, Roman Empire*, vol. 6, 10.
63. Prescott W. Townsend, 'Sextus Catius Clementinus Priscillianus, governor of Cappadocia in AD 238', *Classical Philology* 50 (1955), 41–42; Dietz, *Senatus contra principem*, 122–123 (no. 20a).
64. Haegemans, *Imperial Authority*, 271.
65. *Ibid.*, 257–258, listing the relevant papyri; D.W. Rathbone, 'The Dates of the Recognition in Egypt of the Emperors from Caracalla to Diocletianus', *Zeitchscrift fur Papyrologie und Epigraphik*, 62, 1986, 101–129 – the Gordians are at 109–110.
66. *AE* (1971), 475; M. Avi-Yonah, 'Latin Inscriptions from Ma'agan Michael', *Bulletin of the Israeli Exploration Society* 24 (1959/1960), 236–241; X. Loriot, 'Un milliaire de

Gordien II decouvert pres de Cesaree de Palestine et l'extension aux provinces orientale de l'insurrection de 238 apres J.-C.', *Revue des Etudes Anciens* (1978), 78–84.

67. A. Dieudonne, 'Les monnaies grecques de Syrie au cabinet des medaillies', *Revue Numismatique* 4.32 (1929), 142.
68. *AE* (1996), 1625.
69. Herodian 7.7.5–6.
70. Herodian 8.1.4.
71. Herodian 8.4.1–3.
72. Herodian 8.4.4–5.7; modern accounts are no more than adaptations or elaborations on Herodian's account; see Haegemans, *Imperial Authority*, ch. 6, and Pearson, *Maximinus*, 168–171 (a little fanciful); Arthur Stein, 'Bellum Aquileiense', *Hermes* 65, 1930, 228–235.
73. Herodian 8.4.6.
74. Herodian 8.4.3.
75. See the map in Natale Barca, *Roman Aquileia, the Impenetrable Fortress, a Sentry of the Alps* (Oxford, 2022), 104 (though the description of the siege is pure Herodian).
76. Herodian 8.4.5.
77. Herodian 8.5.3–4.
78. Herodian 8.5.5.
79. Barca, *Roman Aquileia*, map 3.
80. Herodian 8.5.8.
81. Settipani 375; he may have been one of the Twenty.
82. *AE* 1938, 104; Whittaker, Herodian, vol. II, 240 note; not in Dietz, *Senatus contra principem*.
83. Herodian 8.5.8–9.
84. Herodian 8.6.1.
85. Herodian 8.6.2–3.
86. Herodian 8.6.3–4.

Chapter 10

1. Herodian 8.5.9; 8.6.5–6.
2. Herodian 8.6.7.
3. Herodian 8.7.8, and other references.
4. Dexippus, *FGrH* 100, frag 14.
5. The date of this invasion is uncertain; it may have been in 235–236 – either way, it was a sign of more trouble in the future.
6. *HA, Balbinus* and *Maximus* 13.5.
7. *HA, Balbinus* and *Maximus* 2.1–3.1; but the name of the proposer of the compromise, 'Vectius Sabinus', appears to be one of the author's many inventions: Syme, 'Gordianus, Pupienus, Balbinus', in *Emperors and Biography*, 177.
8. Zosimus 12.17; see the coins produced for the two men; but Pupienus is portrayed as Hercules in a statue now in the Louvre (reproduced in Ilkka Syvanne, *Gordian III and Philip the Arab* (Barnsley, 2021), 101 – though he appears to believe the emperor was really seventy-four years old, and that the statue is a physically exact portrait.)
9. Herodian 8.6.7–7.2.
10. Herodian 8.7.3.
11. Herodian 8.7.3–6.
12. Herodian 8.7.7.
13. *HA, Maximus* and *Balbinus* 12.3.
14. Herodian 8.7.2.

15. Herodian 8.6.8.
16. Herodian 8.6.7; *HA Maximus* and *Balbinus* 11.5–7, distorted and exaggerated, as usual.
17. Herodian 8.7.7.
18. Dietz, *Senatus*, no. 75.
19. *Ibid.*, no 18.
20. *Ibid.*, no 81; Dexippus, *FGrH*, frags 20 and 22.
21. Beate Dignas and Engelbert Winter, *Rome and Persia in late Antiquity: Neighbours and Rivals* (Cambridge, 2007), 40; Potter, *Roman Empire at Bay*, 217; Michael H. Dodgeon and Samuel N.C. Lieu (eds), *The Roman Eastern Frontier and the Persian Wars, 226–283, a Documentary History* (London, 1991), 32–33 (using the date 238–239).
22. *HA, Maximus* and *Balbinus* 14.1–4; Herodian 8.8.4.
23. *HA, Maximus* and *Balbinus* 14.3.
24. Herodian 8.4.5; *HA, Maximus and Balbinus* 24.3; the *Historia* seems to have elaborated on Herodian, and so distorted events.
25. So Herodian 8.4.5.
26. Herodian 8.4.6; *HA, Maximus and Balbinus* 14.5–8.
27. Herodian 8.5.7.
28. *Ibid.*; X. Loriot, 'Les Fasti Ostienses et le *Dies Imperii* de Gordien III', *Melanges d'Histoire anciennes offerts a William Seston* (Paris, 1974), 297–312; Maurice Sartre, 'Le Dies Imperii de Gordien III, une Inscription inedited de Syrie', *Syria* 61 (1984), 49–61.
29. Dietz, *Senatus*, no. 30.
30. Ilkke Syvanne, *Gordian III and Philip the Arab*, subtitled his book, *the Roman Empire at the Crossroads* (Barnsley, 2021), which is, given the lack of source material for this very period (238–249), a feat of imagination.
31. *HA, Three Gordians* 23.1.
32. The *Historia Augusta* wanders off into irrelevance: *Three Gordians* 23.2–3.
33. As by Xavier Loriot, 'Les premières années de la grande crise de IIIe siècle …', in *Aufsteig und Niedergang des Romische Welt* II (Munich, 1975), 657–987, at 726–728.
34. *CIL* XIII, 807, from Lugdunum, gives his cursus until 238; also H.-G. Pflaum, *Les carrières procuratoriennes sous le Haut-Empire Romain* (Paris, 19600, 811; Dietz, *Senatus contra principem* 294 for the full cursus.
35. *CIL* 3.4115, gives his *cursus*; *ILAfrica* 322 his origin; Dietz, *Senatus contra principem*, 140–142 (no. 32), with other references.
36. *CIL* 13.11759, a heavily restored text; Dietz, *Senatus contra principem*, 205–206 (no. 69).
37. *AE* (1930), 67; Dietz, *Senatus contra principem*, 165–166 (no. 41); Birley, *Septimius Severus*, 216.
38. Dietz, *Senatus contra principem*, 39 (no. 1).
39. *HA, Three Gordians* 23.4.
40. *CR* 105388; Dietz, *Senatus contra principem*, 192–196 (no. 62) (with several other inscriptions, and the detailed *cursus*).
41. Dietz, *Senatus contra principem*, 209–210 (no. 74); stemma on p. 372.
42. Dietz, *Senatus contra principem*, 128 (no. 25); stemma opposite p. 374.
43. *CIL* 14.3902, 3900, and 8.26212; Dietz, *Senatus contra principem*, 103–109 (no. 17).
44. Dietz, *Senatus contra principem*, 233–245 (no. 81); CIL 3.7606a and 14430 (presumed deletion of his name is uncertain).
45. *AE* 1929, 158; Dietz, *Senatus contra principem*, 210–227 (no. 75 – a long discussion) and numerous inscriptions from Thrace, some with Alexander Severus' name deleted.

46. Dietz, *Senatus contra principem*, 158–160 (no. 39); *ILS* 8841 (Lykia); *CIL* 12.3220 (Nemausus, Narbonensis); Joyce Reynolds, *Aphrodisas and Rome*, Society for the Promotion of Roman Studies (London, 1972), doc. 22.

47. Dietz, *Senatus contra principem*, 156–158 (no. 38).

48. Dietz, *Senatus contra principem*, 40–41 (no. I); *CIL* 13.3162; H.-G. Pflaum, *Le Marbre de Torigny* (Paris, 1960), 7–10.

49. Dietz, *Senatus contra principem*, collected over a hundred names of senators who had lived through the events of 238 and could have been supporters, though his purpose was rather different, to demonstrate continuity from the civilian period through 238 and beyond.

50. Barbieri, 1012, lists a good sixteen of them.

51. Dietz, *Senatus contra principem*, no. 59 'C. Messius Quintus Decius Valeri(a)nus'.

52. Herodian 9.7.3 – 1t.

53. Y. le Bohec, *La troisieme legion Augusta*, Paris 1989.

54. *HA, Three Gordians* 23.4.

55. Barbieri, *Albo*, 1717 and index.

56. Cyprian, *Ad Demetriani* 3–4.

Chapter 11

1. Herodian 8.7.7.

2. P. Southern, *The Roman Empire from Severus to Constantine* (London, 2001), 211–212.

3. Dexippus *FGrH* 100 F 20 and 22.

4. *HA, Balbinus* and *Pupienus* 16.3.

5. Potter, *Roman Empire*, 226.

6. H.-G. Pflaum, *Les procurateurs équestres sous le Haut-Empire Romain* (Paris, 19500, 820.

7. Erased names: *IG Bulg* 641 and 642; Peter the Patrician, frags 8 and 9; Dietz, *Senatus contra principem*, 233–245 (no. 81).

8. *HA, Three Gordians* 26.3–4; Peter the Patrician F 170.

9. *PIR* F 109.

10. Dietz, *Senatus contra principem*, 292–293 for Felicianus' *cursus*; Dietz includes five other men of the same type on 292–296, including Timesitheus.

11. Potter, *Roman Empire at Bay*, 230.

12. Michael the Syrian, *Chronicle*, 5.5, 77–78 in Dodgeon and Lieu, *Roman Eastern Frontier*, 35.

13. *HA, Three Gordians* 28.1.5.

14. *HA, Three Gordians* 29.1.1.

15. *PIR* I 488.

16. The defeat is not mentioned in Roman sources, but it is in the Sasanid inscription called *Res gestae Divi Saporis* from Taksh-i Rustem, ed. and trans. A. Maricq, *Syria* 35 (1953), 245–260.

17. Dodgeon and Lieu, *Roman Eastern Frontier*, 36–45, provide a collection of these contradictions; the Sassanid source is the *Res gestae Dive Saporis*, which has no Roman political axe to grind, but has certainly its own point of view; cf Beata Dignis and Engelbert Winter, *Rome and Persia in Late Antiquity, Neighbours and Rivals* (Cambridge, 2007), 77–80.

18. Ammianus Marcellinus 23.5.7 and 17, an eyewitness testimony of the tomb; Potter, *Roman Empire*, 235–236.

19. Potter, *Roman Empire*, 236–237.

20. *ILS* 510, 512.
21. L. de Blois, 'The Reign of the Emperor Philip the Arab', *Talanta* 10/11 (1978/1979), 12–43.
22. Ammianus Marcellinus 23.5.8; over a century later, the Emperor Julian made offerings there.
23. *Res gestae Divi Saporis* 9–10; Zonaras 12.19 p. 182–183; Dignas and Winter, *Rome and Persia* 119–122.
24. Benjamin Isaac, *The limits of Empire, the Roman Army in the East*, rev, ed. (Oxford, 1992), 361–363
25. Arthur Segal, *Temples and Sanctuaries in the Roman East*, trans. Rebecca Toueg (Oxford, 2013), 187–190, based on surveys by the American archaeological expedition published as *Publications of the Princeton University Archaeological Expedition to Syria*, 1903–1917; Ross Burns, *Monuments of Syria, an Historical Guide*, rev. ed. (1999), 220–223 ('Shahba').
26. Southern, *Roman Empire*, 71 and note 92.
27. 'Prefect of Mesopotamia': *IGR* 3.1201 and 1202, from Philippopolis; '*rector orientis*': *CIL* 3.141495; Pflaum, *procurateurs*, 835.
28. Zosimus 1.19.2.
29. Aurelius Victor 29.2; Zosimus 1.20.2 – but it must be remembered that Philip was generally condemned by these later historians.
30. Aurelius Victor 29.2; Zosimus 1.20.2.
31. Pacatian (*PIR* C 929) had been governor of Syria earlier (*AE* (1933), 227) and had a wide command in the Balkans when he usurped, which may well have been Servianus' original command.
32. Aurelius Victor, *de Caesaribus* 38.10 and *Epitome* 28.2; Eutropius, 9.3; J.M. York, 'The Image of Philip the Arab', *Historia* 21 (1972), 320–332: S. Dusanic, 'The End of the Philippi', *Chiron* 6 (1976), 427–439; H.A. Pohlsander, 'Did Decius kill the Philippi', *Historia* 31, (1982), 214–222.

Chapter 12
1. Syme, *Emperors and Biography*, 195–197; his name: Potter, *Roman Empire at Bay*, 241.
2. Potter, *Roman Empire*, 241–244.
3. *The Roman Imperial Coinage* 4.3, nos. 77–98; J.B. Rives, 'The Decree of Decius and the Religion of Empire', *JRS* 89 (1999), 135–154.
4. He became governor of Moesia Inferior in 234, so his consulship was before that; 233 is thus partly a guess.
5. Barbieri, 1662.
6. Southern, *Roman Empire*, 75.
7. *ILS* 514.
8. Potter, *Roman Empire*, 245–246.
9. Zonaras 12.20; Zosimus 1.23.2–3; Dexippos, *FGrH* 100, frags 25 and 26; A.R. Birley, 'Decius Reconsidered' in E. Frezouls and H. Jouffroy, 'Les empereurs illyriens', *Actes du Colloque de Strasbourg (11–13 Octobre 1990)* (Strasbourg, 1998), 57–80.
10. Dexippos, *FGrH* 100, frag 26.
11. 'Valens Senior' in *HA, Thirty Tyrants*, 20; fully identified in one of Bishop Cyprian's letters (*Ep.* 55.9); Aurelius Victor, *De Caesaribus* 29.2–3.
12. *HA, Thirty Tyrants*, 2 (calling him Cyriades); Ammianus Marcellinus to 3.5.3.
13. Potter, *Roman Empire* 247–248.
14. *Res Gestae Divi Saporis* 10–19, in Dodgeon and Lieu, *Roman Eastern Frontier*, 50–56; also in Potter, *Roman Empire at Bay*, 248.

15. *Sibylline Oracles* 13.147–154; H.R. Baldus, *Uranius Antoninus* (Bonn, 1971).
16. Aurelius Victor, *De Caesaribus* 30.2.
17. *Ibid.*, 2.
18. Zosimus 1.28.1; Eutropius 9.3; Zonaras 12.20 reports on Aemilianus' suggestions.
19. Potter, *Roman Empire at Bay*, 252.
20. Aurelius Victor, *De Caesaribus* 1.31; Zosimus 1.28.1.
21. Zosimus 12.21; Zonaras 1.28.6.
22. Zosimus 1.28.
23. Aurelius Victor, *De Caesaribus* 1.32.
24. Aurelius Victor, *De Caesaribus* 1.31.
25. *Ibid.*
26. Settipani 400–401; Dietz, *Senatus contra principem*, 177–181 (no.49).
27. *HA, Two Valerians* 6.3.
28. R. Syme, 'Emperors from Etruria', *Historia Augusta Papers*, 189–208; he identified Valerian as Etruscan, but also the Ceionius ancestors of Commodus, Pupienus, Decius' wife and perhaps Decius himself, and Trebonianus.
29. Pat Southern and Karen Dixon, *The Late Roman Army* (London, 1996), ch. 2.
30. Such is the implication of the Thirteenth *Oracula Sibyllina*, lines 125–130, and Zosimus 1.27.2.
31. Dodgeon and Lieu, *Roman Eastern Frontier*, 56 (no 3.2.4).
32. Fergus Millar, *The Roman Near East, 31 BC–AD 337* (Cambridge, MA, 1993), 162; J.-C. Balty, Apamee (1986), *CRAI* 1987, 237–238; D. MacDonald, 'Dating the Fall of Dura Europus', *Historia* 35 (1986).
33. Lukas de Blois, *The Policy of the Emperor Gallienus*, Leiden 1976, 26–30; Potter, *Roman Empire*, 257; P. Southern and K.R. Dixon, *The Late Roman Army* (London, 1996), 11–14.
34. Halfmann, *Itinera principum* 237.
35. Aurelius Victor, *De Caesaribus* 33 and 37.

Chapter 13
1. Aurelius Victor, *De Caesaribus* 1.38.
2. Zonaras 12.24; Zosimus 1.37.
3. Zosimus 1.38.
4. *Res Gestae Divi Saporis* 19–26; Aurelius Victor, *De Caesaribus* 32.5; Zosimus 1.36.
5. Zosimus 1.35–36.
6. Southern, *Roman Empire* 97–100; J.F. Drinkwater, *The Gallic Empire* (Stuttgart, 1971).
7. Potter, *Roman Empire at Bay*, 259.
8. Millar, *Roman Near East*, 159–173 and 319–336.

Bibliography and Abbreviations

Abbreviations

AE	*Année Épigraphique*
CIL	*Corpus Inscriptionum Latinarum*
FGrH	*Die Fragmente der griechischen Historiker*
HA	*Historia Augusta*
IG Bulg	*Inscriptiones Graecae Bulgaricae*
IL Africa	*Inscriptiones Latinae Africa*
ILS	*Inscriptions Latinae Selectae*
PIR	*Prosopographia Imperii Romanorum*
RIB	*Roman Inscriptions of Britain*
RMC	Roman
Rupke	Jorg Rupke, *Fasti Sacerdotium* (Oxford, 2008)
Settipani	Christian Settipani, *Continuite Gentilice et Continuite Familiale dans les Familles Senatoriales Romaines a l'Epoque Imperiale* (Oxford, 2000)

Bibliography

Adams, G.W., *The Emperor Commodus, Gladiator, Hercules, or a Tyrant?* (Boca Raton, FL, 2013).

Alfoldy, G., 'Eine Proscriptionsliste in der Historia Augusta', *Historia-Augusta-Colloquium 1968–1969* (Bonn, 1970), pp. 1–12.

Avi-Yonah, M., 'Latin Inscriptions from Ma'agan Michael', *Bulletin of the Israeli Exploration Society* 24, (1959/1960), pp. 236–241.

Aymard, A., 'La conjuration de Lucilla', *REA* 57 (1955).

Baldus, H.R., *Uranius Antoninus* (Bonn, 1971).

Balty, J.-C., 'Apamee (1986)', *CRAI* (1987), pp. 237–238.

Barnes, T.D., 'Philostratos and Gordian', *Latomus* 27, (1968), pp. 581–597.

Barca, Natale, *Roman Aquileia: The Impenetrable City-Fortress, a Sentry of the Alps* (Oxford, 2022).

Bellezza, A., *Massimino di Trace* (Genova, 1964).

Bingham, Susan, *The Praetorian Guard: A History of Rome's Special Forces* (London, 2019).

Birley, Anthony R., *Marcus Aurelius* (London, 1966).

Birley, A.R., 'The Origin of Gordian I', in M.G. Jarrett and B. Dobson (eds), *Britain and Rome, Essays to Eric Birley* (Kendal, 1966), pp. 56–60.

Birley, Anthony R., 'The *coup d'état* of the year 193', *Bonner Jahrbucher* 169 (1969), pp. 24–38.

Birley, Anthony R., *The Fasti of Roman Britain* (Oxford, 1981).

Birley, Anthony, *The African Emperor, Septimius Severus*, 2nd ed. (London, 1988).

Birley, A.R., 'Decius Reconsidered' in E. Frezouls and H. Jouffroy, 'Les empereurs illyriens', *Actes du Colloque de Strasbourg (11–13 Octobre 1990)* (Strasbourg, 1998), pp. 57–80.

Birley, Eric, 'Septimius Severus and the Roman Army', *Epigraphische Studien* 8 (1969), pp. 63–82.

Blois, Lukas de, *The Policy of the Emperor Gallienus* (Leiden, 1976),

Blois, L. de, 'The Reign of the Emperor Philip the Arab', *Talanta* 10/11 (1978/1979), pp. 12–43.

Bohec, Y. le, *La troisieme legion Augusta* (Paris, 1989).

Bowersock, Glen, *Roman Arabia* (Cambridge, MA, 1983).

Brauer Jr, George C., *The Decadent Emperors: Power and Dynasty in Third Century Rome* (New York, 1995).

Brunt, P.A., 'The Fall of Perennis', *Classical Quarterly* 23 (1973).

Burns, Ross, *Monuments of Syria: An Historical Guide*, rev. ed. (1999).

Carson, R.A.G., 'The Coinage and Chronology of A.D. 238', in H. Ingholt (ed.), *Centennial Publication of the American Numismatic Society* (New York, 1958), pp. 181–199.

Champlin, E., 'Notes on the Heirs of Commodus', *American Journal of Philology* 100 (1979), pp. 288–306.

Cheesman, G.L., *The Auxilia of the Roman Army* (Oxford, 1914).

Develin, R., 'The Army Pay-rises under Severus and Caracalla, and the Question of the *Annona Militaris*', *Latomus* 30 (1971), pp. 687–695.

Dietz, K., *Senatus contra Principem* (Munich, 1980).

Dieudonne, A., 'Les monnaies grecques de Syrie au cabinet des medaillies', *Revue Numismatique* 4.32 (1929).

Dignas, Beate & Winter, Engelbert, *Rome and Persia in late Antiquity: Neighbours and Rivals* (Cambridge, 2007).

Dodgeon, Michael H. and Lieu, Samuel N.C. (eds), *The Roman Eastern Frontier and the Persian Wars, 226 –283: A Documentary History* (London, 1991).

Drinkwater, J.F., *The Gallic Empire* (Stuttgart, 1971).

Drinkwater, J.F., *Roman Gaul* (London, 1983).

Fitz, J., 'The Military History of Pannonia from the Marcomannic Wars to the Death of Alexander Severus (180–235)', *A. Arch. Hung.* 14 (1962), pp. 25–112.

Grainger, John D., *Nerva and the Roman Succession Crisis of 96–99* (London, 2000).

Grainger, John D., *Syrian Influence in the Roman Empire* (London, 2018).

Grainger, John D., *The Roman Imperial Succession* (Barnsley, 2020).

Gramatopol, Mahia, 'Decimus Caelius Balbinis cos P.P.', *Latomus* 25 (1966), pp. 824–830.

Grasby, K.D., 'The Age, Ancestry, and Career of Gordian I', *Classical Quarterly* 25 (1975), pp. 123–130.

Haegemans, Karen, *Imperial Authority and Dissent: The Roman Empire in AD 235–238*, Studia Hellenistica 47 (Leuven, 2010).

Haegemans, Karen, 'Representation and Perception of Imperial Power in AD 238, the Numismatic Evidence', in L. de Blois (ed.), *Representation and Perception of Roman Imperial Power* (Amsterdam, 2003).

Halfmann, H., *Itinera principum: Geschichte und Typologie der Kaiserreisen im Römischnen Reich* (Stuttgart, 1986).

Halfmann, H., *Die Senatoren aus dem östlichen Teil des Imperium Romanum bis zum Ende des 2 Jh. n. Chr.* (Gottingen, 1979).

Icks, Martijn, *The Crimes of Elagabalus: The Life and Legacy of Rome's Decadent Boy Emperor* (London, 2011).

Isaac, Benjamin, *The Limits of Empire, the Roman Army in the East*, rev. ed. (Oxford, 1992).

Kolb, Frank, 'Der Aufstand der Provinz Africa Proconsularis im Jahr 238 n. Chr.', *Historia* 26 (1977), pp. 440–477.

Levick, Barbara, *Julia Domna* (Oxford, 2007).

Loriot, X., 'Les Fasti Ostienses et le *Dies Imperii* de Gordien III', *Mélanges d'Histoire Ancienne: Offerts* à *William Seston* (Paris, 1974), pp. 297–312.

Loriot, Xavier, 'Les premières années de la grande crise de IIIe siècle …', *Aufsteig und Niedergang des Römische Welt* II (Munich, 1975), pp. 657–987.

Loriot, X., 'Un milliaire de Gordien II découvert près de Césarée de Palestine et l'extension aux Provinces orientale de l'insurrection de 238 après J.-C.', *Revue des Études Anciennes* (1978), pp. 78–84.

MacDonald, D., 'Dating the Fall of Dura Europus', *Historia* 35 (1986).

Maricq, A. (ed. and trans.), '*Res gestae Divi Saporis* from Taksh-i Rustem', *Syria* 35 (1953), pp. 245–260.

McHugh, John S., *The Emperor Commodus, God and Gladiator* (Barnsley, 2015).

Millar, Fergus, *The Emperor in the Roman World* (London, 1977).

Millar, Fergus, *The Roman Near East: 31 BC–AD 337* (Cambridge, MA, 1993).

Miller, F., 'The Greek East and Roman Law: the Career of M. Cn. Licinius Rufinus', *JRS* 89 (1999), pp. 90–108.

Nutton, V., 'Herodes and Gordian', *Latomus* 29 (1970), pp. 719–728.

Oliver, J.H., 'The Ancestry of Gordian I', *American Journal of Philology* 89 (1968), pp. 345–347.

Peachin, Michael, 'Once More A.D. 238', *Athenaeum* 67 (1989), pp. 594–604.

Pearson, Paul N., *Maximinus Thrax* (Barnsley, 2016).

Pflaum, H.-G., *Les carrières procuratoriennes sous le Haut Empire Romain* (Paris, 1960).

Pflaum, H.-G., *Le Marbre de Thorigny* (Paris, 1960).

Pflaum, H.-G., *Les procurateurs équestres sous le haut-empire romain* (Paris, 1950), p. 820.

Potter, David S., *The Roman Empire at Bay* (London, 2004).

Rathbone, D.W., 'The Dates of the Recognition in Egypt of the Emperors from Caracalla to Diocletianus', *Zeitchschrift fur Papyrologie und Epigraphik* 62 (1986), pp. 101–129.

Rea, J.R., 'O. Leid. 144 and the Chronology of A.D. 238', *ZPE* 9 (1971), pp. 1–19.

Reynolds, Joyce, *Aphrodisas and Rome*, Society for the Promotion of Roman Studies (London, 1972).

Rives, J.B., 'The Decree of Decius and the Religion of Empire', *JRS* 89 (1999), pp. 135–154.

Ross, Stephen, *Roman Edessa* (London, 2001).

Rubin, Z., *Civil-war propaganda and historiography*, Collection Latomus 173 (Brussels, 1980).

Sage, Michael, *Septimius Severus and the Roman Army* (Barnsley, 2020).

Sartre, Maurice, 'Le Dies Imperii de Gordien III, une Inscription inédite de Syrie', *Syria* 61 (1984), pp. 49–61.

Schlieffen, A. von, 'Eine Römische Kaiserstatue in Piräus-Museum', *JOAI* 29 (1935), pp. 97–108.

Segal, Arthur, *Temples and Sanctuaries in the Roman East*, trans. Rebecca Toueg (Oxford, 2013).

Sickle, C.E. van, 'A Hypothetical Chronology of the year of the Gordians', *Classical Philology* 22 (1927), pp. 416–417.

Sickle, C.E. van, 'Some further Observations on the Chronology of the Year 238 A.D.', *Classical Philology* 24 (1925), pp. 285–289.

Southern, Pat & Dixon, Karen, *The Late Roman Army* (London, 1996).

Southern, P., *The Roman Empire from Severus to Constantine* (London, 2001), pp. 211–212.

Stein, Arthur, 'Bellum Aquileiense', *Hermes* 65 (1930), pp. 228–235.

Syme, Ronald, *Ammianus and the Historia Augusta* (Oxford, 1968).

Syme, Ronald, *Emperors and Biography: Studies in the Historia Augusta* (Oxford, 1971).

Syme, Ronald, *Historia Augusta Papers* (Oxford, 1983).

Syvanne, Ilkka, *Gordian III and Philip the Arab* (Barnsley, 2021).

Todd, M., *The Northern Barbarians* (London, 1975).

Townsend, Prescott W., 'The Revolution of A.D. 238, the Leaders and their Aims', *Yale Classical Studies* 14 (1955), pp. 49–105.

Townsend, Prescott W., 'The Chronology of the year 238 A.D.', *Yale Classical Studies* 1 (1928), pp. 231–238.

Townsend, Prescott W., 'A Yale Papyrus and a Reconsideration of the Chronology of the Year 238 A.D.', *American Journal of Philology* 51 (1930), pp. 62–68.

Townsend, Prescott W., 'Sextus Catius Clementinus Priscillianus, governor of Cappadocia in A.D. 238', *Classical Philology* 50 (1955).

Vermeule, C.C., *Roman Imperial Art in Greece and Asia Minor* (Cambridge, MA, 1968).

Vitucci, Giovanni, 'Sulla cronologia degli Avvenimenti del 238 d.C.', *Rivista di Filologia* 32 (1954), pp. 372–382.

Walker, D.R., *The Metrology of the Roman Silver Coinage, III, from Pertinax to Uranius Antoninus*, BAR S40 (Oxford, 1978).

Watson, G.R., *The Roman Soldier* (London, 1968).

Index